Practitioner's Guide to
Ada®

Robert H. Wallace

Intertext Publications, Inc.
McGraw-Hill, Inc. New York, NY

To Paula
      For all the years of loving support.

Library of Congress Catalog Card Number 86-81064

10   9   8   7   6   5   4   3

ISBN 0-07-067922-3

Intertext Publications, Inc.
McGraw-Hill Book Company
1221 Avenue of the Americas
New York, NY 10020

Ada is a registered trademark of the U.S. Government (Ada Joint
    Program Office.
Unix is a registered trademark of Bell Laboratories.

TABLE OF CONTENTS

PREFACE

After being involved with the programming language Ada for the last six years, it has become apparent that many of the "First Wave" books on the subject have been oriented towards teaching Ada as a traditional programming language is taught. Only in the last year have we seen the emergence of books that start to address the needs of the practicing software engineer (i.e. the Practitioner). These "Second Wave" books are still oriented towards teaching Ada in the traditional manner. However, they start off with the assumption that the reader has a strong background in one or more programming languages.

These books address only a small portion of the needs of the practitioner. Most of them focus on Ada as a language, while only touching on the issues associated with the use of the language in real world problems. It is often these issues that are of major concern to the practitioner.

In this book, the orientation is towards addressing the full needs of the practitioner as he or she starts to use Ada. I will cover Ada as a language, but I will also address such Ada-related topics as:

- Ada Oriented Development Environments

- Ada Oriented Design Methodologies

- Ada Policies and Standards

- Ada Products and Vendors

- Sources of Ada-Related Information

- Making the Transition to Ada

- Other Uses of Ada

The scope of this book is much broader than most of the initial books, so the degree of coverage of some topics is limited.

To minimize the impact of this limited coverage, I have used a presentation style that is different from the initial books. In this book, most of the key concepts, issues, or questions related to the application of Ada are presented in tabular form. This format has two benefits. First, it reduces the amount of text needed to cover a topic. Secondly, it defers the detailed information from the main line of text. This allows the reader to regulate the level of detail he or she wants to see at any point in time. An additional benefit of this format is that the important aspects of a topic can be easily located through the table of contents.

This tabular format has been used in the description of Ada itself by using tables to summarize such concepts and features as data typing and statement types. These tables are supplemented with a large number of examples organized into example blocks that again give the reader all the benefits of a tabular presentation format.

The final aspect of the book deals with the style of presentation of the non-language topic areas identified above. Many of these topics will affect the practitioner in different ways depending on the organizational constraints that he or she must work within. With this in mind, it is impossible for me to give a single or even a limited number of answers to the possible questions that various issues will raise. Instead of offering you a single answer, I have tried to present the issues associated with a topic area, provide guidance to assist in addressing the issues, and identify the sources of further information on a topic or issue.

The scope, presentation formats, and the presentation style used in this book are the results of six years of closely observing the evolution of Ada, trying to apply Ada, and teaching over 1000 classroom hours of Ada and Software Engineering to practitioners. This book is really the result of the questions and issues of which I became aware during this six-year period.

A book of this type could not have been written without the help and encouragement of many individuals, as well as those people who have written articles, books, and reports that served as the primary information sources for this book.

This book would not have taken the form that it has if it were not for the questions and concerns of the Ada and Software Engineering classes I taught at the Naval Underwater Systems Center in Newport, R. I., and New London, Conn.

Another group that served to encourage me in the darker months and were always ready to act as sounding boards for the ideas presented in this book were my co-workers at SofTech's Newport, R.I. office. I want to particularly thank Mark Rinfret, Anna Larson, Jack Rienzo, and Mary Lopes for putting up with many of my ideas and for helping me to put them in their final form.

Finally, I want to thank my wife Paula, son Shawn, and daughter Erin for their encouragement and support. Without their understanding and help this book would never have seen the light of day.

1. INTRODUCTION TO THE ADA EFFORT

It has been estimated that the Department of Defense (DoD) alone is currently spending over $4 billion per year on embedded system software, and there
are countless billions more being spent by industrial and commercial
organizations on similar software. This money is going towards activities
that include the design, development, acquisition, management, and
operational support of software. Any activities which demand such an intense
amount of investment must be fraught with problems. The most elementary
of these problems is related to the exponential growth in the functionality and
required performance of the software portions of systems. This is coupled
with the almost antiquated practices employed today within industry in the
development of that same software. The problems with software today are
typically associated with what some call the "Software Crisis."

Much of the current interest in Software Engineering over the last 10
years has been motivated by the Software Crisis. In various references to the
Software Crisis [14, 21, 33, 34], we find comments like the following:

- Software, if it is ever delivered, is never delivered on time!

- If the software is delivered, it never works according to
  expectations.

- Why does software cost 10 times the amount that it was initially
  estimated to cost?

- Why is software so unreliable?

- Why does it cost 100 times more to maintain a piece of software than it did to develop it in the first place?

These comments may not be applicable to all software, but they can be applied to a fair percentage of the software developed over the past 20 years. Over the past ten years, the Software Crisis has cost the Department of Defense alone tens of billions of dollars.

The causes of the Software Crisis have been identified by many individuals and have some of the following observable characteristics:

- The complexity of the applications being attempted are well beyond the scope of the management and technical tools/techniques that are currently in use.

- The failure of organizations to consider the full life cycle implications of software, its development, its maintenance, and its evolution.

- The lack of trained practitioners who can engineer software.

- The continual reinventing of the wheel; that is, creating software with identical functionality on each new project, since software in general has not been reusable.

- The proliferations of languages and dialects that are often poorly matched to the needs of the applications.

- The failure of most languages, tools, and computer architectures to support the application of sound engineering practices to the development of software or a system in general.

- The lack of interest and desire on the part of some organizations to improve their methods of developing software.

Addressing the causes of the Software Crisis has become the challenge of the 1980s. Much of the groundwork that allows us to confront the crisis, was laid out during the late 1970s with the start of the Ada Effort. The Ada Effort, as illustrated in figure 1-1, extends beyond a simple language definition activity

**Modern
Software
Engineering
Methods**

The
Ada Effort

**Common
Support
Environment**

Ada, the Language

Ada Effort Focus

- Reduce the Cost of Developing Systems

- Increase the Portability of Software

- Increase the Portability of Software
  Developers

- Increase Productivity

- Increase Reliability and Maintainability

- Support the Management of Complexity
  and Change

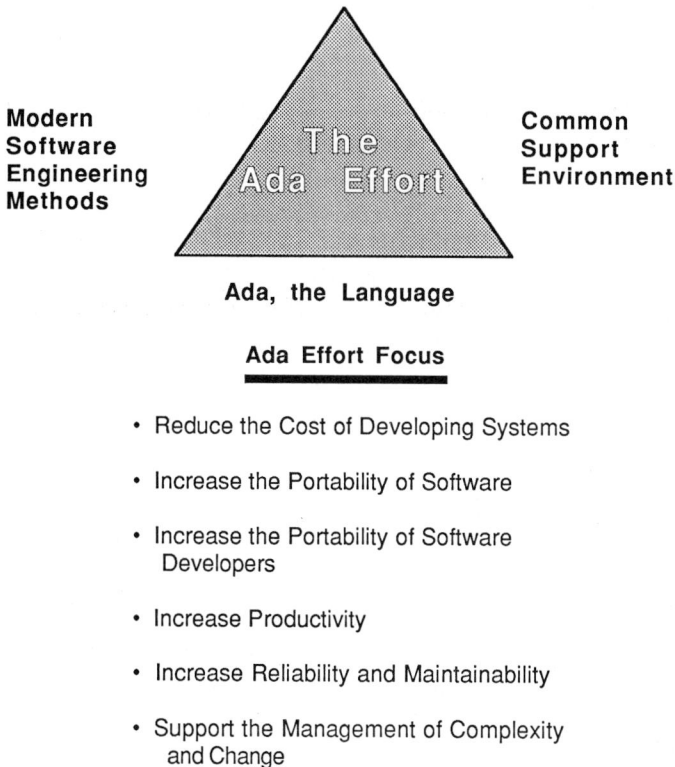

Figure 1-1   **A View of the Ada Effort**

well into the realm of how software is developed and maintained. It is oriented towards helping control the cost and improving the quality of software by
encouraging the application of modern software engineering practices. The
Ada Effort is an attempt to attack the key issues associated with the Software
Crisis. This attack has been spearheaded by the DoD with the support of
hundreds of other organizations all over the free world. To put the Ada
Effort into context, we have to understand the history of the effort, as well as
how the results of its various elements attack individual aspects or causes of
the Software Crisis. The remainder of this chapter focuses on the history of

the Ada effort, while later chapters attempt to identify how various elements of the Ada Effort attack, in part, the Software Crisis.

A Short History of the Ada Effort (1974-1985)

To address its Software Crisis, the DoD started a set of software oriented initiatives to focus the technical and management resources of government, academia, and private industry on the improvement of the tools, techniques and practices used in the development and maintenance of software [6, 23, 24, 52].

The first focus of these initiatives was the development of a standard programming language that resulted from the realization that such a standard was needed to help keep software costs in check. Analyses performed during the period of 1974 to 1976 projected cost savings as high as $24 billion over 30 years. This could be directly attributed to embedded computer programming language standardization. The cost savings would primarily be in the form of cost avoidance.

In 1974, as part of this first initiative, it was thought that a common programming language with the necessary characteristics would be feasible. Further, such a language was within the current state of the art. In pursuit of this, a comprehensive set of requirements was developed through a definition review process within the governments of the United States and allied countries, as well as industry and academia. Over 26 existing languages were selected to be evaluated in the review process. These languages varied from ones that were in production use to languages that were strictly research vehicles. All 26 languages were evaluated for their support of the preliminary requirements identified in the review process. The result of the set of evaluations was that none of the existing languages satisfied the requirements sufficiently to serve as the single common DoD language. The evaluations and their supporting analyses further determined that:

- A single common language was desirable and necessary.

- Such a common language could be developed and standardized if required.

- Several of 26 languages evaluated could serve as the basis for the definition of this new common language.

Based on these conclusions, the DoD undertook a competitive international procurement for the design of a single language that would meet the stated requirements and would be based upon one or more of the following languages: Pascal, PL/1, or ALGOL.

During 1977, the procurement process started with the selection of four independent designs for a common DoD language, which at that point was referred to as DoD-1. During this period, the requirements for the language evolved as would be expected. In early 1978, the four designs, each designated by a color, were reviewed by over 400 individuals from all over the world. Included in the review were representatives from industry, the military, government agencies, and academia. Based on this review, the field of candidate language designs was reduced to two.

The two selected language designs, both based on Pascal, were allowed to proceed on the long path to a workable language definition and finally implementation. In parallel with these design activities, the DoD was going through the process of finalizing the requirements for the language. In early 1979, the two designs were again reviewed in the process of preparing for the selection of a single language.

At about this time, the final name, Ada, for the DoD common language was suggested by Jack Cooper of the Navy Material Command. Up to this point the working name for the language, as you recall, was DoD-1. But some individuals involved in the development process thought DoD-1 was too militaristic and would not gain acceptance in commercial and industrial sectors.

The choice of Ada for the name of a programming language was quite appropriate. It was the name of the first programmer, Augusta Ada Byron, countess of Lovelace and the daughter of the poet Lord Bryon. Ada was a mathematician, who has been credited with working for Charles Babbage on his Difference and Analytic Engines. To many, these are considered to be the first programmable computers. Ada is recognized as the first programmer because of her suggestion of how Babbage's engines could be programmed in a manner similar to that used for the Jacquard loom. Ada became the language's official name in May 1979, when the language designed by a joint European/United States team, the developers of the Green Language, was selected to be implemented.

After the selection was made, the language was tested through an extensive review process in which over 2000 experts in the computing field were allowed to comment on the language definition. Comments were solicited on the language definition contained in a preliminary language reference manual which evolved into the current Military and ANSI standard for Ada. In July of 1980, a revised reference manual replaced the preliminary one. This marked the end of the language design effort.

The definition of Ada was modified over the next few years as the compiler developers and the review teams found implementation problems with the language. This tweaking process continued through 1982. In January of 1983, the DoD and the ANSI standards organization released the *Reference Manual for the Ada Programming Language, ANSI/MIL-STD-1815A* [60], which represents the current definition of the language.

The Ada Effort actually involved more than the design and establishment of a common programming language. By design, the language was intended to directly support sound, modern software engineering concepts and practices. Since one of the key software engineering principles states that a language by itself is not sufficient, the language must also be supported by an automated environment as well as software engineering methodologies that provide the tools and techniques needed to develop, maintain, and evolve software over its lifetime. Recognizing the importance of environments and methodologies to the ultimate success of the common language effort, several parallel initiatives were started during the design of the language.

The first of these initiatives was the creation of modern software development environments which directly supported Ada. These Ada Programming Support Environments (APSE) were intended to support the organizations involved in the development of software as well as to maintain the data critical to the management, development, testing, and evolution of software.

The DoD funded two APSE developments; the Ada Language System (ALS) and the Ada Integrated Environment (AIE). Both environments were intended to meet a set of requirements stated in a document known as the STONEMAN which sets out the requirements for an APSE. As of November 1985, only the ALS has been delivered and it is currently going through an evolutionary process which involves some limited production usage, maintenance, and performance improvements. Ada oriented environments will be discussed more fully in Chapter 3.

The final aspect of the Ada Effort has not been all that well focused; it is the area of Ada oriented methodologies. Here, a large number of individuals and groups are interested in developing and applying various methodologies to address the problems of developing software. Some of these efforts are sponsored by private industry, U. S. and allied governments as well as academia. This is the area in which much of the true promise of the overall Ada effort will be achieved in the future. This topic will be discussed later in Chapter 7.

The real benefits of the Ada effort, illustrated in figure 1-1, have not been achieved. We are just at the beginning of the application of the results of 10 years of development activities that have only recently made available usable implementations of Ada. It may be 20 years before we can actually sit back and assess whether the Ada Effort has really addressed the Software Crisis. But being practical people, we can't wait for Ada to be proven. We must start now and prepare ourselves, our organizations, and our customers for the effective utilization of the efforts to date. It is only through the use of the results of the Ada Effort that we will ever bring its promise to bear on the causes of the Software Crisis.

The purpose of writing this book is to help you, the practitioner, to apply the Ada Effort results to your real world problems. To this end, the chapters that follow focus on answering some key concerns and questions about the Ada Effort and its effects on the way one develops and maintains software. Some of the key concerns and questions this book will attempt to answer include:

- What is Ada?

- What can I use Ada for?

- How does Ada compare to Pascal, C, or FORTRAN?

- What is an Ada Programming Support Environment?

- How do I select the right environment or toolset for my organization?

- What is the meaning of all these Ada-related DoD policies and what effect will they have on me?

- If I'm going to use Ada, where can I get training, a compiler, and consulting services?

- Where can I get more information about Ada and how do I keep up to date with the Ada Effort as it evolves?

- How do I help my organization make the transition to Ada?

- What issues and pitfalls must be addressed when I am considering the design, implementation, and managing of software being developed in Ada?

Because all practitioners in the field of software engineering labor under definite time constraints, the remainder of this book shall be devoted to the answering of these questions in the clearest and most concise manner possible.

2. Ada as a Language:
An Introduction

The goals of the Ada Effort have always been to develop a common language as well as to develop the tools (and the supporting methods) that address the needs of the software community that build "mission critical" military systems. This limited view of the application domain for the Ada Effort is far too restrictive for the language that evolved from the DoD's desires for a common programming language. The application interest in Ada is not limited to those who develop weapon systems, but is international and multi-industrial. This wide range of application interest should not be that surprising since the demands for real-time application-critical software have expanded out from DoD applications to such categories of systems as:

- Telephone Switching

- Factory Automation

- Process Control

- Electronic Fund Transfer

Each of these categories of systems has a need for a standard language that directly supports the development of reliable and maintainable programs that have a high degree of concurrency or could take advantage of real time processing if it were available to them.

The features of Ada that will be covered later in this chapter and appendix A are oriented towards addressing the needs of these diverse applications as well as some applications that may surprise you. The following random list is intended to illustrate the uses of Ada that overlap the traditional military, industrial, and commercial boundaries that languages in the past have suffered with or from:

- Implementation language for Real Time, Numerical Computation Intensive, Signal Processing , and/or Hardware Control applications

   — Communication Systems
   — Navigation Systems
   — Robotic Control Systems
   — Chemical Process Control Systems
   — Nuclear Power Plant Control Systems
   — Weapon Delivery Systems
   — The New Space Station
   — Worldwide Electronic Fund Transfer Systems
   — Air Traffic Control System
   — Radar, Sonar, Optical Sensor Processing Systems

- Implementation language for Data Management systems

   — Battlefield Management System
   — Database Management Systems
   — Information Management Systems

- Implementation language for Simulator and/or Stimulator systems

   — Warfare Gaming Systems
   — Flight Simulators
   — Onboard Trainers
   — Prototyping Environments
   — Modeling Systems
   — Graphics Systems

- Design description language for any of the above systems

   — System Design Languages
   — Programming Design Languages

- Hardware description language for Very Large Scale Integrated Circuits

    — Hardware Description Languages
    — Hardware Modeling and Simulation Languages

Although there is no single data source that one can point to today, the number of systems that can use Ada is far greater than the number of systems that use any other single programming language today. This makes Ada potentially the most important software implementation vehicle in the near future. Thus, it warrants our close attention. The remainder of the book focuses on the important aspects of the Ada Effort and the issues one must address when dealing with Ada. We hope to provide the reader with an understanding of Ada and how it fits into his unique application and organization domain, and how to effectively make use of Ada and the products of the Ada Effort.

The Underlying Requirements of Ada

The whole Ada Effort has its origin in the Common High Order Language Program, a DoD sponsored activity started in 1975. This activity had as its original goal the definition of a single common higher-order language for the various military departments. Through the efforts of a working group of representatives from the various DoD departments, a set of requirements evolved which were used to design and guide the evolution of the Ada language. How the requirements evolved is an interesting story but is not within the scope of this book. We are going to focus on the eventual requirements that were documented in the *Requirements for High Order Programming Languages, STEELMAN*, 1978 [58] . This Department of Defense document, often referred to as "STEELMAN" was the result of nearly three years of effort on the part of the working group and others who had put thousands of hours into the review of the evolving requirements. The STEELMAN document had the following characteristics :

- Requirements were stated to be as quantifiable as possible.

- No implementation specific features were to be included.

- Goals as well as specific requirements were to be addressed.

The technical requirements for Ada can be put into six major goal categories. These categories require that any DoD common language:

1. Must be suitable for embedded computer system development.

2. Must be suitable for the design, development, and maintenance of reliable software for systems that continually evolve over their extended lifetimes.

3. Must be complete, unambiguous, and machine independent.

4. Must not impose execution or efficiency costs in applications due to unused or unneeded generalities.

5. Must provide the base in which effective and useful software development and maintenance environments can be developed.

6. Must be based upon good modern software design practices.

At the highest level, these goals form the primary constraints on the language design that we today call Ada. Table 2-1 through table 2-13 summarize the full set of requirements and constraints placed on the design of Ada. This summary highlights the significant requirements and follows the presentation order used in the STEELMAN document. Upon reviewing the requirements, we hope it is apparent that they are really quite detailed. They are based on the need that the language designers must be provided with a fairly complete statement of the requirements in order to address the somewhat unique application domain that Ada is destined to serve. In addition, these requirements evolved over a period of time and are intended to help address the Software Crisis, or at least a major portion of it.

Also included in this set of tables is an indication of those requirements that proved to be difficult to implement. This indication is proved by underlining the specific requirements. We have also noted those few requirements that were not fully implemented in the final language design.

Consideration of the requirements for Ada is important since the requirements were derived from the first full scale analysis of the programming language requirements of an application domain. In the past, most languages just happened; a sequence of try-it, fix-it steps. In the future, it will be interesting to see what effect this requirements analysis has on the stability and usability of Ada for the applications it was intended to serve.

TABLE 2-1 STEELMAN REQUIREMENTS

GENERAL DESIGN CRITERIA:
OVERALL CRITERIA ON THE LANGUAGE DESIGN

REQUIREMENTS	DESCRIPTION
Generality	— provide generality only to the extent needed to support embedded computer applications
Reliability	— the language should aid in the production of reliable programs — error prone features must be avoided — compilers should not attempt to correct programming errors
Maintainability	— the language should promote ease of program maintenance — emphasize readability — encourage user documentation of programs — require explicit specification of programmer decisions
Efficiency	— the language features should have simple and efficient implementations
Simplicity	— the language should be simple, but not simplistic — build on a minimum number of underlying concepts
Implementability	— the semantics of a feature should be well specified and understandable so that it can be implemented and its interaction with other features can easily be predicted
Machine Independence	— the language should not dictate the characterstics of the target machine or operating system

	— facilities should be provided that allow programs to take advantage of the characteristics of the target machine
Complete Definition	— language should be completely and unambiguously defined - *not fully achieved in language design*

TABLE 2-2 STEELMAN REQUIREMENTS

GENERAL SYNTAX:
UNDERLYING RULES FOR ALL LANGUAGE FEATURES

REQUIREMENTS	DESCRIPTION
Character Set	— programs should be able to be written in a 55-character subset of the ASCII character set — additional characters can be used but must be able to be expressed as a sequence of the 55-character set
Grammar	— use form syntax — must be simple, uniform and easily parsed
Syntactic Extensions	— the user should not be able to introduce or define new syntactic forms or precedence rules
Mnemonic Identifiers	— the language must allow user meaningful mnemonic identifiers — abbreviations are not allowed — a break character within an identifier must be allowed
Reserved Words	— reserved words should be restricted to those that introduce special syntactic forms or as delimiters
Numeric Literals	— built-in decimal literals should be supported — no implicit rounding or truncation of numeric literals should occur

| String Literals | — built-in facility for fixed length string literals that are interpreted as one dimensional arrays of characters |
| Comments | — comments should be introduced by a special sequence of characters and terminated by the end of a line |

TABLE 2-3 STEELMAN REQUIREMENTS

TYPES: SUPPORT FOR DATA REPRESENTATION AND STRONG TYPING

REQUIREMENTS	DESCRIPTION
Strong Typing	— the language should be strongly typed — the types of all variables, components, expressions, functions, and parameters should be determinable by a compiler
Type Conversion	— the language should distinguish between the concepts of type, subtype, and representation — no implicit type conversion
Type Definition	— new data types should be definable within a program
Subtype Constraints	— subtype should include one or more of the following constraints: range, precision, scale, index ranges, and user-defined constraints — the value of a subtype constraint for a variable may be specified when the variable is declared
Numeric Values	— provide distinct types for exact as well as for approximate computations
Numeric Operations	— built-in functions for conversions between numeric types

— support normal arithmetic and relational
  operators

Numeric Variables — the range of numeric variables must be specified in
  a program and is to be interpreted as the minimum
  range to be implemented and as the maximum
  range needed by the application

Precision — the precision of each expression result and variable
  in an approximate computation must be specified in
  the program
— the above specification should be interpreted as the
  minimum accuracy to be implemented

Implementation — approximate arithmetic should be implemented
  using the target machine's actual precisions, radix,
  and exponent range
— built-in functions should provide access to the actual
  precisions, radix and exponent range used by an
  implementation

Integer Numbers — integers should be treated as exact numeric values
— integer modulo and integer division should be
  provided

Enumeration Type Definitions — definable by enumerating its allowed
  values
— values may be identifiers or characters

Enumeration Operations — relational, successor, predecessor, position in
  defined sequence, first allowed value, and last
  allowed value

Boolean Type — predefined

Character Types — character sets should be definable as enumeration
  types
— may contain graphic as well as control characters
— the ASCII character set should be predefined

Composite Type Definitions — include arrays and records whose
components can be of any other data type

Component Specifications — all components must have an explicit data
type specified within the program

Operations on Composite Types — component selection, assignment and a
constructor operation

Array Specifications — arrays with different dimensions or component
type should be different types
— the range of subscript values for each dimensions
should be specified in the program
— subscripts should be either integer or enumeration
types

Operations on Subarrays — built-in operations on one-dimensional
subarrays should include assignment, catenation,
and value access

Variants   — should be able to define record types with
alternative component structures

Tag Fields   — each variant of a record must have a nonassignable
component that discriminates between variants
during program execution
— tag fields should be altered only by full record
assignment

Indirect Types   — types whose elements are indirectly accessed
— elements of an indirect type should remain allocated
as long as it can be referenced by the program

Operations on Indirect Types — a constructor operation which each time it is
executed creates a distinct element of the type
— operation to select between different elements and
select any component in the substructure
associated with the definition of the type

Bit Strings — it should be possible to define types whose elements are one-dimensional Boolean arrays represented in maximally packed form

Bit String Operations — construction, membership, equality, complement, intersection, and union operations should be automatically defined for each Bit String type

Encapsulated Definitions — an encapsulation may contain declarations of anything that is defined in a program

Effect of an Encapsulation — may be used to inhibit external access to implementation properties of the definition

Own Variables — variables declared in an encapsulation should remain allocated and retain their values throughout the scope in which the encapsulation is instantiated

---

TABLE 2-4 STEELMAN REQUIREMENTS

EXPRESSIONS: BASIC FEATURES OF ALL EXPRESSIONS

REQUIREMENTS	DESCRIPTION
Form of Expression	— parsing of correct expressions should not depend on the types of their operands
Type of Expressions	— the language must allow the explicit specification of the type of an expression in those cases where its type can not be determined by its context
Side Effects	— side effects are allowed but with restrictions
Allowed Expressions	— expressions of a given type can be used anywhere that a constant and variable of that type is allowed
Translation Time Expressions	— are permitted wherever literals of the expression type are permitted

Operator Precedence Levels — precedence level should be specified, they cannot be altered by the user and should not depend on the types of the operands

Effect of Parentheses — explicit parentheses should dictate the association between operators and operands

---

TABLE 2-5 STEELMAN REQUIREMENTS

CONSTANTS, VARIABLES, AND SCOPES

REQUIREMENTS   DESCRIPTION

Declarations of Constants — all types must support constants
— translation and allocation time assignments of values to constants should be allowed

Declarations of Variables — variables must be explicitly declared
— the type of a variable must be specified and determinable at translation time

Scopes of Declaration — everything declared should have a defined scope (i.e., the portion of program text in which it can be referenced) determinable at translation time

Restrictions on Values — procedures, functions, types, labels, exception situations, and statements should not be computable or assigned to variables

Initial Values   — there should be no default initial values for variables

Operations on Variables — assignment and implicit value access operations should be automatically defined for each variable

TABLE 2-6 STEELMAN REQUIREMENTS

CLASSICAL CONTROL STRUCTURES:
SUPPORT FOR STRUCTURED CONTROL CONSTRUCTS

REQUIREMENTS	DESCRIPTION
Basic Control Facility	— a minimun number of simple control mechanisms should be built in, each providing a single capability
	— nesting of all control structures should be allowed
Sequential Control	— a control mechanism should be provided
Conditional Control	— should permit the selection of alternative control paths based on the value of a Boolean expression, on a computed choice among labeled alternatives, or a true condition in a set of conditions
Short Circuit Evaluation	— there should be infix control operations for conjunction and disjunction of Boolean expressions
Iterative Control	— there should be an iterative control structure
	— iterative control may be exited at any number of places
	— iteration through a succession of integer type or enumeration type values should be allowed
Explicit Control Transfer	— there should be a mechanism for control transfer but it should not be possible to transfer out of closed scopes, into a narrower scope or into control structures

TABLE 2-7 STEELMAN REQUIREMENTS

FUNCTIONS AND PROCEDURES

REQUIREMENTS	DESCRIPTION
Definitions	— functions should be definable which return values to expressions — procedures should be definable which can be called as statements — multiple functions and procedures may be denoted by the same identifier provided they differ in the number or types of parameters
Recursion	— functions and procedures should be callable recursively
Scope Rules	— global identifiers should be determined lexically, not by the dynamic calling sequence of procedures or functions
Function Declarations	— the type of the result of a function must be specified when the function is declared — functions may return any type
Formal Parameter Classes	— the directions of parameter passing should be explicitly defined for all parameters
Parameter Specification	— types of parameters must be specified — corresponding formal and actual parameters must be of the same type
Formal Array Parameters	— the dimensions of a formal array parameter must be specified in a program and determinable at translation time, but the determination of subscript ranges can be deferred until execution time

TABLE 2-8 STEELMAN REQUIREMENTS

INPUT-OUTPUT, FORMATTING, AND CONFIGURATION CONTROL

REQUIREMENTS   DESCRIPTION

Low Level Input-Output — there should be a few low level operations that send and receive control information of physical channels and devices

User Level Input-Output — the language design should give calling format and general semantics for a recommended set of user level input-output operations
— operations should be provided to work with sequential and random access files

Operating System Independence — the language should not require the presence of an operating system

Resource Control   — there should be low level operations to interrogate and control physical resources that are managed by built-in features of the language

Formatting   — there should be operations to convert between the symbolic and internal representation of all types that have literal forms in the language

TABLE 2-9 STEELMAN REQUIREMENTS

PARALLEL PROCESSING:
SUPPORT FOR REALTIME AND CONCURRENT PROCESSING

REQUIREMENTS   DESCRIPTION

Parallel Processing   — it should be possible to define parallel processes, each instance of which will have a name

Implementation	— the facility for parallel processing should be designed to minimize execution time and space
	— processes should have consistent semantics whether implemented on a single computer, a multiprocessor or multiple computers
Scheduling	— the built-in scheduling algorithm should be first-in-first-out within priorities
	— a process may modify its own priority
Real Time	— it should be possible to access a real time clock
	— in any control path it should be possible to delay until at least a specified time before continuing execution
Asynchronous Termination	— it should be possible to terminate another process.
Passing Data	— it should be possible to pass data between processes that do not share variables
	— it should be possible to delay such data passing until both the sender and receiver have requested the transfer
Signaling	— it should be possible to set a signal without waiting for it to be acknowledged as well as wait on the occurrence of a signal

TABLE 2-10 STEELMAN REQUIREMENTS

EXCEPTION HANDLING:
SUPPORT FOR ERROR DETECTION AND HANDLING

REQUIREMENTS	DESCRIPTION
Exception Handling Facility	— there should be an exception handling facilty to respond to error situations detected in

declarations, statement execution, or user defined error conditions

— exceptions should add to execution time only if they occur

Error Situations — a wide variety of typical error situations were identified

Raising Exceptions — there should be an operation for raising exceptions

— raising an exception should transfer control to an exception handler (rules for propagating exceptions were given as requirements)

Exception Handling — there should be a control structure for discriminating between exceptions that occur in a specified statement sequence

Assertions — it should be possible to include assertions into a program - *not fully achieved in language design*

Suppressing Exceptions — it should be possible to individually suppress the execution time detection of exceptions within a given scope

---

TABLE 2-11   STEELMAN REQUIREMENTS

REPRESENTATION AND OTHER TRANSLATION FACILITIES: USER LEVEL CONTROLS OVER EXECUTABLE CODE

REQUIREMENTS	DESCRIPTION
Data Representation	the language should permit but not require programs to specify a physical representation for the elements of a type which will have no effect on the logical properties of the data type

Translation Time Facilities — it should be possible to interrogate properties of data types, programs, and the operating environment from within a program

Interface to Other Languages — there should be a machine independent interface to other programming languages *not fully achieved in language design*

Optimization   — program must advise the translator, on an optional basis, on the criteria for optimization of either space or time

TABLE 2-12 STEELMAN REQUIREMENTS

TRANSLATION AND LIBRARY FACILITIES:
SUPPORT FOR LARGE-SCALE DEVELOPMENT

REQUIREMENTS	DESCRIPTION
Library	— there should be an easily accessible library of generic definitions and separately translated units — all predefined definitions should be in the library
Separately Translated Units	— it should be possible to build executable images from separately translated units within a library — it should be possible to export definitions from one separately translated unit to another
Generic Definitions	— a definition and instantiation facility for parameterized types, functions, procedures and encapsulations should be provided

TABLE 2-13 STEELMAN REQUIREMENTS

SUPPORT FOR THE LANGUAGE:
HOW THE LANGUAGE DEFINITION IS TO BE CONTROLLED

REQUIREMENTS	DESCRIPTION
Defining Documents	— the language should have a complete and unambiguous defining document - *not fully achieved in language design*
Standards	— there will be a standard definition — there will be procedures for certification of translators conformance to the standard
Completeness	— translators must implement the standard definition
Software Tools	— statements made in the requirement document indicated that software tools to support the development of Ada programs must be developed using a similar approach to that taken in the definition and design of the language.

In the course of designing a new language, the stated requirements are important, but equally important are the specific goals that the design team had in mind as they went through the design process. In Ada's design we are lucky that these design goals were actually written down in the Ada Language Reference Manual. The specific Ada design goals identified included:

- **Improve program reliability**
    - emphasis is on readability
    - the compiler should do as much checking as possible
    - use more "English-like" constructs
    - avoid error-prone constructs
    - enforce compiler checking even in the case of separate development

- **Simplify program maintenance**
  - — emphasis is on readability
  - — support a high degree of modularity that allows independent development and maintenance

- **Treat programming as a human activity**
  - — keep the language as simple as possible (Ada is based on a small set of easily understood concepts: data abstraction, information hiding, and strong typing)
  - — integrate concepts in a systematic and consistent manner
  - — use language features that are intuitive to the user of the language
  - — support the current decentralized and distributed nature of development and maintenance that exists today
  - — allow programs to be assembled from independently developed pieces
  - — allow people to approach problems in a new way
  - — build on features and concepts that encourage the use of sound software engineering practices.

- **Avoid inefficient features**
  - — make sure that every construct is implementable on the current generation of machines and using current technologies
  - — reject constructs that are excessively costly from an efficiency standpoint

- **Build on existing language features where possible**
  - — extensive review of existing language in common use
  - — extensive review of preliminary and three competitive language designs

- **Design for a specific application domain**
  - — embedded computer systems

As you can see, there is (and should be) an overlap between the STEELMAN requirements and the design team's stated goals. But, when taken in combination, you see that Ada is really based on a sound set of requirements and is designed with some specific goals in mind. This is unusual in our industry today. As I describe the features of the language in the upcoming sections, reflect back on the requirements and the goals in order to get a feeling for the motivation for the inclusion and format of the features. For background on individual features, I suggest that you review the *Rationale for the Design of the Ada Programming Language* [79]. This is a well written discussion of Ada features which focuses on the reasons for features instead of a description or specification of those features. Some care should be taken when reviewing the rationale document as well as any Ada document written before 1983. They typically covered early versions of Ada which have changed somewhat in the final 1983 standard.

An Introduction to Ada Features

Ada, as you will see in this chapter, is a feature-packed language. Some individuals even criticize it for being overly complex, due to this richness of features. Hopefully, after reading this chapter and appendix A, you will make up your own mind concerning the complexity of Ada. All this aside, we will begin the discussion of Ada features by first giving a quick rundown of the full set of features. A more in-depth coverage of the features can be found in appendix A. This rundown follows the form of the summary provided in the *Ada Language Reference Manual* but in a somewhat more compact arrangement. Boldface type is used to highlight the first occurence of a word or phrase that has a very specific meaning in Ada.

All **Ada programs** are composed of one or more **program units** that can be **compiled separately**. An Ada program can make use of language features that allow the construction of a program from a collection of **library program units** which may consist of user defined units, language predefined units and environment defined units. These library program units may include any combination of the following:

- **Subprograms (Functions or Procedures)** — define executable algorithms or **operators**.

- **Packages** — define collections of various program entities.

- **Tasks** — define potentially parallel computations.

- **Generics** — define parameterized forms of packages, procedures, and functions that act as templates.

Each of these program units consists of two parts:

- **Specification** — containing the information required by other program units to allow them to use that program unit.

- **Body** — containing the implementation details which are not visible to those using the program units.

The basic features of the various program units are:

- Subprograms express algorithms and come in two forms: procedures and functions.

- Subprograms may have **parameters** that allow information to be passed to/from the subprogram and the calling point.

- Procedures in general are used to express a series of actions.

- Functions are used to compute a value, as an operator would.

- Packages can be used to define a common pool of data or data types, a collection of related program units, or an abstract data type.

- Packages allow the writer of the package to specify what is to be **visible** to the user of a package and what is to be hidden.

- Tasks, which can execute in parallel, allow the programmer to express the natural concurrency in his application.

- Specifications and bodies can be compiled separately.

- The bodies of program units generally have two parts: a **declarative part,** which defines the entities that are used in the program unit, and an executable part, which defines the executing sequence of statements of the program unit.

- The body of a program unit can have an associated set of
  exception handlers that may be used for error condition
  recovery or other error handling requirements of the application.

The declarative part of a program unit associates names with the declared
entities that the program unit will use. These entities can include a data type, a
constant, a variable, a nested subprogram, a nested package unit, a nested task
unit or a generic unit.

The sequence of statements in the executable part of a program unit are
executed and are made up of any combination of the following statement
types:

- **Assignment** — sets the value of a variable to the computed value
  of an expression.

- **Procedure Call** — invokes the execution of a subprogram.

- **Case** — allows selection of the next sequence of statements to be
  determined by the value of an expression.

- **If** — allows selection of the next sequence of statements to be
  determined by a condition.

- **Loop** — specifies that a sequence of statements should repeatedly
  be executed while a condition exists or for a specified number of
  times.

- **Exit** — allows the unconditional or conditional exiting of a loop.

- **Block** — allows the introduction of local entities that apply only to
  the enclosed sequence of statements.

- **Raise** — generates a programmer-defined error condition (i.e., an
  exception).

Every object in Ada, either a **variable** or **constant**, has a **data type** that
specifies the allowed set of values for that object, as well as the allowed set of
operations that may be performed on or with those values. The data type
concept is refined to allow for **subtypes**, that further **constrain** the allowed
set of values of an object. Ada supports a wide range of data types including:

- **Integer types** — used for exact computations.

- **Floating point types** — used for computations requiring a large dynamic range and can live with a **relative error bound**.

- **Fixed point types** — like floating point but have an **absolute error bound**.

- **Enumeration types** — defines an ordered set of distinct values (i.e., enumeration **literals**).

- **Array types** — a composite structure of objects of a single other data type that is selected by indexing.

- **Record types** — a composite structure of objects of one or more data types, each of which is selected by its component name.

- **Access types** — allows the construction of linked list structure by designating other objects of another data type with a pointer.

- **Private types** — used to conceal the structural details of a data type that are externally irrelevant to its use in program units.

Relative to data types, Ada allows the programmer to specify various runtime characteristics of the data type such as address, number of bits, and memory layout through the use of **representation clauses**.

Ada does support Input-Output through the use of language defined packages that provide textual as well as binary formated disk, tape, and device I/O. Also supported is low level access to the underlying target machine devices if needed.

Appendix A focuses on further exposing you to the features of the language. The discussion is oriented more towards enlightening the current or future Ada user rather than teaching the beginner. The actual learning of the language is best done in a "hands-on" educational environment rather than in the restricted framework of a book like this. The discussion in appendix A will present each Ada feature or concept in a concise manner. Presented for each feature or concept is:

- A quick overview of the feature or concept

- A set of examples that illustrates the feature's proper usage.

Most features and concepts are described through the use of a collection of tables and figures that highlight the key aspects of the feature or concept being described. The examples included here were derived from the Ada Language Manual, several textbooks, and the course material from the U. S. Army's Ada Curriculum [3, 20, 45, 60, 64-70]. In addition, the examples are annotated with comments identifying usage information on a feature as well as potential pitfalls in usage.

The remainder of this chapter attempts to put all of the Ada features into a common perspective. The manner chosen to present this perspective is to provide a detailed comparison between Ada and other languages with which you might be familiar.

A Comparison of Ada and Other Popular Languages

This section provides a comparison between the features and characteristics of Ada and three other popular languages; Pascal, C and FORTRAN. The comparison is based on the work by J. V. Cugini of the National Bureau of Standards which analyzed many popular languages to provide guidance in the selection and use of such languages [19]. The evaluation criteria used covered a wide range of the aspects of general purpose languages. What we have done is to condense the comparison to a table, table 2-14, which provides a feature-by-feature comparison. To help in the interpretation of the meaning of a feature or characteristic, table 2-15 provides the relevant definitions. In table 2-14, we have used boldface type to indicate values of the evaluation factors that would be considered to shine a favorable light on a particular language relative to a specific characteristic.

Ada is a powerful, yet expressive language, which addresses a wide range of application needs. Ada is the most expressive of the general purpose languages we could pick for applications today and in the near future.

Ada by itself can be viewed as only one of the tools that practitioners need to attack and hopefully solve the Software Crisis. Ada encourages us to apply good Software Engineering principles as we develop new applications. Even with this, Ada by itself does not provide the complete set of tools. What we need in addition are sound engineering methodologies supported by good development environments in order to fully address the issues associated with the Software Crisis. Other chapters of this book will provide you with an insight into these other areas of the Ada Effort.

TABLE 2-14   COMPARISON OF ADA AND OTHER PROGRAMMING LANGUAGES

LANGUAGE FEATURES	ADA	C	FORTRAN	PASCAL
SYNTACTIC STYLE				
Free Format	**Yes**	**Yes**	No	**Yes**
Label Forms	**Name**	**Name**	Number	Number
Maximum Identifier Size	**Line Length**	8	6	**Line Length**
Undeclared Variables	**No**	**No**	Yes	**No**
Program Style Orientation	**Reader**	Writer	Writer	**Reader**
CONTROL OF EXECUTION				
Structured Programming	**Yes**	**Yes**	Partial	**Yes**
Blocks	**Yes**	**Yes**	No	**Yes**
Recursion	**Yes**	**Yes**	No	**Yes**
Generic Procedures	**Yes**	No	No	No
Exception/Error Handling	**Yes**	No	No	No
Concurrency	**Yes**	No	No	No
CONTROL OF DATA				
Automatic Variables	**Yes**	**Yes**	Yes	**Yes**
Static Variables	**No**	Yes	Yes	**No**

Language Features	ADA	C	FORTRAN	PASCAL
Array Initialization	Yes	No	Yes	No
Array Comparison	Yes	No	No	No
Records				
Records/Structures	Yes	Yes	No	Yes
Record Assignment	Yes	No	No	Yes
Record Comparison(equality)	Yes	No	No	No
Variable/Dynamic Format	Yes	No	No	Yes
Other Data Types				
Character	Yes	Yes	Yes	Yes
String	Yes	Yes	Yes	Yes
Logical/Boolean	Yes	Yes	Yes	Yes
Enumeration	Yes	No	No	Yes
Pointer	Yes	Yes	No	Yes
Sets	No	No	No	Yes
Internal Representation Control	Yes	No	No	No
I/O and Files				
Sequential Files	Yes	Yes	Yes	Yes
Direct Access Files	Yes	Yes	Yes	No

LANGUAGE FEATURES	ADA	C	FORTRAN	PASCAL
User Allocated Variables	Yes	Yes	No	Yes
Register Variables	No	Yes	No	No
External Data	Yes	Yes	Yes	No
User Defined Types	Yes	Yes	No	Yes
Type Checking	Yes	No	No	Yes
User Defined Operators	Yes	No	No	No
Degree of Flexibility	High	Moderate	Low	Moderate

NUMERIC DATA

	ADA	C	FORTRAN	PASCAL
Integer	Yes	Yes	Yes	Yes
Floating Point	Yes	Yes	Yes	Yes
Fixed Point	Yes	No	No	No
Complex	No	No	Yes	No
Basic Operators	Yes	Yes	Yes	Yes
Numeric Functions	Few	None	Many	Some
Numeric Libraries	Few	Some	Many	Some

ARRAYS

	ADA	C	FORTRAN	PASCAL
Dimensions	Unlimited	Unlimited	7	Unlimited
Subscript Type	Discrete	Integer	Integer	Discrete
User Defined Lower Bounds	Yes	No	Yes	Yes
Array Assignment	Yes	No	No	Yes

LANGUAGE FEATURES	ADA	C	FORTRAN	PASCAL
OTHER FACTORS (DEGREE OF SUPPORT)				
Low Level I/O	**Yes**	No	No	No
APPLICATION DOMAIN (DEGREE OF SUPPORT)				
Business	Low	Low	Low	Low
Math/Science	Moderate	Low	**High**	Moderate
Operating Systems	**High**	**High**	Low	Low
Real Time	**High**	Low	Low	Low
Education	Moderate	Low	Moderate	**High**
Team Developments	**High**	Low	Low	Low
Reliability	**High**	Low	Low	Moderate
Portability	**High**	Moderate	**High**	**High**
Execution Efficiency	Moderate	**High**	**High**	Moderate
Large Program Developments	**High**	Moderate	Low	Low

TABLE 2-15 COMPARISON CATEGORIES

SYNTACTIC STYLE

Free Format
— Does the language allow the placement of source text freely in the source image?

Label Forms
— What notation is used for statement labels?

Maximum Identifier Size
— Are the names used within a program limited to a specific number of characters?

Undeclared Variables
— Does the language allow undeclared variables?

Program Style Orientation
— Is the basic style of the language oriented towards making the source code more readable or writable?

CONTROL OF EXECUTION

Structured Programming
— Does the language support the "structured programming" control constructs?

Blocks
— Does the language allow you to mark off sections of code that are treated as a single statement?

Recursion
— Does the language support the ability of a procedure or function to call itself?

Generic Procedures
— Does the language provide a mechanism so that procedures can be written in a manner such that multiple copies of the code can be created, each varying by a set of parameters?

Exception/Error Handling
— Does the language have the ability to have control transferred to special section of code to handle anomalous conditions that result during program execution?

Concurrency
— Can the language be used to express multiple asynchronous threads of control?

Numeric Libraries — How many off-the-shelf libraries of numerical routines are available?

<u>ARRAYS</u>

Dimensions — How many array dimensions are supported?
Subscript Type — What data types can be used as array subscripts?
User Defined Lower Bounds — Can the programmer specify the lower bounds for a subscript?
Array Assignment — Is the whole array assignment provided?
Array Initialization — Can the programmer initialize the value of an array with a single expression?
Array Comparison — Can two arrays be compared for equality and inequality in a single expression?

<u>RECORDS</u>

Records/Structures — Does the language provide for the creation of data structures with multiple components which do not all have to be of the same data type?
Record Assignment — Is whole record assignment provided?
Record Comparison(equality) — Can two records be compared in a single expression?
Variable/Dynamic Format — Does the language allow the format of a record to vary during execution?

<u>OTHER DATA TYPES</u>

Character
String — What other data typing facilities are available?
Logical/Boolean

Automatic Variables — Are new copies of local variables within procedures and functions generated on each call to the procedure or function?

Static Variables — Does the language allow the variables to maintain the same value between calls to a procedure or a function?

Use Allocated Variables — Does the language support pointers?

Register Variables — Does the language allow the programmer to indicate the variables that should be maintained in registers?

External Data — Does the language allow the programmer to create global data that is sharable between multiple procedures or functions?

User Defined Types — Does the language allow the definition of new abstract data types?

Type Checking — Are data type characteristics checked during execution to insure proper usage?

User Defined Operators — Can the programmer reuse the operator symbols when writing functions on new data types?

Degree of Flexiblity — How flexible are the data declaration facilities of the language?

Integer — What predefined data types are provided?

Floating Point

Fixed Point

Complex

Basic Operators — Are all the normal expected operators provided for the predefined data types?

Numeric Functions — How many numeric functions above and beyond the basic ones are provided?

Enumeration

Pointer

Sets

Internal Representation Control — Can the programmer force the mapping of the data items to a particular underlying machine representation?

I/O AND FILES

Sequential Files — Does the language provide access to sequential files, the moral equivalent of tape?

Direct Access Files — Does the language provide access to random access disk files?

Low Level I/O — Can the programmer directly access low level hardware interfaces?

APPLICATION DOMAIN (DEGREE OF SUPPORT)

Business — What application areas is the language useful for?

Math/Science

Operating Systems

Real Time

Education

OTHER FACTORS (DEGREE OF SUPPORT)

Team Developments — To what degree does the language directly support a team oriented development strategy?

Reliability — To what degree does the language provide features that are aimed at making programs more reliable?

Portability — To what degree does the language provide features that are aimed at making programs easier to move from one machine to another?

Execution Efficiency — How efficient relative to assembly language is the executable code?

Large Program Developments — To what degree does the language provide features that are aimed at supporting very large applications?

3. ADA ENVIRONMENTS

As described in Chapter 1, the Ada Effort can be characterized as more than just a language development. It also encouraged the development of software engineering methodologies as well as the development of programming support and software engineering environments. This chapter highlights several of the critical aspects of Ada oriented environments that would be of concern to a software engineering practitioner. The specific aspects to be covered include:

- The general characteristics of an Ada oriented environment

- The primary categories of Ada oriented environments

- Guidelines for selecting an Ada oriented environment

Before we get into the characteristics of an Ada oriented environment, one should have a clear definition of what is meant by an environment, when used in the context of software development and maintenance. There are several good working definitions of an Ada oriented environment in the literature, but the one we will use here is:

> *An Ada Environment is the set of methods, techniques, procedures, tools, and equipment needed to develop, maintain and evolve Ada application software over the full lifetime of that software.*

Note that the scope of this definition is larger than one would traditionally use for a programming support environment. This broader definition is important to consider, not because such an environment can be bought off the shelf today, but because we must consider the consequences of any compromises we make in establishing a workable environment today.

As highlighted in Chapter 1, the DoD has been the prime mover in the definition of what a near-term Ada oriented environment should be. In their definition process, the emphasis was placed on specifying and some day requiring that all DoD sponsored software be developed and maintained on an Ada Programming Support Environment (APSE). The requirements for such an environment were spelled out in "STONEMAN" Requirements for Ada Programming Support Environments [59]. This document provided a model for discussing the requirements as well as stating the individual requirements for each element of the model. It is this basic model that we use in this discussion of the aspects of environments of concern to the practitioner using Ada.

A Model for Ada Environments

In order to view environments, we must have some form of model for a general environment in mind. This model would be used whenever we are trying to understand a single environment or compare several different environments. To aid in your understanding, we are going to introduce a model that represents many of the common features of an Ada programming environment. The model proposed is based on models found in the literature [59, 75], although some liberties have been taken with them.

The model we proposed is a layered model (see figure 3-1) which builds on the model in STONEMAN, but allows us to look at an environment from a static as well as a dynamic viewpoint. From a user's perspective, an environment could be looked at as a layered structure that consists of the following four layers:

Command Language Layer: the primary interface between the environment and the user. It is only through this interface that he or she perceives and uses the capabilities of the environment.

Toolset Layer: the set of tools which provides the user with the capabilities to create and maintain Ada application software. Access

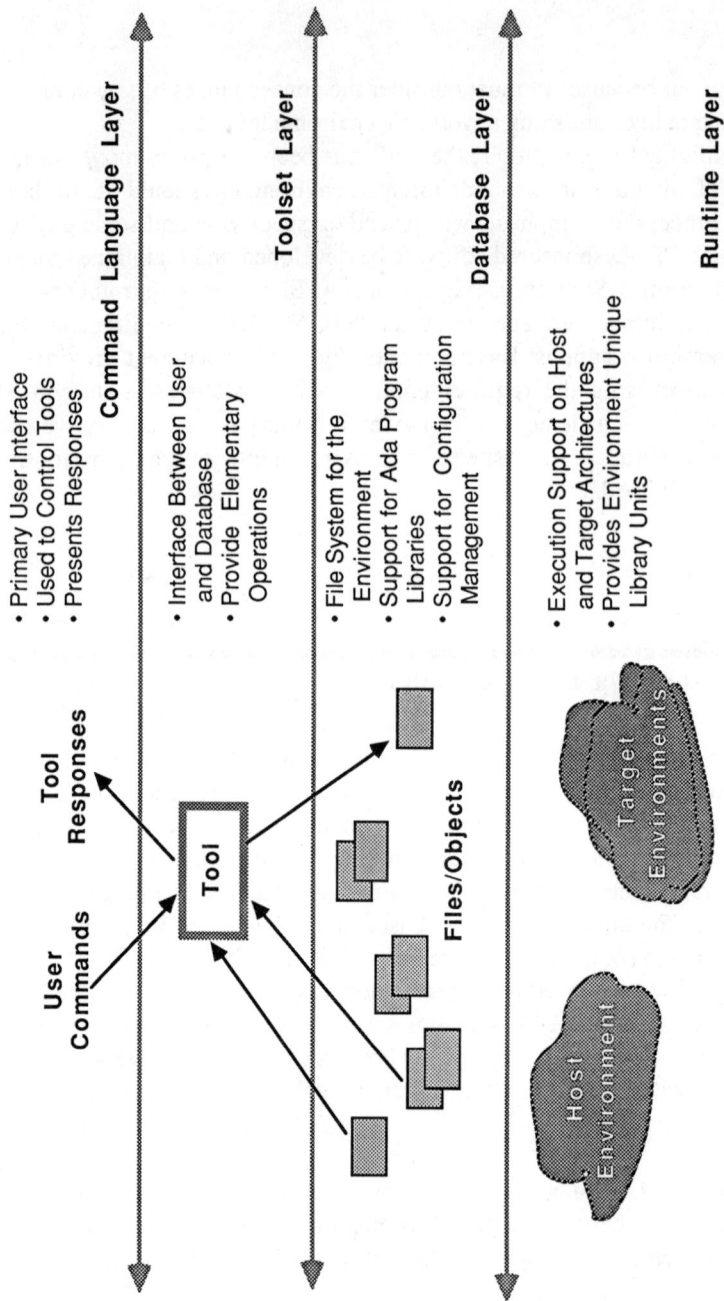

Command Language Layer

- Primary User Interface
- Used to Control Tools
- Presents Responses

Toolset Layer

- Interface Between User and Database
- Provide Elementary Operations

- File System for the Environment
- Support for Ada Program Libraries
- Support for Configuration Management

Database Layer

- Execution Support on Host and Target Architectures
- Provides Environment Unique Library Units

Runtime Layer

User Commands

Tool Responses

Tool

Files/Objects

Target Environments

Host Environment

Figure 3-1   An Ada Oriented Environment Model

to these tools is only through the interface provided by the Command Language Layer

Database Layer: the repository of the information that must be maintained in order to create an Ada application. It could be as simple as a flat file system or as complex as a fully relational database management system.

Runtime Layer: the actual execution environment that runs the application code.

Figure 3-2 indicates the use of the model to describe a scenario using an existing Ada environment, the Ada Language System (ALS) [42, 75]. The scenario is a change to an Ada package body that requires no recompilation of a dependent unit. In addition, it shows the execution of the resulting object code on the machine on which the code was developed.

Three primary categories of environments seem to be in use today. These are:

Integrated: an environment which supports a full set of tools and database features so that all of the tools work together in a well defined manner with no user-perceived interface problems

Toolkit: an environment made up of a set of well defined tools that may not use a common database, but on the whole can be used with a minimum of tool interface problems

Collection of Tools: an environment that is made up of a collection of tools which share minimal commonality, thus introducing considerable interfacing problems.

In one sense, these categories of environments could be looked at as discrete points on a line. This line represents the degree to which the user can perceive interface problems associated with the use of an environment. For instance, we would expect that an integrated environment would make the process of compiling, linking, and downloading to the target machine a sequence of operations, each of which could be executed with a single command. In the case of a Collection of Tool environment, we would expect that the user would have to compile, then run an independent tool which translates the object file to some other format. This other format is what the

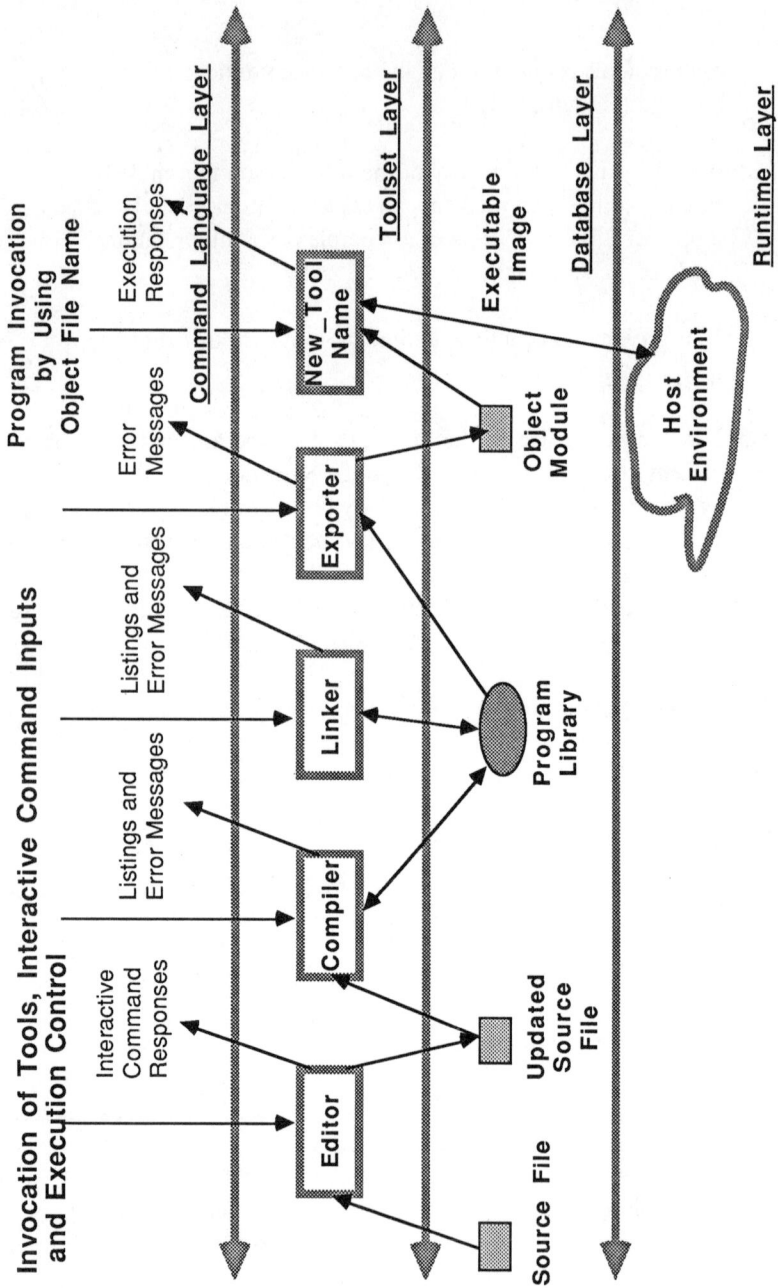

Invocation of Tools, Interactive Command Inputs and Execution Control

Program Invocation by Using Object File Name

Execution Responses

Command Language Layer

Error Messages

Listings and Error Messages

Listings and Error Messages

Interactive Command Responses

Toolset Layer

New_Tool Name

Exporter

Linker

Compiler

Editor

Executable Image

Object Module

Program Library

Updated Source File

Source File

Database Layer

Host Environment

Runtime Layer

Figure 3-2   Sample Operational Scenario

linker is expecting. The linker output would, in turn, have to be further translated in order to download an executable image to the target machine.

The categories of environments identified above are fairly general and in some sense are meant to be the first criteria used, when selecting an Ada oriented environment. Based on your organization's goals, budget constraints, and level of prior investment in environments, you are going to look only at a limited number of environments and in a lot of cases only environments within a certain category. Once you have restricted your selection in this manner, then you are ready to make a selection or just evaluate a single environment for use in your organization. The remainder of this chapter provides you with a set of questions that can be of help in addressing the full range of issues an organization should consider in making an environment selection.

Guidelines for Selecting an Environment

One of the problems facing practitioners in our field is the selection of the development and support environment for a project or an organization. Many constraints are placed on the practitioner which prevent him or her from making the "right" selection. These constraints come in many forms and from many directions at once. These may consist of some of the following:

- Limited budgets

- Must run on existing hardware and operating system

- Selection must be made immediately

- General guidance for selecting an environment is not readily available

No book is going to help you with the first two constraints, but the last two can be at least partly addressed by a set of well formulated guidelines which you can customize for your purposes. It is with this in mind that we have included in this chapter a set of guidelines for the selection of an Ada oriented environment. The guidelines that are provided are a compilation of guidelines found in the literature [18, 35, 47].

The framework used in these guidelines is built on the models developed earlier in this chapter with one addition which will cover the non-technical aspects of environment selection. This framework breaks the guidelines into five major groupings that include:

- Command Language Guidelines

- Toolset Guidelines

- Database Guidelines

- Runtime Guidelines

- Other Selection Criteria

The guidelines below have been organized into these groups. To help put each group of guidelines into perspective, we have included the relevant requirements from STONEMAN as a preface to the actual guidelines. Most of the Guidelines are derived from the Evaluation Criteria/Questionnaire for Ada Compilers and the Ada-Europe Guidelines for Ada Compiler Specification and Selection [18, 35].

Command Language Guidelines

The following STONEMAN derived requirements apply to the Command Language Layer:

- Use uniform protocols and conventions when providing communications between users and tools

- Provide an Ada-like command language

Table 3-1 lists the questions that can be used to establish a selection criteria which is considered appropriate for the command language layer.

TABLE 3-1 COMMAND LANGUAGE SELECTION GUIDELINES

---

1. Does the command language for the environment address the requirements specified in STONEMAN as summarized above?

2. What is the maximum number of users who can invoke the compiler simultaneously without degrading the performance of interactive editing and other operations? Note that you must determine what level of degradation is acceptable.

3. Can tools be invoked interactively, in batch mode and through command language scripts?

4. Is background execution of tools supported? How is it supported?

5. How accurately are error messages positioned to where they occur, in compilation and in the execution of other tools?

6. How clear are the error messages?

7. Can the user control the level of error conditions that will cause a compilation to abort?

8. What classes of messages are produced by the primary tools in the environment?

9. What documentation is provided to the user and is it available on-line?

Toolset Guidelines

The following STONEMAN-derived requirements apply to the Toolset Layer:

- Must support the development of Ada Programs, in particular separate compilation

- Write tools for portability; use Ada wherever possible

- Provide uniform error handling

- Provide comprehensive "help" facilities

- Provide the following tools as a minimum:

  — text editor
  — prettyprinter
  — language translator(s)
  — linkers
  — loaders
  — set/use analyzers
  — control flow static analyzers
  — dynamic analyzers
  — file administrator
  — configuration manager

The Toolset selection guidelines, provided in table 3-2, are primarily in the form of questions that one should ask during the selection process. Most of the guidelines here are oriented towards the selection of an Ada compiler which to most of us is the biggest unknown when we are selecting a development environment.

TABLE 3-2   **Toolset Selection Guidelines**

---

1. Does the environment provide sufficient coverage of the toolset layer requirements from STONEMAN as stated above?

2. What are the host/ target pairs supported by the environment?

3. Are multiple languages handled in an integrated manner?

4. What object code formats are supported?

5. Is sufficient version and history information maintained or listed with compilations to allow recreation of any object code from source files (assuming they still exist)?

6. What compiler options are allowed?

7. Can the user control listing formats? Examples of formats would include:

   — source text
   — prettyprinted source text
   — cross references
   — suppression of private part of packages
   — machine/assembly code

8. Is the compiler intermediate language, if generated, and other compiler/linker generated information available with sufficient documentation to allow new tools to use it?

9. Can source text be recreated from the outputs of the compiler, linker, and/or loader?

10. Are all defined Pragma properly handled?

11. What is the time for error detection and recovery?

12. Under what error conditions will the tools produce executable object code?

13. What target independent optimizations are performed and what is the expected impact of each class of optimization on code size and execution times?

14. What control does the user have over optimization?

15. What is the compilation speed for

   — syntax checking only,
   — front-end syntax and semantic checking only, and
   — full compiles with object code generation?

16.   What is the speed of listing generation?

17.   What is the maximum number of

—   errors detectable on a single line or compilation unit,
—   source lines in a single compilation unit,
—   compilation units allowed in a single file or database,
—   object,
—   symbols allowed per compilation unit,
—   literals allowed in an enumeration type,
—   operands in an expression,
—   withed units,
—   tasks that can be in existence, and
—   tasks that can be activated for a single program?

19.   What is the maximum length of a source line?

20.   What compiler features would be considered above and beyond that which is specified in the LRM?

Database Guidelines

The following STONEMAN derived requirements apply to the Database Layer:

- Act as the central repository of all information associated with a project throughout the project life cycle

- Offer a flexible storage facility for all tools

- Access to every object, a separately identifiable collection of information, by its distinct name

- Permit the creation and maintenance of relationships between objects

- Permit the user to designate several database objects as forming a "version group" with the ability to designate a preferred version, access the entire group, and access a single version within that group

- Provide a mechanism by which all objects needed to recreate a specified object will continue to be maintained as long as the specified object itself remains in the database

- Provide the ability to create partitions within the database and associate general access controls to them

- Provide direct support for the Ada Program Library

- Provide access controls to the object level commensurate with supporting a project team through the lifetime of a project

- Allow management information reports to be generated from the information stored in the database

- Provide for long-term archiving of objects

- Preserve the consistency of the information and relationships contained in the database

- Provide attributes on every object that record the manner in which an object was produced

- Use attributes to categorize objects and define the access rights to each object

Table 3-3 lists the questions that can be used to establish a selection criteria which is considered appropriate for the database layer [36].

TABLE 3-3 DATABASE SELECTION GUIDELINES

1. Does the environment provide sufficient coverage of the Database layer requirements from STONEMAN as stated above?

2. Does abnormal termination of any tools that manipulate a program library leave the program library in an inconsistent state?

3. What safeguards are implemented for protection and recovery of the database from user, tool, and/or system equipment introduced failures?

Runtime Guidelines

The following STONEMAN derived requirements apply to the Target Runtime Sublayer:

- Source level testing and debugging on the host and target shall be done with equivalent facilities.

- Provide a virtual interface to the host's operating system on which all inter-tool communication and the database layer are built on to aid in portability of the APSE to various host machine configurations.

Table 3-4 lists the questions that can be used to establish a selection criteria which is considered appropriate for the runtime sublayer.

TABLE 3-4   RUNTIME SELECTION GUIDELINES

1. Does the environment support the STONEMAN requirements as stated above?

2. Are there any restrictions on unchecked conversions or deallocation?

3. Does the compiler, as an option, generate automatic traceback of the execution of statements, procedures, or other program units?

4. Are efficient parameter passing and calling conventions utilized?

5. Will the compiler as an option generate debug code that tracks variable changes and produces time/frequency statistics?

6. What are the restrictions on the use of representation specifications?

7. How is the performance of the executable code impacted by

    — use of select alternatives,
    — idle tasks,
    — the ordering of entry clauses in a select statement,
    — number and size of tasks,
    — size and type of parameters passed, and
    — number of select alternatives?

8. Can the Ada scheduler or dispatcher starve a task?

9. What is the minimum size of the runtime system? Are optional runtime system configurations supported?

10. What effect does optimization have on execution time?

11. What performance comparisons of Ada programs vs. other languages exist for this environment?

12. What is the maximum precision supported by the environment?

13. What is the demonstrated performance of the host and/or target configurations supported? Note: use the benchmarking approach identified in the next section as a guide for selection of appropriate benchmarks.

14. Are hardware dependencies clearly identified in the documentation?

15. What is the assumed memory model for the host and/or target configurations?

16. Does the environment support distributed or multiprocessor targets?

17. Under what conditions are NUMERIC_ERROR, PROGRAM_ERROR, and STORAGE_ERROR raised?

Other Selection Criteria

The following STONEMAN principles were meant to provide guidance to the developers of Ada Programming Support Environments:

- The structure of an APSE should be based on a few simple concepts, to ease understanding and encourage use.

- An APSE should support all project personnel through the entire software life cycle.

- Both system and project portability should be provided to the maximum extent possible.

- An APSE should facilitate the development and integration of new tools as well as the improvement and updating of existing tools.

The list of questions in table 3-5 are meant to provide additional criteria to aid you in the selection of an Ada oriented environment. These questions may be the determining factor as to which environment you use, since these questions are typically asked by those individuals who control the purse strings. As we all know, those who holds the purse strings often have the last (and sometimes the only) word in the selection process.

TABLE 3-5   OTHER SELECTION CRITERIA GUIDELINES

1. To what level does the environment address the general goals identified in STONEMAN as summarized above?

2. Have there been any major software developments that have used the environment? Note: get references that can be checked.

3. What is the configuration management plan for the environment and who is responsible for its implementation?

4.   How are user trouble reports for the system, tools and documentation handled and resolved?

5.   What is the cost of acquiring the environment? Does the cost include

— installation,
— maintenance support,
— update services,
— multiple CPUs or sites,
— licensing fees, and
— hot-line services?

6.   Are design specifications and requirements documents available?

7.   Is an LRM appendix F included in the documentation and are all implementation dependent features properly documented?

8.   Are there any proprietary restrictions on the environments and user developed tools that make use of environment features?

9.   Is source code available for tools, interfaces, etc?

10.   What test procedures are available to validate installation initially and after each version or update installation?

11.   How are updates and releases handled and what requirements on updating exist in order to be considered within the scope of the maintenance agreement?

12.   Does the validation test report indicate any implementation limitations inconsistent with your proposed application?

Using Benchmarking in the Selection Process

Several of the selection criteria above require that some level of performance assessment be done in order to determine if the environment will meet your real requirements. Depending on what you are interested in, this performance assessment can be accomplished using one or more of the following techniques:

— Benchmarking
— Simulation
— Analytic Modeling

Of primary interest here is the use of benchmarking, since it is the most universally accepted and misused approach to performance assessment. In addition, there is a wealth of benchmarks that one can build on.

Within the context of this book, benchmarking is the process of running specific tests that exercise a single feature or mix of features of a programming language, an operating system, a hardware configuration, or some combination of the three. The tests themselves are called benchmarks, some of which do "useful" processing, while a majority of them are contrived programs optimized for the purpose of the test, but do no real "useful" processing.

A typical benchmark will be oriented towards measuring the time duration of a section of processing and will often use the internal timing capabilities of the system under test to measure the performance of the system. Repeated execution of the benchmark code and averaging of the execution times measured is often done. This is to eliminate variations inherent in the use of the system's timers which measure the performance of the system itself.

Benchmarking can be used to assist in language, implementation, operating system, and/or processor selection by allowing a feature-by-feature comparison to be made between competing languages, implementations, operating systems, and/or processors. Benchmarking can also be used to evaluate the best language (operating system, etc.) for a certain class of applications such as those that are I/O, string manipulation, or number crunching intensive.

When one considers the use of benchmarking to assess performance of an Ada implementation, you must carefully select the framework in which the assessment will take place. This framework is important since it provides a set of reference points from which you can classify the various benchmarks that will be used in the performance assessment. The framework used here is a conceptual model that represents an Ada implemented system as an eight layer structure in which each layer provides a set of basic services used by higher layers. This conceptual model is very much like communication protocol layers, but not used as formally as they are. The conceptual model is useful since it provides a way of classifying benchmarks.

Benchmarks can be classified by the layer or layers they exercise. Such a classification provides insight into the degree of coverage (i.e., how many layers are exercised and to what degree they are exercised) that one can expect from a particular set of benchmarks.

The conceptual model used here includes the following layers (highest to lowest) [74]:

1.   **System Design Layer**: the highest layer which is concerned with issues such as man-machine interface, allocation of functionality to subsystems, etc. This layer is typically not exercised by benchmarks.

2.   **Application Architectural Layer**: this layer deals with the real world application at hand and is the most important layer. It is interesting that this is often the only layer which the user of an Ada implementation has any control over since it is usually the only place where the users are allowed to make performance trade-offs or adjustments. The factors that affect performance at this layer can include:

     — Partitioning of the application into tasks
     — Design technique used
     — Algorithm design
     — Data vs. program text tradeoffs

The benchmarks for this layer are typically an instrumented prototype of the real application with actual processing often replaced with a workload that only wastes time.

3.   **Compilation Layer** — this layer includes the following performance determining factors which are often overlooked in typical benchmarking:

     — Level of optimization
     — Memory model assumed by the compiler/linker
     — Generated code efficiency

This layer is often completely hidden from the application developer. It is something he/she has no control over. Benchmarking targeted at this layer is often used to identify inefficient language features that one should avoid in a particular implementation.

4. **Ada Language Feature Layer** — this layer includes the set of features that this particular application makes use of. This layer includes such performance determining factors as:

— Basic statement execution times
— Task activation times
— Procedure overhead
— Elaboration times

A majority of the benchmarks found in the literature are oriented towards this layer.

5. **Runtime Environment Layer** — this layer includes features found in the runtime environment and in the operating system on which the runtime environment is implemented. This layer includes the following performance determining factors:

— Context switching time
— Procedure calling overhead
— Memory management
— Nature of the environment (distributed, multiprocessor, etc)
— Buffer sizes
— Disk caching
— Scheduling algorithms

This layer can have a major affect on the performance of an Ada implemented system. It is also the one in which we as developers have little or no insight since the Ada language designers and the compiler writers have hidden these factors from us.

6. **Processing System Architecture Layer** — this layer is intended to represent the interconnection of hardware elements that make up the machine on which the software application will run. The performance determining factors for this layer include:

— Number of processors

— Processing support functions (floating point units, memory management units, etc.)
— Memory bus bandwidth
— Memory hierarchy
— I/O bandwidths

7. **Instruction Set Layer** — this layer consists primarily of the instruction set of the processor or processors that make up the processing elements of the system. Included in this layer are such performance determining factors as:

— Instruction execution times
— Address determination times
— The match between the instruction set and the programming language

The way the performance of this layer is determined is through the use of an instruction mix for the application. This works well for COBOL and FOR-TRAN applications written for existing machines since we have a large volume of compilations we can analyze. This is not true for Ada applications today. Using existing data and extrapolating it for an Ada implemented system is downright dangerous, since the results would be highly questionable due to lack of a significant experience with Ada.

8. **Hardware Design Layer** — this is the lowest layer in which all of the other layers are built. The performance determining factors in this layer include:

— Hardware device technology (ECL, STTL, CMOS, NMOS, etc.)
— Number of bits in the processor data/address paths
— Number of hardware registers
— Basic processor clock rate
— Memory access times

With such a framework established, it should be apparent that the assessment of the performance of an Ada implemented application is not a simple process of running a single benchmark program or determining what the clock rate of the CPU is. It is a process that must be undertaken with the same care one undertakes in designing an application. One must understand what is being measured, how it is being measured and what factors are interacting when the measurements are made. If one does not understand this, then the results of the performance assessment are questionable at best. The danger lies not in the production of inaccurate results; it is in the fact that others latch onto performance figures and use them out of the framework in which they are valid. This typically raises havoc within a project's organization and industry as a whole. Just look in any computer journal over the last five years and you will see a continuous debate going on about the performance of the XYZ processor vs. the ABC processor based on data the measurements of which were made in a context long since lost.

All this discussion is leading somewhere. The reason for concern about a model is that we needed a framework in which to put the various benchmarks that appeared in the literature. By placing the benchmarks within this framework, we hope to help you select a set of benchmarks which will be useful to you in the assessment of the performance of an Ada implementation. The referenced benchmarks are available through the Ada Information Clearinghouse (see chapter 5). Included with each of these referenced benchmarks is a brief description of the benchmark, identification of its source, and the model layers it is primarily oriented towards [50]:

TABLE 3-6 SUMMARY OF ADA ORIENTED BENCHMARKS

Name: ACKERMAN.ADA   **Source:** Ada Fair 1984
Applicable Layers: 4 and 5
Feature or Aspect Measured: calling overhead

Description: Ackerman's function is used to measure procedure calling overhead. The function is recursive which includes testing for zero as well as incrementing and decrementing of integers.

Name: BOOLVEC.ADA   **Source:** Ada Fair 1984
Applicable Layers: 4 and 7
Feature or Aspect Measured: logical operation times

Description: Measures the time for the "and" operation on a boolean vector.

Name: CHAR_DIR.ADA   **Source:** Ada Fair 1984
Applicable Layers: 5
Feature or Aspect Measured: direct I/O file operation times

Description: Measures the time required to perform various file operations
using the Direct_IO package with Characters.

Name: CHAR_ENUM.ADA   **Source:** Ada Fair 1984
Applicable Layers: 5
Feature or Aspect Measured: enumeration I/O times

Description: Measures the time required to perform various file operations
using the Text_IO and Enumeration_IO packages.

Name: CHAR_TEXT.ADA   **Source:** Ada Fair 1984
Applicable Layers: 5
Feature or Aspect Measured: Text_IO file I/O times

Description: Measures the time required to perform various file operations
using the Text_IO package with Characters.

Name: CONPROD.ADA   **Source:** Ada Fair 1984
Applicable Layers: 4 and 5
Feature or Aspect Measured: task performance

Description: Measures tasking performance using the buffering task example
in chapter 9.12 of the Ada Language Reference Manual. Both a producer
and consumer task are used, as well as Text_IO to Standard Input and
Output.

Name: FLOATVEC.ADA   **Source:** Ada Fair 1984
Applicable Layers: 4 and 7
Feature or Aspect Measured: floating point operation times

Description: Measures the time required for adding the elements of a large
floating point vector.

Name: FRIEND.ADA   **Source:** Ada Fair 1984
Applicable Layers: 3
Feature or Aspect Measured: compilation warnings

Description: Determines how friendly the Ada compiler is with regard to warning about the use of uninitialized objects, exceptions which will always be raised, and warnings about code that should have been removed by optimization.

Name: INTVEC.ADA   **Source:** Ada Fair 1984
Applicable Layers: 4 and 7
Feature or Aspect Measured: simple operation time

Description: Measures the time required for adding the elements of a large integer vector.

Name: PROCCAL.ADA   **Source:** Ada Fair 1984
Applicable Layers: 4 and 5
Feature or Aspect Measured: procedure calling overhead

Description: Measures the time required for simple procedure calls with scalar parameters.

Name: QSORTPAR.ADA   **Source:** Ada Fair 1984
Applicable Layers: 2, 4 and 5
Feature or Aspect Measured: tasking timing

Description: A tasking implementation of a Quicksort algorithm, used primarily to compare a traditional sequential implementation with the tasking implementation. Up to fourteen tasks can be created in the process of implementing the sort.

Name: QSORTSEQ.ADA   **Source:** Ada Fair 1984
Applicable Layers: 2, 4 and 5
Feature or Aspect Measured: used for comparison with QSORTPAR

Description: Traditional implementation of a Quicksort algorithm.

Name: RENDEZ.ADA   **Source:** Ada Fair 1984
Applicable Layers: 4 and 5
Feature or Aspect Measured: simple rendezvous timing

Description: Measures the time required for a simple rendezvous.

Name: JUGGLING   **Source:** Ada Validation Office
Applicable Layers: 2, 4 and 5
Feature or Aspect Measured: task timing

Description: A multiple subunit program that exercises the following Ada
features: tasking, selective waits, families of entries, exceptions, subunits,
and separate compilations.

Name: IO_TEST   **Source:** Ada Validation Office
Applicable Layers: 2, 4, 5 and 6
Feature or Aspect Measured: I/O capabilities of Ada System

Description: Exercises both the Sequential_IO and Direct_IO capabilities of
an implementation.

Name: DHRYSTONE   **Source:**   Communications of the ACM,
                                              October 1984,
                                              Volume 27,Number 10,
                                              pages 1013-1030.
Applicable Layers: 4
Feature or Aspect Measured: statement mix timing

Description: A statement mix that is representative of higher level
programming languages, includes:
- •53% assignments
- •32% control statements
- •15% procedure, function calls

100 statements are executed and balanced with respect to statement type,
operand type, and type of access (global vs. local vs. constant).

These benchmarks are considered representative of those generally available from the literature. As with any benchmarks, before you use these, make
sure you understand what is being measured, how it is being measured, and
under what conditions the results will be useful.

4. ADA POLICIES
AND RELATED STANDARDS

This chapter focuses on the major policies and standards that affect what Ada is, who is required to use it, and how one knows it's Ada when one buys it. The primary areas that will be covered are the Ada language standard, DoD directives, and DoD policies. The rationale for covering these areas is that many practitioners will be required to use Ada in the future due to policies and standards that currently exist, but have not been well described or have potentially been misrepresented before. In addition, several of the standards and policies directly affect the definition of the language as well as the testing a compiler must go through in order to be considered an implementation of Ada. From the discussion in this chapter hopefully you will understand what is required by an Ada implementation and, more importantly, what is not.

Much of the discussion in this chapter is involved with DoD policies and standards which, to some individuals, may not be directly relevant. For these individuals, the important aspects of this chapter are the discussion of the language standard, validation policy, and trademark policy.

Language Definition Standard

It should be apparent by now that Ada came out of a DoD sponsored definition and development effort. But what may not be apparent is the fact that the DoD has standardized the language by documenting its definition in the form of a military standard. This standard, the *Reference Manual for the Ada Programming Language ANSI/MIL-STD-1815A,* dated January 1983, is the single definition of the programming language. No dialects, subsets, or supersets of the language can bear the name Ada in the United States.

The stated scope of the standard is to specify the form and meaning of program units written in Ada with the primary purpose being to promote the portability of Ada programs to a variety of systems. The language standard, often called the Language Reference Manual (LRM) specifies, in fourteen chapters, three annexes, and three appendices :

- The form of a program unit.

- The effect of translating a program unit.

- The effect of executing a program unit.

- The ways in which program units can be combined to form Ada programs.

- The predefined program units which an implementation must provide.

- The allowed variations within the definition of the language.

- How an implementation must document such variations.

- What violations to the standard an implementation must detect.

- The effect at translation and/or execution time of these violations.

- What violations to the standard an implementation need not detect.

This list is interesting, but what is even more interesting is what the LRM does not specify:

- The means by which a program unit is translated into an executable image.

- The means by which execution is invoked or controlled.

- The form and contents of various program listings.

- The effect of executing programs that have violations in them which an implementation is not required to detect.

- The size of the object code generated by an implementation.

- The execution speed of that object code.

- The relative execution time of language features.

The last three items are the most interesting, since they state that an implementation of Ada can conform to the standard, but may not be useful in real applications. Several of the earliest implementations of the Ada standard were actually useless for anything but the smallest of test cases, at least from the practitioner's standpoint. The concern is not whether the standard should or should not have specified the performance aspects of an implementation, but that the users of an implementation should approach the selection of an Ada implementation with care. Conformance with the standard is not sufficient grounds to select an implementation.

MIL-STD-1815A also has been accepted by the American National Standards Institute (ANSI) as a standard. This combined standard has been sent to the International Standards Organization (ISO) for the establishment of Ada as an International standard. This standardization effort continued until September of 1984, when an ISO subcommittee voted to make the LRM a Draft Proposed standard, getting it one step closer to international standardization.

A side effect associated with the definition of Ada as a standard is that it forced the Language Reference Manual to be written in the manner in which most military standards are: as a "legal" document which makes it unusable as a learning vehicle.The LRM is a well written reference document oriented towards concisely defining the language which is vital to you if you are going to develop an Ada compiler, teach advanced Ada courses or win money from bets on Ada trivia, *but don't try to learn the language from it.*

Compiler Validation Process

The standard described above defines the language, but when it comes time to determine if an implementation conforms to the standard, we need some form of test to determine conformance. This form of test is provided by what is known as the Ada Compiler Validation Capability (ACVC) which, in simple terms, is a test suite. It can be run by a compiler developer or a validation agency to determine if an implementation conforms to the standard. All Ada compilers to be used in the United States, and which wish to use the name Ada, must pass this suite of tests.

The ACVC test is really expected to be performed twice: once internally by the compiler developer, at which point he certifies that he has passed all the tests that apply to his implementation; and a second time by representatives of the Ada Validation Facility, who formally validate the conformance to the standard. These two steps are referred to as Prevalidation (formerly called Certification) and Validation. The process is governed by policies that cover what version of the test suite to used and under what conditions validation certificates are issued.

The ACVC test suite is an evolving set of tests that reflect the current interpretation of the language definition. As such, the test suite, at any point in time, may contain errors and/or implementation dependent feature assumptions. These facts complicate the validation process since an implementation developer can challenge tests. This makes the test suite that is used for any particular implementation unique from those used in the validation of other implementations.

What this means to the practitioner is that he or she can not rely on the test suite version numbers to determine that two implementations are identical. If this is important to you, then the only way to compare two implementations is to do a detailed analysis of the Validation Test Reports prepared by the Ada Validation Facility. Of the more than 2000 tests in the current version of the test suite, only 100 or less are typically challenged.

The ACVC test suite was designed with the intent of detecting particular errors of omission and commission in an implementation. But in using this design strategy, the ACVC test developers created a set of tests which are only useful for determining conformance to the standard.This point may not seem that important at first. However, to some people in the field it would have been more desirable to have a formally controlled test suite which could be used to demonstrate the features of Ada and in the performance assessment of an implementation.

But no such luck.

The classes of tests in the test suite are determined by their pass/fail criteria [53]. The six classes of tests are identified in table 4-1.

TABLE 4-1   VALIDATION TEST CLASSES

Class A: pass if no errors are detected at compile time.

         — used for detecting language supersets
         — execution of test code not necessary

Class B: pass if all errors are detected at compile time and no legal statements are detected as errors.

         — illegal programs
         — not executable

Class C: pass if the test completes execution and does not report failure.

         — executable self-checking programs

Class D: have no clearly defined pass/fail criteria.

         — capacity tests
         — results used to indicate potential limitations of an
           implementation

Class E: have no clearly defined pass/fail criteria.

         — used to determine how an implementation handles
           ambiguities in the language definition
         — results do not determine validity of an implementation
           they only provide information

Class L: pass if errors are detected prior to the execution of the main program unit.

         — illegal programs whose errors are typically detected at link

---

Of the six classes of tests, only the results from Class D and E are of any real use to the practitioner since these would give him or her information about the capacities and potential limitations of a particular implementation. Aside from these uses, the ACVC tests and the fact that an implementation is validated gives no insight into the usefulness of an implementation. Don't be fooled by the formalism of the testing/validation process. Its objectives are to determine conformance, not usefulness; *that is still the user's job.*

Language Use Directives and Policies

As one would expect, the use of Ada is being encouraged by the DoD since they have been the prime movers of Ada until recently. To "encourage" the use of Ada, the DoD, through the Office of the Secretary of Defense, has issued several directives and policies related to the use of Ada as well as other programming languages for software developed for and by DoD components (i.e., Navy, Army, Air Force, DoD Agencies, etc.) One of these directives, DoD Directive 5000.31, "Computer Programming Language Policy," was approved as an interim policy by Dr. Richard D. DeLauer, Under Secretary of Defense for Research and Engineering, in a memorandum dated 10 June 1983 [56, 57]. This memorandum is often referred to as the "DeLauer Letter." Attached to the memorandum was a draft copy of the directive which was in the final phases of formal coordination and publication.

The following summarizes the contents of the memorandum:

- Ada is approved for use consistent with the approved Ada introduction plans of individual DoD components and the validation requirements of the Ada Joint Program Office (AJPO).

- "The Ada programming language shall become the single, common programming language for defense mission-critical applications."

- Ada shall be used on all Advanced Development programs as of 1 January, 1984.

- Ada shall be used on all Full-Scale Engineering Development programs as of 1 July 1984.

Upon first reading of this memorandum one would conclude that as of July 1984 most of the new DoD programs would be using Ada. But that is far from what happened. From our perspective, very few defense programs have jumped on the Ada bandwagon, even as we enter 1986. This may seem inconsistent with the directive above, but what is often overlooked in a first reading is the statement, "for use consistent with the Ada introduction plan for the individual components." This statement says that it is up to the individual DoD components to determine under what conditions Ada can be used. An example of this would be the Navy's policy up until recently that a new program had to get a waiver in order to use Ada instead of a waiver for why they should not use Ada.

The point we are trying to make here, maybe too indirectly, is that the use of Ada is really controlled by the individual services and agencies and that directives such as DoDD 5000.31 and its successor, DoDD 3405.xx, are only stating the direction in which the services and agencies are heading, but they do not control the timing and the sequence of steps needed to make it a reality.

The strategy for introducing Ada will vary with the nature, needs, and the capabilities of each individual DoD component. Since several of the services are currently committed to other languages and support environments, we are going to see a gradual migration of DoD applications over to Ada. This migration will depend in part on the availability of stable and moderately high performance environments as well as the development of Ada oriented organizational support infrastructure within government, academia, and industry. It is our feeling that these things are just beginning to happen and that in 1986 we will begin to see the first real commitments being made to Ada.

Ada Trademark Policy

In order to prevent improper use of the name Ada and to restrict the normal subsetting and supersetting of the programming language, the DoD applied for and was granted trademark status for the name Ada. "Ada" is a registered trademark of the U. S. Department of Defense. Authorization for the use of this trademark is controlled by the Ada Joint Program Office (AJPO), Office of the Under Secretary of Defense for Research and Engineering. As such, the AJPO has granted to the general public free (i.e. at no cost) use of the trademark Ada when used in accordance with the guidelines in table 4 -2 [54].

TABLE 4-2   ADA TRADEMARK GUIDELINES

— The trademark "Ada" shall not be utilized as part of any other name or composite term, or the name of any product offered for sale unless licensed in writing by the AJPO.

— The preferred appearance of the trademark Ada shall be capital 'A' followed by lower case 'd' then 'a'.

— The word "Ada" should not be used alone in text without the word "language" or similar noun following it unless the context makes clear that it refers to the single programming language defined by the standard.

— In any published material, the first appearance of the term "Ada" must be properly acknowledged and include the statement "Ada is a registered trademark of the U. S. Government (Ada Joint Program Office)." {The AJPO guidelines also identify where the statement is to appear, the minimum font size, and the type of symbol (®) used to acknowledge the trademark. }

— Describing, advertising, or promoting a language processor as an "Ada" processor is equivalent to making a voluntary statement of conformance to ANSI/MIL-STD-1815A dated January 1983.

— The term "Ada" can be used for language processors that don't completely conform to the standard, provided that there is a precise, easily visible statement of their non-conformance at the same time and in the same context in which the term appears.

These guidelines are important for those individuals who will be using the term "Ada" in any published work. A more novel use of these guidelines is to use them as a source for good trivia questions. Some examples could be:

- How many times in the last year has The New York Times improperly used the word Ada?

- How many variations of the Ada trademark statement are there in the Proceedings of the Ada International Conference, Paris 14-16 May 1985?

Well, some of us will go to any lengths to get "good" trivia questions.

Other standards and guidelines will affect the manner in which we develop application in Ada, but are really beyond the scope of this book [25]. But we feel it is necessary to at least provide you with a list of some of the more important ones here. Table 4-3 summarizes the key standards and guidelines that fall in this category.

TABLE 4-3   **ADA USAGE RELATED STANDARDS**

DOD-STD-2167	**Defense Software Development** — covers the process of developing software for defense applications.
DOD-STD-2168	**Software Quality Evaluation** — covers the quality assurance procedures to be used in developing software for defense applications
DOD-HDBK-287	**Defense System Software Development Handbook** — provides guidance as to the use and tailoring of DOD-STD-2167 and other standards to the particular system and organization's needs

5. WHO'S WHO IN ADA

In this chapter we will provide you with a roadmap into the Ada world, its repositories of information, services, and products. At first this seemed like a very straightforward chapter to write for, over the past six years, I have collected two filing cabinets full of miscellaneous Ada related information from hundreds of sources. So all that seemed necessary was to condense that down to a manageable number of tables. Well, that didn't happen. Upon reviewing the material, it became apparent that most of the information has a finite lifetime associated with it. Specific Ada products like compilers will evolve over time by supporting more targets or hosts and by their degree of integration with the other elements of the environment. The time frame over which this will occur can be less than a year. These short time intervals make it difficult to include the specific targets supported by a compiler today.

The need to provide information that does not suffer from such a short lifetime is a dilemma. Therefore, in this chapter we are focusing on two somewhat distinct areas:

- Sources of Information — identifying the time stable sources of information about various aspects of the Ada Effort.

- Current and Future Trends — identifying the types of products and services available today and in the near future.

In both of these areas, I have tried to eliminate the time sensitivity of the information by summarizing and generalizing the data that is available in the open literature.

Sources of Ada Related Information

In the Ada community we have a multitude of sources for the information needed to support us in almost any aspect of an Ada application from research projects to policy issues. The real problem is that there are too many sources for the practitioner to deal with. Practitioners cannot spend 80% of their time reading thirty to forty Ada related publications, articles, conference proceedings, and The New York Times to find the answers to a few very specific questions they may have. This section is an attempt to give the practitioner pointers on Ada information sources so those specific questions can be answered more quickly. Possible information sources include:

- Organizations — agencies and committees established to address various issues related to Ada.

- Publications — journals that appear on some regular basis.

- Conferences — conferences, seminars, and tutorials of various durations that specifically address some aspect(s) of Ada.

- On-Line Sources — computer informational databases that cover Ada related topics and issues.

- Vendors — vendors of Ada related products and services

We have been selective about the sources of information highlighted here. Our interest is to provide useful sources of information to the practitioner. The principle organizations that serve as sources of information on Ada related areas are identified in tables 5-1 through 5-5 .

TABLE 5-1 INFORMATION SOURCE:
         THE ADA JOINT PROGRAM OFFICE (AJPO)

The AJPO has the overall responsibility for managing DoD's efforts to implement, introduce, and provide life cycle support for the Ada language, environments and methodologies. One of the primary roles of the AJPO is to support the transferring of Ada technology to the Ada community. In this role, the AJPO has established or sponsored other organizations and services identified in this chapter.

> Ada Joint Program Office
> 3D139
> The Pentagon
> Washington, D.C. 20301-3081

TABLE 5-2 INFORMATION SOURCE:
THE ADA INFORMATION CLEARINGHOUSE (ADAIC)

AdaIC is an AJPO established organization which collects and disseminates information and manages the collection and distribution of documentation on all aspects of the Ada Language and other DoD sponsored initiatives. The specific services provided include:

- A public computer database that announces recent activities and general information about the Ada Effort. All information can be accessed through commercial and military network services (TELENET or MILNET). The database currently covers the following areas:
  — DoD software initiative contracts
  — Upcoming Ada meetings
  — Ada, ALS, and AIE status
  — Up-to-date Ada oriented bibliography
  — Up-to-date Implementation/Environment matrix
  — On-line reference manual
  — Usage guidelines

- A Catalog of Resources for Education in Ada and Software Engineering (CREASE) which identifies the various forms and sources for Ada-related education and training; covers textbooks through computer aided instruction.

- An online Ada mailing list of individuals within the Ada community to encourage communications between individuals and organizations about all aspects of Ada.

- An Information Packet which has evolved over time. In some sense, it's an Ada Starter Kit covering such things as Ada history, trademark policies, and miscellaneous aspects on the use of Ada.

- A bimonthly newsletter (AdaIC) which highlights recent events in the Ada community and identifies additional sources of Ada related information.

The clearinghouse is possibly the single most important source of Ada related information available today.

Ada Information Clearinghouse
Suite 300
4550 Forbes Blvd.
Lanham, M.D. 20706

TABLE 5-3   INFORMATION SOURCE: SPECIAL INTEREST GROUP FOR ADA OF THE ASSOCIATION FOR COMPUTING MACHINERY (ACM) (SIGADA)

SIGAda is a technical group of the ACM which provides its members with a forum to discuss the technical aspects of Ada including usage, environments, standardization, and implementation. SIGAda provides the following services and publications to its members:

- Technical symposia and conferences on Ada related issues and research. Conferences are held quarterly as well as on a non-regular basis. The conferences provide the technical forum for Ada researchers, users, and vendors. Here they can share their work in an informal manner.
- A bimonthly publication (Ada Letters) which covers all aspects of the Ada Effort. Topic areas covered over the last year include:
  — Highlights of new products
  — Upcoming conferences and meetings

— Call-for-Papers
— Technical articles on usage and the implementation of Ada
— Ada policy statements
— Environment Matrix
— Education and training sources
— Design language developments
— Overview of current contracts
— Reports for various working groups who specialize in Runtime
      Support Environment, Education, etc.

SIGAda is the best source of non-DoD Ada-related activities, development, and research. It also provides good insight into "what's up" in the DoD Ada community.

SIGAda
Association for Computing Machinery, Inc.
11 West 42nd Street
New York, N.Y. 10036

**TABLE 5-4   INFORMATION SOURCE:
STARS APPLICATION TEAM (A-TEAM)**

The STARS A-Team is the DoD sponsored Software Technology for Adaptable, Reliable Systems (STARS) Application Area Coordinating Team [55]. The overall objective of STARS is to improve the quality of mission critical software while reducing the cost of the software over its lifetime. The A-Team is focused on developing:

• Application Specific Reusable Components
• Testing Procedures for Components
• Development and Usage Methodologies for supporting the
  application of components
• Automated Library Systems to support the distribution and use of
  components.

These focuses are addressed by DoD activities that include Workshops, Prototyping and Capability Demonstrations.

STARS Program Office
3D139
The Pentagon
Washington, D.C. 20301-3081

**TABLE 5-5   INFORMATION SOURCE: NATIONAL SECURITY
INDUSTRIAL ASSOCIATION (NSIA)**

NSIA is a national organization of industrial, research, legal, and educational organizations. It is dedicated towards maintaining close working relationships between industry and government, promoting understanding between organizations, and encouraging research and application of technology within government, industrial, and research communities.

One of the major program areas for the NSIA is demonstrated by the work of the Software Committee, which is chartered to interface with the major software initiative activities of the U.S. Government. These include:

- The Software Technology for Adaptable, Reliable Systems (STARS)
- The Software Engineering Institute (SEI)
- The Ada Program (AJPO)
- NASA's Space Station Initiative
- DARPA's Strategic Computing Initiative
- The Strategic Defense Initiative (SDI or STAR WARS)

The Software Committee also maintains relationships with industrial software initiatives:

- Microelectronics and Computer Technology Corporation's Software Technology Program
- Software Productivity Consortium

The NSIA sponsors conferences, participates in the review of programs, and develops white papers on issues of concern to industry as well as government.

National Security Industrial Association
1015 15th Street, N.W.
Washington, D.C. 20005

In addition to these sources of information, several computer information databases exist that provide access to Ada related information. The other databases are identified in tables 5-6 and 5-7 .

TABLE 5- 6   INFORMATION SOURCE:
DIALOG INFORMATION SERVICES

Dialog Information Services is an information retrieval service that provides access to over 175 databases, many of which address the needs of the scientific and engineering communities. Access to Dialog is through commercial computer networks and is typically provided as a service to a company, not an individual. Access to the databases is through an information retrieval query language that supports multiple word/phrases searches of the databases at various levels including full abstract text searching. The specific databases of interest to the Ada practitioner include:

- National Technical Information Service (NTIS) — abstracts and provides bibliographic citations of reports and publications of government related research and development. A typical month in 1985 would have five to seven Ada-related citations abstracted. This service is also available through NTIS directly in the form of a weekly abstract newsletter, *NTIS Computers, Control and Information Theory Newsletter.*

- Dissertation Abstracts International — an index of more than a half million doctoral and master's theses from U.S and Canadian universities and colleges. On an average, over 50 theses are written each year about Ada related research issues.

- Conference Papers Index — an index that abstracts the proceedings of over 1000 conferences a year. In 1985, there were over 50 conferences which covered various aspects of the Ada effort.

- Computerized Engineering Index (COMPENDEX) — abstracts over 3,500 scientific/engineering professional and trade journals as well as technical reports and books. This index provides a view into a multitude of journals produced by organizations like the IEEE, ACM, or IEE as well as other trade journal and newspapers produced all over the world.

The Dialog service is not for everyone as it is costly to use. But often, it may be the most direct manner to get your hands on a wealth of information available in a limited amount of time.

> Dialog Information Services, Inc.
> 3460 Hillview Avenue
> Palo Alto, CA 94304

TABLE 5- 7 INFORMATION SOURCE: THE ADA REPOSITORY

The Ada Repository is an on-line service that provides a collection of general Ada information, Ada programs, tools, and educational material free to users of the Defense Data Network (DDN). The repository has two basic purposes. First, to promote the exchange and use of Ada programs and tools, including software "components." Secondly, to promote Ada education within the community by providing several working examples of programs in source form for people to study and modify. It is also expected to distribute public domain Ada packages in the future. Users are encouraged to submit any information, particularly programs, that they think would be useful to others in the Ada community.

Access to the Ada Repository is presently restricted to DDN users. To determine whether you can access it, contact the Ada Clearinghouse (above) since they are in touch with the operators of the repository and the user community as well as the network controlling agencies.

The on-line sources identified above are not the only computerized sources for Ada related information. Several computer networks also provide either bulletin boards or special groups who focus on Ada related issues. Some of the more popular computer science and engineering networks oriented include:

- ARPANET/MILNET- DoD sponsored research oriented networks used primarily by those involved in government sponsored research and development.

- USENET- an informal network of UNIX™ users that encourages the sharing of developments in the UNIX community on a broad number of subject areas.

- CSNET- similar to ARPANET but not restricted to DoD sponsored researchers.

Commercial personal computer networks also have limited special interest groups related to Ada. In the future, such networks could be used as one of the major vehicles for distributing Ada "components." Only time and the copyright laws will tell when this will be a major part of our industry.

As one would expect, the interest in Ada has caused an Ada oriented industry to spring up over the last few years. This industry is made up of many new businesses as well as several of the more established members of the computer industry. The size of the Ada oriented industry by 1990 has been estimated as greater than $10 billion. This is difficult to prove today, but even an industry half that size is worth being involved in, if one can assume a leadership role in it.

To help put the industry into perspective as it sits today (early 1986), we have tried to summarize the players in the industry and the types of products/services they provide by giving the following general information in table 5-8:

Company Name and Address — (most of this information is taken from advertisements that have appeared over the last few years, so some of the data may have changed by the time this book has been published)

™ UNIX is a Trademark of Bell Laboratories.

Product and/or Service Categories — the product and service categories that the companies address are below. The order in which the category codes appear are used to indicate, in my opinion, vendor's principal focus.

Notes — an indication of any special products or services that may or may not be obvious from the general categories identified.

Table 5-8 can be used to help identify the potential sources of products and services that may be needed in one's development of Ada applications. The Product and Service categories include:

Application {A} — products that are typically used standalone or as part of an application environment made up of other applications.

Consulting {C} — consulting services oriented at aiding in the application and/or transition to Ada.

Environment {E} — products that support the development and maintenance of Ada applications.

Package {P} — products that could be used as part of an application such as a component or major subsystem of that application.

Special Product {S} — products that don't fit nicely into the A, E, or P categories above.

Training {T} — courses, seminars, computer aided instruction, and other educational services or products that provide training in the language, environments, or methodologies directly related to the use of Ada.

TABLE 5- 8: VENDORS OF ADA PRODUCTS AND SERVICES

COMPANY	PRODUCTS/SERVICES	NOTES
AdaSoft Inc.	**A** T	- computer aided training
9300 Annapolis Rd.		- DBMS application package
Lanham, MD. 20706		

Computer Corp. of America   **A**   - DBMS in Ada
Cambridge, Mass. 02142

Computer Representatives Inc.   **A**   - relational DBMS written in Ada
5333 Betsy Ross Drive
Santa Clara, Calif. 95052

Intellimac Inc.   **A** S E   - provide a high performance
Rockville, MD 20850   environment
    - business applications in Ada
    - mix Ada/LISP development tools

EVB Consulting Design   **C** T   - both Ada and Object Oriented
451 Hungerford Dr.   consulting and training
Rockville, MD 20850

Intermetrics   **C** E T   - developers of the AIE
733 Concord Ave.   - provide integrated PDL and
Cambridge, Mass. 02138   documentation tools

Systems Designers Software Inc. **C** E   - a 1750A cross compiler
Woburn, Mass. 01801

Advanced Computer Tech.   **E**   - microprocessor Ada cross
16 East 32nd St.   compilers
New York, N.Y. 10016

Alsys Inc.   **E** T C   - multiple host/target environments
400 Totten Pond Rd.
Waltham, Mass. 02154

Data General Corp.   **E** T   - full toolset for DG computers
4400 Computer Drive
Westboro, Mass. 01580

DDC International   **E**   - multiple host/target compilers
Lyngby, Denmark

Digital Equipment Corp.   **E**   - toolset for Ada development
Maynard, Mass. 01754

Gould Inc.   **E**   - supports Gould processors
6901 W. Sunrise Blvd.
Fort Lauderdale, Fla. 33313

Irvine Computer Sciences Corp. **E**   - retargetable compilers
18021 Sky Park Circle
Irvine, Calif. 92714

Loral Corp.   **E**   - provides environments for ROLM Ro
Im Mil-Spec Div   computers
One River Oaks Place
San Jose, Calif. 95134

Rational   **E S**   - high performance environment
1501 Salado Dr.   for Ada development support
Mountain View, Calif. 94043   - integrated environment

SofTech Inc.   **E C T** - developers of the ALS
460 Totten Pond Rd.   - developers of Army Ada
Waltham, Mass. 02254   Curriculum

Symbolics Inc.   **E P**   - provides full support for Ada and
11 Cambridge Center   LISP
Cambridge, Mass. 02142

Tartan Labs.   **E**   - multiple host/target compilers
Pittsburgh, PA 15213

TeleSoft   **E P T** - supports multiple hosts/targets
10639 Roselle St.   - developing reusable Ada
San Diego, Calif. 92121   packages

Verdix Corp.   **E**   - supports multiple hosts/targets
7655 Old Springhouse Rd.
McLean, Va. 22102

Xinotech Research, Inc.   **E**   - template oriented editor for Ada
520 2nd Avenue S.E.
Minneapolis, Minn. 55414

Computer Thought Corp. Plano, Texas 75074	**P** E	- tools and packages to support AI applications in Ada
Harris Corp. Government Info. Sys. Div. Fort Lauderdale, Fla. 33309	**P** E	- developing GKS graphics package
Infotrans 300 Orchard City Dr. Campbell, Calif. 95008	**S** T	- provides a library of Ada products which members can evaluate and/or purchase through them
Tachyon Corp. 2725 Congress St. San Diego, Calif. 92110	**S**	- on-line Ada manual and simulator
Control Data Corp. Minneapolis, Minn. 55414	**T** E	- PLATO based computer aided training (multiple groups)

What should be apparent from table 5-8 is the number of companies currently providing tools and environments, particularly compilers. This should be expected, since without the tools, other aspects of the industry cannot flourish. The other dominant category of products and services includes training-related services that range from short courses to computer aided education.

The trend that is not apparent yet, but should start to materialize soon, is Ada standalone applications and standard packages. These aspects of the industry should begin to appear in 1986 and by 1990 will be the dominant aspects of the Ada oriented industry. If one included DoD contracting for software (which should be considered part of the application and/or package business) it may already be the dominant aspect.

So where are the future opportunities for the Ada Industry? The following list is a summarization of some opportunities listed by category:

Application- DoD, industrial, and some limited business applications
— Weapon Systems
— Process Control Systems

— Distributed Business Applications
— Communications

Consulting- services to support the application of Ada
— Ada Transition Planning
— Independent Verification and Validation
— Product Evaluations and Marketing Support
— Technology and Methodology Transfer

Environment- compilers, tools, and fully integrated environments to support microprocessor and mainframe applications.
— Distributed Environments
— Distributed Target Runtime Support Systems
— Application Configurable Runtime Support Systems
— Multi-Language Development Environments
— Methodology Driven Environments
— Full Life Cycle Support Environments
— Ada/AI Mixed Environments
— Productivity Enhancing Tools

Package- packages for vertical "niche" markets as well as general purpose utility packages
— Graphic Packages
— Vertical Market Packages
— Scientific/Engineering Utilities
— DBMS Kernels
— Man-Machine Interfaces
— Signal Processing Packages

Special Product
— Environment Performance Accelerators
— High Performance Ada Oriented Computer Architectures
— Ada Oriented Database Machines

Training- more than 100,000 individuals may require training over the next 10 years in Ada, Environments and Methodologies.
— Computer Aided Instruction Systems
— Video Media Courses
— Conventional Classroom Instruction

6. Making the Transition to Ada

Making the transition to Ada in any size organization or project is filled with its ups and downs and, all too often, only downs. The reactions of the organization to such a transition are mostly negative and in some cases downright hostile. Why should making the transition to Ada solicit such a reaction? We all know of the potential benefits of Ada. Many have written about them, so why shouldn't others accept a minor disruption in their lives and joyfully receive Ada with "open arms"? These are not easy questions to answer for those with a technical background. They require us to deal with "people problems," not just "technical problems." There are no transcendant answers to these questions. However, after several years of observation, reading, and an attempt at bringing an organization through an Ada transition, we can make the reader aware of the issues involved and give some real guidance on how to make such a transition.

When considering the transition to any new technology two kinds of issues must be addressed:

- Perception — The users of the new technology must perceive the benefits in terms of their own needs.
- Actuality — There must be a sound match between the user's needs and the new technology.

We all know that the process of achieving acceptance for something must include satisfying a real need of the user, in this case the software engineering practitioner. Factors such as cost of the transition are also important, but in most cases are considered to be part of the real needs of the users (i.e., to a practitioner, if a technology is not affordable then it doesn't satisfy a real need).

This chapter will focus on the identification of the critical issues that should be addressed in the transition to Ada. As in the other chapters of this book,we will attempt to put these issues within a framework to enhance their useability to the reader. With this in mind, we need a structure in which to describe the issue. We have selected three somewhat overlapping models in which to describe the transition to Ada [2, 22, 49]. These include:

- A "Technology Transfer" model

- A classical "Training" model

- A "People Management" model

When treated together, these three models accurately reflect the set of issues that must be addressed in an organization's transition to Ada.

Ada Transition - The Technology Transfer Model

Treating the transition to Ada as a "Technology Transfer" activity is a fairly natural approach. To most people, Ada can be considered a new technology to be added to their current bag of technology tricks. Many have written about the issues associated with the transfering of new technology and in the process have identified generic issues associated with the transfer that can be directly applied to the transition to Ada. The following discussion highlights these issues.

ISSUE: Should Ada as a technology be "pushed on" or "pulled into" an organization? — "What do you mean they will not buy it? It has all these great features. Everyone should love it." This statement is often heard when one is involved in the process of "pushing" a new technology into an organization. The problem here is that the individuals pushing the technology do not consider the reaction that the organization will have to such activities. In most cases, you can not identify the reasons for the resistance to new technologies. We often discount the resistance as being the reactions of the "uneducated masses." But looking deeper, one finds a multitude of reasons that include some of the following:

- Feelings of being left out of the decision making process — in particular, on decisions that affect the way one will do his or her daily work.

- Lack of understanding of the effect the new technology will have on one's job.

- Fear that those involved in the technology transfer will take over key positions within the organization.

As these reasons indicate, pushing Ada onto an organization will, in general, not be successful. The primary force for the technology transfer must come from within the organization or from the people who currently own the problem, not from a corporate committee or research group dictating the transfer. One must work from within the organization to stimulate a pulling process, thereby making the technology (i.e., Ada) more acceptable to the organization.

ISSUE: Any technology transfer takes place over an extended period of time. — Technology transfer can not occur instantaneously, even though some would like it to happen that way. It occurs over an extended period of time. To be effective over this long haul, we must rely on informal communications between the groups involved in the technology transfer which may include marketing, research, development, management, and support groups. The use of informal communications is important since formal communications typically result in the NIH (Not Invented Here) syndrome, which treats any work outside of one's own group as inferior and is most apparent when a technology transfer takes an extended period of time. Effective technology transfer can be viewed as a process of gradually winning over the organization to the new technology. In the process of winning over the organization, the future roadblocks to the transfer can be identified and addressed in a controlled manner.

ISSUE: Scaling up a small scale pilot project to a full scale development use of Ada is loaded with pitfalls. — Most technology transfer efforts use some form of pilot project as a vehicle for assessing the technology and its possible effects on an organization. Such pilot projects are important to aid in our understanding of the technology, but we often need to try to extend the lessons learned in the pilot to the much larger projects or situations. A typical pilot project may have a single individual working on a small application, one that does not have to work over an extended period of time and has little or no documentation requirements. This individual is typically a "technologist" who is very interested in the technology and may even have a background in that technology. This type of pilot project falls short of satisfying the needs of the organization because the scale and nature of the pilot project is generally not consistent with the scale and nature of the projects the whole organization deals with. Most organizations that will use Ada develop large applications under tight documentation and timing constraints, possibly using large numbers of individuals who exhibit a wide variation in skills, knowledge, and interests. This is a completely different set of conditions than those which the pilot project is under. The net result is the inability to directly apply the results of the pilot project to support the technology transfer.

A pilot project can be effective in the technology transfer process if the project is well planned and executed. The key factor is planning. It must consider the ability of the organization to scale up the pilot to a large project by addressing the following:

— management issues
— resources
— development strategy

The pilot project should be planned and executed as a miniature of a large project. The large project's documentation and timing constraints, appropriately scaled down, must be applied to the pilot project. More than a single individual should be involved, and a mixture of skill levels should be used in the execution of the plan. After completing the project, the organization should be able to look at the pilot project's results and any lessons learned as one looks at the architectural model of a building. It should be a miniature project that can be manipulated, thus allowing the organization to test, probe, and assess how easily the pilot can be scaled to a larger project. To do this, one must understand the technology well enough to allow the control of the scaling up process to be successful. Also one must select a pilot project application in which Ada can be applied with a limited extension of the organization's current techniques.

ISSUE: Cultural differences do exist between the groups involved in the transition to Ada and will affect the outcome of the transition. — All too often, the individuals responsible for initially assessing the use of Ada within an organization come from a Research or Advanced Development group and have a computer science background with a limited number of years of "real world" experience. On the other side of the technology transfer are the development groups which are made up of individuals with engineering backgrounds, often not from an academic environment but from years of solving real world problems under a large number of constraints. This background difference is one of the roots of the cultural difference between the groups and can result in open hostility during the process of transferring the technology (i.e., Ada).

This cultural difference is typically most visible when one considers the tools the two groups have access to on a daily basis. The research oriented groups have the advanced tools and computer facilities that are used for experimenting with new technologies and small scale prototype applications. Considerations like performance, resource sharing and the quality of the tools are not the primary concern of this group. On the other hand, the development groups are using production oriented tools and facilities that are always overloaded. They must often schedule their work around the availability of facilities. It is not unusual for the development groups to see response times to interactive commands measured in minutes rather than the tenths of seconds that the research groups may be familar with. This assumes they can use interactive commands at all; many practitioners see response times for single compilations measured in days or even weeks due to the production nature of the process of developing software in their organization. The believability of the technology being transferred is always questioned by the development group in light of these differences in tools and facilities. This may be the main reason why, in the past, some organizations have failed to make the transfer of a technology successful.

In the process of transferring a technology like Ada from within or from outside, an organization must consider all of the cultural differences between the groups involved in the transfer. We have only identified one above, but others exist, since other groups or subgroups may be involved in the transfer process. These include:

- Functional Management

- Corporate Management

- Support Groups

- Quality Assurance

- Project Management

This list could go on for several pages. Differences in background, education, current work assignment, and nature of work environment will affect the transition process to Ada. To be successful, one must address these cultural differences directly and assess any group's reactions to the transition within the context of these cultural differences. In general, for a successful technology transfer, all groups involved in the transfer must be considered.

Ada Transition — A Classical "Training" Model

Yet another approach to the transition to Ada is to consider it only as a training problem. To most people, this simply requires the selection and institution of a training curriculum within the organization. This is often the view that management has, and all too often, management thinks the best approach to training is "On The Job Training." This approach has never really been successful but may have appeared to have succeeded since the projects that used it succeeded. If this method were analyzed, we would find that "On the Job Training" actually had no positive effect on the success of the projects.

Training in Ada is available from multiple sources. But here we will consider the issues associated with the use of training as an approach to making the transition to Ada within a project or organization. Specific issues are identified below.

Issue: An Ada training program must be tuned to the intended audience. — Effective training programs are always the ones that have been customized to the audience which, in this case, is an organization that is making the transition to Ada. This customization must address the needs of all groups involved in the process of developing software. This means that the training program must address the needs of the following subgroups in the organization as a minimum:

- Project management

- System Engineers

- Software Architects

- Designers

- Programmers

- Quality assurance

- Development support staff

- Integration/Test Engineers

Because Ada affects the way we think about the software being developed as well as the way we implement it, we have to get more people up to speed than we did with previous languages.

Since we have diverse groups of individuals that need training, it should be obvious that a single course will not satisfy the training needs of an organization making the transition to Ada. Generally speaking, each group needs its own course, even though some of the material used may be common. The format of presentation may vary for the different groups depending on the type of involvement the group will have with Ada when it is applied. Management and systems engineering groups may be given courses that are primarily lecture, while designers and programmers would best benefit from courses that have many practical exercises, preferably using an Ada environment. In all formats, the examples used within a course should be relevant to the application types that the organization develops.

Issue: An Ada training program must integrate software engineering concepts with the exposure of language features. — In Chapter 1, we introduced you to the Ada Effort and hopefully you now realize that Ada is more than just another programming language. It should be apparent that Ada has been built on a set of software engineering concepts that are oriented toward the production of reliable, maintainable, and understandable software systems. Due to this fact, when one teaches Ada, consideration must be given to these software engineering concepts as well as to the language features. In one sense we must teach the Ada mindset which requires us to shift our current views of what a programming language does.

Issue: You will need remedial and advanced courses in any effective Ada training program. — When you consider the future needs for software, it should be apparent that the current software engineering workforce will not be able to satisfy the needs of DoD and industry. This gap between the size of the available workforce and the future needs will force or draw many individuals into software engineering positions who do not have an engineering or computer science background. Many of these individuals will come with some exposure to computers through a high school or college course in BASIC or FORTRAN, but with no formal or real world training or experience, particularly in realtime software. It is therefore important when selecting a curriculum that you address the needs of the newcomers to the field. This requires that a wide range of courses or training opportunities have to be made available including remedial as well as advanced coverage of the language. Again, it is important to remember that any courses on Ada must provide equal emphasis on software engineering concepts and language features since most of the newcomers will have little or no background in either area.

Issue: Training and the application of that training should be timed as closely together as possible. — Timing of training is critical in the success of any training program. In general, it is best to provide the training at the point immediately before the individuals will need to apply it and provide it so it does not interfere with any ongoing work. This ideal timing never seems to occur in the real world, so some compromises must be made. One reasonable approach to the timing problem seems to be to break the training into three phases which include the following:

- Introductory Phase — a period of time before the actual need for the organization to make the transition to Ada. During this phase, introductory courses and seminars are used to raise the awareness of the organization.

- Basic Phase — a period at the beginning of the time when the organization starts to use Ada. During this phase software engineering and the elementary and intermediate level Ada courses would be given. It is at this time that remedial courses would be given.

- Advanced Phase — a period during the application of Ada. During this phase, advanced features of Ada would be covered in detail to a limited number of individuals who are preparing to use these features.

One implication of this phasing is that you may be able to use outside courses and seminars in the Introductory phase, but you would find them difficult to use for the other two phases due to the custom nature of the training needs in these phases.

Ada Transition — A "People Management" Model

Treating the transition to Ada as a people management activity helps us to look at some of the reasons why transitions can fail even though we may have addressed the technological transfer and training aspects successfully. As the following issues will highlight, this particular model of the transition to Ada is concerned with the management of the individuals involved in the transition. In general, these issues will be the most difficult to address since most of us who are technically oriented do not have the background and/or the inclination to address the issues. The issues included here represent only classes of issues that must be addressed. In most organizations they will take slightly different forms.

Issue: Address the true concerns within the organization directly. — Having been involved in transition to Ada, I have heard the "thousand and one" reasons why an organization cannot use Ada. Examples of these reasons include:

- "It can't be done in Ada."

- "Ada is too inefficient to be used for my application."

- "The selected Ada implementation is poorly matched to our needs."

- "We tried it on a different compiler/language/CPU and it was inefficient."

- "I read somewhere that it was inefficient."

- "Ada does not allow me to use 'COMMON' and my application is full of 'COMMON'."

- "In C (i.e., the programming language) I can write the same program in one-half the time."

These are all reasons that individuals have given for not supporting the transition to Ada, or blocking it outright. If one looks at these reasons quickly, you see that most individuals are opposed to Ada from the standpoint of efficiency or apparent lack of features of another language that they are familar with. Efficiency and familarity are good issues to be considered when making the transition, but they should not be the only issues considered.

Aside from the obvious meaning of these stated reasons for opposing the transition, looking deeper you will typically find hidden reasons for an individual's stated objections. Some of the hidden reasons or agendas could include one or more of the following:

- "I can't figure out how to do it in Ada."

- "I don't understand it."

- "I won't let you force me to use it."

- "Nobody from research is going to tell me how to do my job."

- "I don't have time to learn it."

These hidden reasons occur most often because of a lack of awareness within the organization of what Ada is and how it is going to affect the organization as well as the individuals within the organization. The key to a successful transition to Ada is in the hands of the management of the organization. They must be constantly aware of the true concerns of the organization. A strong management team is needed in order to make this transition happen successfully. This team must be able to temper the reluctance as well as the enthusiasm of the individuals involved in the transition with objectivity and understanding.

Issue: Estimation of an Ada project is a problem since no rule of thumb or experience base is available to draw upon. — Project management and the technical leaders within an organization are typically the ones who do the initial planning and estimation associated with any new projects in an organization. If the new project is similar to a previous project then they usually rely on one or more "rules of thumb" and past data to support them in the estimation and planning process. With the introduction of Ada into an organization most of these "rules of thumb" no longer apply. For most organizations past data is not readily available. This makes the estimation and planning process nearly impossible and has been used by some as a reason for opposing the transition to Ada.

To address this seemingly impossible situation, the organization must first realize that it is not business as usual and that possibly special measures should be taken. These special measures will vary from organization to organization, but could include:

- Assigning an Ada Transition Champion to guide the organization through the transition period.

- Planning the project at a greater level of detail, being careful to identify the risk areas and the areas where gaps in data exist.

- Monitoring the project to verify the actual performance of the project against the planned performance. Where differences exist, one should resolve them by adapting the plan, but recording the differences to serve as data for future projects.

- After completion of the project, do a project post-mortem to collect data and hopefully one or more "rules of thumb" that can be used on future projects.

Most of these points are common sense, but within many organizations they are forgotten in the heat of the transition to a new technology like Ada.

Issue: The conflicting goals of the managers, designers, programmers, and support groups must be weighed when planning a transition to Ada. — The goals of the various individuals and groups involved in the transition to Ada must be understood if the transition is to be successful. When considering the goals of the individuals, it is often convenient to divide goals into three categories:

- Quality Goals

- Productivity Goals

- Control Goals

In determining an effective people management approach to the transition, one must be aware of the priorities that individuals place on each of these categories of goals. This is important since the priority of goals will determine the manner in which individuals will interpret data and respond to problems or changes. Note that a functional manager may oppose the transition to Ada because he feels that it will affect the degree of control he has over his portion of the organization. This is partly due to the goal priorities of a functional manager (first Control, then Productivity, and finally Quality). The technical leader for a project has the opposite ordering of priorities (first Quality, then Productivity, and finally Control).

What all this really means is that we must sell the individuals involved in a transition on the attributes of the transition to Ada that benefit them and directly support their own personal goals in accordance with their priorities.

Hopefully, in this discussion we have made it clear that the process of successfully getting through an Ada transition is made up of what seems a relatively straightforward situation of addressing the key issues that are important to one's organization. There is no magic to being successful in such an activity. It just takes the right combination of motivated individuals, who are willing to learn and understand what is going on around them. Table 6-1 summarizes the issues listed above and attempts to order them according to importance and identify who within an organization should address them. Table 6-2 provides some helpful hints and reminders to aid you in the planning and implementation of a transition to Ada within your organization.

TABLE 6-1: ADA TRANSITION ISSUES

ISSUE ORDERED BY PRIORITY	ADDRESSED BY
• Address the true concerns within the organization directly	Transition Champion All Managers

- Cultural differences do exist between the groups involved in the transition to Ada and they will affect the outcome of the transition.

  Transition Champion
  Functional Managers

- The conflicting goals of the managers, designers, programmers, and support groups must be weighed when planning a transition to Ada.

  Transition Champion

- Scaling up a small scale pilot project to a full scale development use of Ada is loaded with pitfalls.

  Transition Champion
  Project Leaders

- An Ada training program must be tuned to the intended audience.

  Functional Managers

- An Ada training program must integrate software engineering concepts with the exposure of the language features.

  Functional Managers

- Training and the application of that training should be timed as closely together as possible.

  Project Leaders
  Functional Managers

- You will need remedial and advanced courses in any effective Ada training program.

  Functional Managers

- Estimation of an Ada project is a problem since no rule of thumb or experience base is available to draw on.

  Project Leaders

- Should Ada as a technology be "pushed on" or "pulled into" an organization?

  Senior Manager

- Any technology transfer takes place over an extended period of time.

  Transition Champion

TABLE 6 - 2 HELPFUL HINTS TO AID THE TRANSITION TO ADA

- Know who must be sold on the transition and who you have to drag into it.

- Plan for success but learn from any failures along the way.

- Planning is the key to the success of any transition. Focus on the following:
  — setting standards
  — eliminating roadblocks
  — eliminating hidden agendas
  — making the planning process visible

- Make any plans and any pilot projects as visible as possible to get others involved and get them to "buy in."

- Use short awareness-raising discussions to ease tension and apprehension associated with the transition.

- Gain early support or at least a non-interference attitude from the management involved in the transition.

- Do as much in house training as possible.

- Use of textbooks and videotapes for training in Ada is not enough.

- Learning Ada from the Ada Language Manual (MIL-STD-1815A) is a disaster waiting to happen.

- Use outside courses and seminars only to provide an overview, not as the primary means of training.

- Create a multi-disciplined team to handle the transition process.

- Systematically expose the organization to Ada and software engineering through seminars, reviews, demonstrations, etc.

- Give potential users of Ada access to an Ada capability after some limited training. This may backfire, if the Ada capability provided performs marginally or is buggy.

- Get a champion to sell the organization on the transition. This champion should have the following attributes:

  — a detailed knowledge of Ada
  — a detailed knowledge of software engineering
  — a knowledge of the organization
  — must be an insider
  — must have been self-selected

7. ADA DESIGN AND IMPLEMENTATION METHODOLOGIES

Whenever we start a new project, we are often forced to fend for ourselves relative to the specific approach to use to address a new situation and its associated problems. This is the way in which most of us will face the application of Ada on a project. We will all bring to this new challenge our prior experiences which suggest to us various approaches. These may or may not be appropriate for the situation at hand. Since we are dealing with a new technology, we must wonder if there are other approaches that could be used more effectively to address the problems at hand.

The need to select an approach for applying Ada is not unique. The need is interesting since the language itself, as well as the worldwide interest in it, has encouraged many individuals and organizations to modify existing design methodologies or to develop new ones for use with Ada. These new approaches to the problems are documented in a myriad of technical articles written over the last 10 years. This chapter provides the following:

- An overview of several Ada oriented design and implementation methodologies.

- A review of the issues that one must consider when designing or implementing with Ada.

This chapter completes the discussion of the three major elements of the Ada Effort: Ada the Language, Ada Oriented Environments, and Ada Oriented Methodologies.

Before describing the various methodologies and issues associated with the design and implementation of an Ada application, we will set the stage for the remaining discussion by introducing the process, products, and underlying principles in the design and implementation of software.

A working definition for design:

Design is a process that translates stated software requirements into a blueprint or model of the software which, when implemented, will satisfy those requirements. Design is often broken into two phases: architectural design and detailed design.

Design consists of the following types of activities:

- Allocating functional requirements to a design structure, the modules, and interconnections that make up the software.

- Identifying the functions that must be performed by each part and subpart of the design structure.

- Presenting the structure and functions in a format that is consistent with the organization's needs and documentation guidelines.

- Verifying that performance, reliability, maintainability, and reusability constraints will be met by the structure and functions proposed.

From its definition, design can be viewed as a modeling process which leaves out or defers certain details about the software that is being developed. This is done to give the coders something to do in the implementation phase. The level of detail provided in design will vary depending on the methodology in use, the nature of the application, and the tools, languages, and methods to be used in the implementation of the software (i.e., Coding and Testing). Even within design we have varying levels of details to be concerned with. In Architectural Design we are concentrating on the structure and form of the software, while in Detailed Design we are focusing primarily on the detailing of functions that fit into the structure.

In general terms, the designer must deal with the global issues associated with the development of the software at hand and he or she must:

- Defer implementation decisions as long as possible.

- Try to "hide" many of the decisions made inside of modules (i.e., the parts and subparts of the software design).

- Be concerned with overall structure more than selection of language statements and features.

- Specify what algorithms and control flows must be implemented.

- Define as fully and cleanly as possible the interface between the modules (i.e., the interconnections between modules).

- Communicate between other members of the team including analyst, implementers, and management.

The design and implementation processes are often constrained by such things as budgets, schedules, and imposed standards. In the real world, these con-straints often dictate the manner in which design is performed. The budget and schedule constraints typically force us to compromise the design process, since to many individuals in management, design does not produce anything tangible. To these individuals, only implementation (Coding and Testing) shows any actual results. They often push directly into Coding, sometimes bypassing design entirely. To avoid this trap one must make design a process that produces a tangible result: a set of products that indicates that progress is being made to the end goal, which is the delivery of the software. It is therefore important that the design methodologies which one uses produce useable, understandable, and progress measuring products.

Our description of design and implementation so far implies that it is a sequential process of well defined steps that leads us from the stated requirements of the software to a final delivered product. This is a simplistic view since, in reality, design and implementation are part of an iterative process in which we proceed to expose problems or errors in what was done before. Sometimes this requires us to modify the structure of the design or some of the assumptions/decisions made, both of which force us to reapply one or more of the steps of the process.

The iterative nature of the process is something that frustrates management. Most managers view software design and implementation as a manufacturing process: in go the requirements (the raw materials) and out comes the working software (the end product). Each step in the process is well understood and is visited only once. This view is far from reality, and constrains us more than we would like to admit. With this in mind, we must make sure that the methodologies we use in design and implementation make the process understandable and visible to management as well as to the individuals performing the activities.

In general, the underlying principles that are associated with software engineering and the design and implementation processes, in particular, include those identified in table 7-1 [37].

TABLE 7-1 DESIGN AND IMPLEMENTATION PRINCIPLES

• **Structuring** — the manner in which parts and subparts relate to form a whole. The goals of structuring in design and implementation are:

  — reduction of complexity
  — increasing understandability

• **Modularity** — a rational and purposeful manner of achieving structuring. Modularity when applied to design and implementation imposes a purpose on the manner in which we provide structuring. The goals of modularity are:

  — to make the interfaces between parts of the structure explicit
  — to divide the design or implementation into parts which could be developed independently

• **Abstraction** — controlled suppression of details, highlighting of essential details, suppressing the non-essential details. Abstraction aids in the understanding of the aspects of interest by controlling the level of detail we need to see in order to achieve understanding. The goals of abstraction relative to design and implementation could be considered to be the same as those for modularity. In many methodologies, abstraction is used as the criterion for achieving modularity.

• **Hiding** — purposefully making certain details or design decisions unaccessible. Hiding, like abstraction, could be viewed as a criterion for achieving modularity. It provides us with guidance as what to make visible (as in the interface to a module) and what we should hide inside of the module. The details to be hidden could be selected based upon:

— likelihood of a detail changing (if it is likely to change, hide it in a module to minimize the effect of the change)
— complexity of the detail

- **Separation of Concerns** — physically collecting related things and separating unrelated things. Separation of Concerns is intended to reduce the impact of change in a design or implementation as well as providing the criteria by which one can find the answers to one's questions about a design or implementation. The information that one should separate includes:

— Functionality from behavior
— Input/Output bit representation from logical meaning
— Expected changes from stable items
— Input/Output mapping from functionality

To summarize, the software engineering principles of Structuring, Modularity, and Abstraction are oriented towards reducing complexity, which will enhance our understanding of the design or implementation. In addition to this, the principles of Modularity and Hiding as well as Separation of Concerns are oriented toward limiting the impact of change on a design or implementation. Since the purpose of this chapter is to discuss various approaches to design and implementation, we will leave the general discussion here but as we introduce the various methodologies, we will try to identify the principles that they support and the degree to which these principles are supported.

There are three distinct aspects of a methodology that must be considered. These three aspects are:

Process — the planning, directing, and executing of the operations or activities that make up the methods you are applying.

Representation — the form or format of the information which is used to convey the results of the operations that make up the methods.

Guidance — assistance that the methodology gives in getting you started, going from one step of the process to the next, judging the quality of the results, and knowing when you are done.

The reason for focusing on the three aspects of a methodology is that many of the methodologies that have been adopted for supporting design and implementation in Ada only address one or two of these aspects. As such, they need to be supplemented with aspects from other methodologies in order to address the full needs of a practitioner.

In this chapter we will discuss design methodologies in very general terms. Table 7-2 identifies the specific methodologies to be covered in this chapter. The emphasis is on those methodologies that hold real promise in being successfully applied to Ada applications. By identifying the methodologies in this way, we hope it will allow you to mix and match the processes, the representations, and the guidance of the various methodologies as you see fit.

The methodologies covered in this chapter are only representative of the methodologies available and potentially adaptable to the needs of an Ada design and implementation effort. The general literature is a good source for more on these other methodologies.

TABLE 7-2 ADA ORIENTED DESIGN METHODOLOGIES

METHODOLOGY	PROCESS	REPRESENTATION	GUIDANCE
Object Oriented Design	•	•	•
Jackson System Design	•	•	•
System Design In Ada		•	•
Program Design Language		•	
Design/Coding Guidelines			•

A Quick Summary of Design Methodologies

In this discussion, we have included as methodologies some approaches that do not satisify some of the more rigid definitions of a methodology. This seems appropriate since no single methodology fully addresses the needs of the practitioner. As one approaches the design of an application, one must build a methodology either from the ground up or, more realistically, combine elements of existing methodologies or these "psuedo" methodologies. Table 7-2 points out those aspects that these pseudo methodologies address, and those they do not. After describing several methodologies, we will cover a "demonstration methodology" which indicates how one could combine parts from several of the methodologies.

Object Oriented Design

Object Oriented Design is a design methodology described by G. Booch that cannot be credited to a single individual [6, 7, 8, 63]. It really evolved out of the work of several individuals. Object Oriented Design, as a design process, focuses on the structure of an application as one would see it if one looked only at the abstract objects that make up the application and the operations on those objects. By focusing on the objects, it does not follow the more traditional view that an application's structure should be derived from a top-down decomposition of the functions that must be performed by that application. Object Oriented Design can be applied in a top down manner. In that case, it would follow the natural way in which the objects or data of the application decompose instead of the way in which the functions decompose.

Because of the process one uses when one applies Object Oriented Design, it is currently limited to small or medium scale application efforts (less than 30,000 lines of code). If one were to use the methodology for large applications, it is suggested that it be used in conjunction with another methodology which is applied to break the application into smaller chunks. Then one should apply the Object Oriented Design process to each chunk independently. In one sense, Object Oriented Design could be looked at as an intermediate design methodology, one that sits between architectural design and detailed design. The real advantage of Object Oriented Design to the practitioner is that it is intuitive and can be used very easily to take advantage of many features of Ada which may not be useable when one approaches the design using other methodologies.

Object Oriented Design supports all aspects of a methodology which we identified above. Its heaviest focus is on the process aspect. Object Oriented Design is built on a three step process identified in table 7-3.

TABLE 7-3 PROCESS STEPS OF OBJECT ORIENTED DESIGN

- **Definition of the Problem**

    — State the problem to be solved in a single sentence.
    — Organize and clarify any given information about the problem.

- **Development of an informal "Strategy" for the Problem Domain**
    — State in a single paragraph "a solution" to the problem above.

- **Formalization of the Strategy**
    — evolve the informal strategy to an Ada structural design by:
        a. Identifying the application objects and their attributes.
        b. Identifying the operations on these objects.
        c. Establishing the interfaces to the objects and operations.
        d. Implementing the operations in Ada.

Using this process, the application's logical abstract data types fall out automatically. The process also relies heavily on the software engineering principles of abstractions and information hiding. These principles directly support the specification of the interfaces to the objects and their associated operations.

The representations used by the Object Oriented Design methodology include a graphical notation for expressing the structure and interactions between elements of the design and a full syntax Ada program design language. The graphical notation was developed to highlight the interfaces of the elements that will make up the design. This notation has been built upon by others such as R.J.A. Buhr in his *System Design with Ada* methodology [11]. Due to the similar purpose of the two notations, I plan to describe only one of them, which will be described in a later section using figure 7-1.

In an *Object Oriented Design Handbook* for Ada Software [63], a considerable amount of design and implementation guidance is given to the designer in the application of Object Oriented Design. The guidance consists of guidelines, suggested deliverables at each step in the process, and quality assessment information. This guidance is given in small increments associated with the description of each of the process steps and substeps.

Jackson System Development

The Jackson System Development (JSD) Methodology evolved out of the work by M. Jackson on software requirements analysis, design, and programming methods during the middle to late 1970's [15]. JSD is not a "top down" methodology as other methodologies of that time frame were. JSD is based on observation that most "good" system or program structures reflect the structure of the data. Design is just a process of exposing the data structure inherent in the problem at hand and then transforming that data structure into a system or program structure.

JSD is a multi-level design method that starts at the point where the problem is vague and our concerns are with defining and delimiting the subject matter more closely. From this point we develop a model of the real world situation. Then we transform that model into a design and finally, into an implementation.

The process of JSD is well established and is in common use in Europe. It is used primarily for administrative system development, but it has also been used on several realtime systems. The process used by the designer consists of developing a specification and implementation that can be outlined as a set of steps. These steps are identified in table 7-4.

TABLE 7-4 PROCESS STEPS OF JACKSON SYSTEM DEVELOPMENT

- **Entity Action Step** — limit the scope of the real world problem at hand by listing the entities (the things that make up the real world) for the area of interest and identifying the actions on those entities with which the system will be concerned:

  — entities include people and things, as well as organizations.

  — a selection criteria is used in the identification of relevant entities and actions. See guidance discussion below.

  — the list of entities and actions acts as a glossary of terms in the real world that will be used to specify the functions of the system.

- **Entity Structure Step** — for each entity, order the actions that are performed upon or by the entity. The ordering, on the basis of time of occurrence, is indicated using a graphical representational notation.

  — an entity can perform or suffer under an action.

  — actions may have time ordering dependencies which are required by the real world

  — a structure diagram is developed for each entity that explicitly states the time ordering of actions and the relation of those actions to this entity and other entities.

  — the structure diagram represents each entity as a sequential process which performs a set of actions.

- **Initial Model Step** — develop a process model for the real world problem based on the results of the previous steps.

  — the goal of this step is to specify the system as a simulation of the real world.

  — for each entity above, or more accurately, for each sequential process above, there will be a process in the system which will be executed by the computer or computers.

  — the link between a real world process and the model process is a data stream which is a series of messages from an entity. There is a message for each action to be performed.

  — a System Specification Diagram (SSD) is produced that represents the model process which expresses the relationships between the real world inputs/outputs and model processes as well as among model processes.

  — supplementing the System Specification Diagram is a structured textual specification.

- **Function Step** — specify functions that produce the system outputs. Additional processes may be introduced during this step.

— from the model, identify and specify the functions that produce the required outputs.

— elaborate SSDs and structured textual specification.

• **System Timing Step** — consider the scheduling requirements of the processes that would affect the correctness or timeliness of the system outputs.

• **Implementation Step** — this step involves the selection of data structures and program units that will properly implement the entities and processes specified above.

The process outlined in table 7-4 fits well with Ada, because the process highlights the structural parts of the system which require implementation as tasks. In some of the "top down" methodologies, we can only take advantage of subprograms and packages as our structuring mechanisms.

In terms of guiding the process, Jackson's System Development, provides guidance for each step in the process. To illustrate the nature of the guidance in the Entity Action Step, the criteria for selecting entities and actions would be:

• Actions take place at a point in time, not over an extended period of time.

• The actions to be identified must be the actions that take place in the outside world, not the internal actions of the system.

• An action must be considered to be atomic in that it cannot be decomposed into subactions.

• An entity must be a real world entity.

• An entity must perform or suffer under actions in a significant time ordering.

Additional guidance in the form of examples and issues/concerns is given throughout Jackson's book [29].

System Design with Ada

A methodology that evolved out of several other methodologies (including Structured Design and Object Oriented Design) is the *System Design with Ada* methodology. This name is derived from the name of the primary reference on the methodology, a book by R.J.A. Buhr of Carleton University [11]. We select this methodolgy not so much for its uniqueness as for the fact that it provides a very useful design notation or representation for expressing the architectural design of an Ada program, as well as additional design guidance that is not found elsewhere. In addition, this methodology is one of the few that is being automated today. We will review the automation aspects later.

System Design with Ada provides a top-down approach to the architectural design aspects of an Ada application. It does this through the use of a graphical design notation which maps very closely to features of the Ada language. This notation and the guidance given in usage of Ada features is the essence of the System Design with Ada methodology.

The methodology has be characterized as "object oriented structured design" in which the objects are the components that make up the structure of the application or system. These components are viewed by the designer as "black boxes," for all that is visible to him is the interface specification. The component's internal organization and details are hidden. This view is totally consistent with the program-unit view in Ada. As such, this makes Ada a natural language for implementing a design represented using this methodology. The ties to Ada are even closer since the classes of black box components used are graphical representations of the Ada features.

The interconnection of the components, as well as the individual components, serves as the vehicle for communicating the design, much like a blueprint communicates a hardware design. Since Ada supports the nesting of program structures, it would be expected that any design notation or methodology should take advantage of this to allow the design to evolve in a topdown manner using step-wise refinement. The System Design with Ada methodology supports this directly by allowing the designer to create a set of "blueprints" that may represent the application as a single structure. Then one can create additional "blueprints" which express the inner workings of the top level design. This process can be repeated for each new level, until the designer has completely specified the design.

This top down view is not the only one supported by this methodology. A mixed top down/ bottom up view is also supported, just as with Ada. The bottom up view allows the designer to specify components that provide services to one or more other components.

The System Design with Ada methodology does not propose a particular formal design process, but relies more on providing a good representational scheme (a design notation) and guidance to the designer in the application of Ada to real world problems. The methodology in some sense is process-independent in that it could be used with any of the other methodologies that explicitly support a design strategy. Better still, it could be used as a common ground on which various design processes could be used together to address real world system designs in which no single strategy could be used to attack all possible problems. The design processes for which this methodology seems suited include:

- Object Oriented Design

- Structured Design

- Data Driven Design

Although it is not a formal process, a basic process can be identified, particularly when one considers the automation of the methodology currently going on. The process could be viewed as the elementary interactions between the designer and the tools that automate the methodology. This basic process can be represented by a sequence of phases identified in table 7-5.

TABLE 7-5   PROCESS PHASES OF SYSTEM DESIGN WITH ADA

Phase 1. Structure Definition : In this phase the designer graphically enters the structure of the design, using a set of icons that can be viewed as black boxes representing Ada structures (tasks, packages, subprograms, etc.) which are interconnected in the same manner as a schematic would be used to interconnect hardware components. This structure is refined by expanding upper level structures into lower level structures using the same iconic notation.

Phase 2. Temporal Interface Behavior: This phase supplements the structure developed above by specifying the temporal behavior of the various task interfaces and the task interaction. This allows the analysis of the overall application performance without having to completely define the internal structure of the design, thereby directly supporting an incremental design process.

Phase 3. Specification of Internal Sequencing Rules: This phase involves the detailing of the internal temporal sequencing rules for the design. This phase could be viewed as temporal flowcharting in which we are concerned with the sequencing associated with the design, not the details of the functions or algorithms to be implemented.

Phase 4. Program Strip Definition: The result of the previous phases is a structure which can be translated by the environment into an Ada source code in which the structural and temporal sequencing/task interaction is fully developed. Only the functional and algorithmic nature of the program needs to be filled in.

The phases outlined in table 7-5 are supported with graphical entry/editing and analysis tools which will evolve over the next few years (assuming continued interest in the project) into a well integrated environment that will serve as a true Ada architectural design assistant.

From the standpoint of providing a detailed design process, the System Design with Ada methodology is lacking. But that is not what it was intended to provide. The most important aspects of the methodology are the design notation introduced and the general design guidance provided.

The System Design with Ada Design Notation has been described as a "Pictorial System Description" technique in which the architectural design of the application is expressed as a set of pictures that reflect the structures as well as the control and dataflow between those structures. Figure 7-1 summarizes the design notation as described in Buhr's book. Also included in figure 7-1 is a legend that defines the basic terms and concepts used in the notation.

The System Design with Ada methodology provides guidance to the designer which includes:

- Metaphors on tasking and the rendezvous concepts of Ada.

PACKAGES

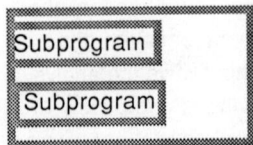

• Packages with Interfaces
  Explicitly Shown
• Procedural as well as
  Non-Procedural Interfaces

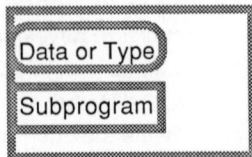

Subprogram

Subprogram

Data or Type

Subprogram

TASKS

Entry

Entry

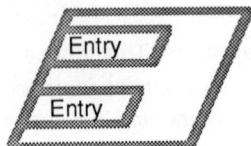

• Tasks with Entries Explicitly
  Shown
• Variations are Provided to Show
  all Forms of Entries Allowed
  in Ada

SUBPROGRAMS

Subprogram

• Either a Procedure or Function

UNCOMMITTED MODULES

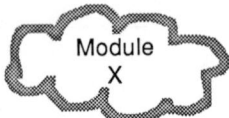

Module
X

• Used to Show a Program Structure
  in which the Exact Form has not been
  Selected Yet

ACCESS CONNECTIONS

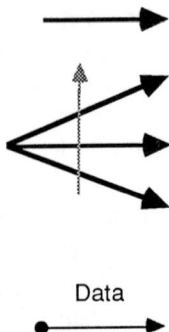

• Explicitly Shows Access between
  Program Structures
  - Subprogram Call
  - Task Entry Call
  - Data Access
• Ordering of Calls typically Top
  to Bottom
• Annotations used to Show Other
  Orderings

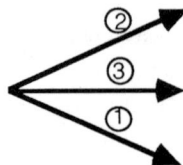

②

③

①

DATA

Data

• Data Structures can be Shown
• Parameters that flow across
  Access Connections are also
  Shown

Data

Figure 7-1   **System Design With Ada - Basic Notation**

- The identification of a set of canonical, structured system parts that can be used to build a design. These parts are characterized and guidance is given as to when they should and shouldn't be used.

- Techniques for expressing typical structure interaction mechanisms, using the system parts above, that may be required in an application.

- Techniques for mapping the parts above to Ada code fragments that would implement them.

- Identification of issues that one must consider when using tasking.

- Modularity and packaging techniques usable for various classes of systems.

Due to the limited scope of this book, it is difficult to cover the guidance provided by the methodology in any more detail. For those who are interested, I would refer to R.J.A Buhr's book *System Design with Ada* [11]. In this book he provides detailed guidance through a well defined set of examples that were developed using the methodology.

Almost as important is the current effort being made to automate the methodology. This effort is focused on the development of the Carleton Embedded System Design Environment (CAEDE) which is an experimental Ada oriented design environment that supports the generation and use of the design representation aspects of that methodology [12, 13]. The work is being performed by the Department of Systems and Computer Engineering, Carleton University, Ottawa, Ontario, Canada. The environment consists of a design database, an "Iconic" design entry system, and design tools which work together to support the development of application in Ada. Implemented in Prolog, the environment tools can be used by a designer to:

- Perform Structured Analysis/Design at the architectural design level, not at the system requirements level.

- Perform Performance Analysis of the Design.

- Develop a Graphical Representation of the Design.

- Generate Ada Source Code in a partially automated manner.

CAEDE was built on a set of underlying principles that serve as good guidance in any design effort. Table 7-6 summarizes the most important of these principles.

TABLE 7-6 PRINCIPLES OF CAEDE THAT SUPPORT THE DESIGN PROCESS

- A design environment should assist in the creative process of design and should be guided by a well understood methodology.

- Use graphical representations to provide a framework for the designer to express himself as well as to allow him to reason about the system being developed.

- The gap between the design representation and the coded program should be kept to a minimum.

- A design environment must support the incremental design of the system from three perspectives: structural, temporal, and functional.

The principles identified in table 7-6 established the framework for the CAEDE implementation which assists the designer in learning the methodology and designing in general, as well as serving as a design assistant. This allows the designer to focus on the creative aspects of the design process.

Program Design Language

A Program Design Language (PDL) is a textual language which must be precise enough to describe software while being expressive enough to allow you to express a design with it. This loose definition would rule out English as a good PDL. English lacks the precision, even though it does have the required expressivenes. The natural form of language that seems to fit this definition best is a programming language. The problem up until recently has been that general purpose languages lack the expressiveness even though they are precise. In order to use them as a PDL, we have to supplement them with some form of structured comments. With Ada available, we finally have a general purpose programming language that is expressive enough to describe all aspects of a software design.

A Program Design Language that supports the types of application which Ada is intended to address must directly support:

- Abstraction

- Decomposition

- Information Hiding

- Stepwise Refinement

- Modularity

Most of these were part of the stated requirements for Ada, which makes Ada a good fit for a PDL. In addition to supporting these broad principles, a PDL must document the resulting design in a manner which has most of the following qualities:

- Must be <u>readable and understandable</u> by all individuals involved in the design process.

- Must be a <u>complete, concise, precise, and structured</u> representation of the design.

- Must be <u>verifiable and traceable</u> relative to the stated system design requirements.

A PDL must be expressive enough to allow algorithms, program structure/modularity, data structure, design constraints, and design decisions to be documented in a structured yet understandable manner [5, 31].

Many Ada oriented PDLs have been proposed and are in common use today. These range from language subsets to language supersets [16]. When one looks at the support, training, management, and cost issues of maintaining another language in addition to Ada, it should be obvious that a PDL based on full sytax Ada is the best compromise between the subsetting and supersetting indicated above. By using full Ada we have available to us the full capabilities of an Ada environment to analyze, maintain, and manage our designs as well as our code.

Using full Ada requires placing restrictions on the manner in which designs are to be represented. To highlight this, consider the early stages of detailed design when one does not know the exact condition that will be used to select between two alternate processing algorithms. One would like to express it something like this:

```
if the size of x and z are compatible then
        do algorithm 1
else
        do algorithm 2
end if;
```

This is far from legal Ada, so in a full syntax Ada PDL we would be required to use comments to express this in the following manner:

```
if Size_of_X_and_Z_Compatible then
        -- do algorithm 1
else
        -- do algorithm 2
end if;
```

This PDL statement cannot be compiled without errors, but it conforms to the syntax rules of the language and it indicates that the condition in the "if" statement must be computed in some manner that results in a Boolean value.

In a full syntax Ada PDL, comments and standard comment forms are used to convey information that is not readily expressable directly in Ada due to the timing or the nature of the information. The use of comments to express this information may have a side effect that benefits the design process in the long run. In design we are often expressing unformed and vague ideas. If we use some construct other than a comment, we may forget that this idea was not fully formed and proceed without exploring it fully. Also, no language designer (including a PDL designer) is going to have enough insight to provide all of the needed constructs to address the diverse applications that will be designed in the future.

The final point relative to the use of a PDL concerns where it fits into the overall development process. A PDL in some sense is just another form of programming language and should be used in those places where a programming language would fit naturally. This most obvious place in the development process would be during detailed design where we elaborate the structural design of the software to provide sufficient detail to code from. This is the only place for a PDL as it is defined here.

Some individuals will recommend using it early in the development process to express the architectural design or even the system design. Both of these are inappropriate places for a PDL for the following reasons:

1. System and Architectural Design are concerned with expressing structure. A textually oriented language is difficult to use to express structure or the relationships between structures.

2. System Design is often performed by individuals who have direct application experience. Often they have not had much experience with Ada or other programming languages and would find it difficult to adapt to a PDL at this level.

3. System Design includes more than specifying software functions and structures. It requires description of hardware and personnel and their relationship to the system as a whole.

In general, a PDL can be used effectively within the context of other methodologies, but typically its use should be restricted to the detailed design portions of the development process.

Design/Coding Guidelines

Any complete methodology would address the issues of how one takes the bag of tricks at hand and apply them to the problem at hand. Often the best way to address these issues is to have a set of guidelines that instruct you or provide you with evaluation criteria that you can use during the activities associated with the design or implementation process. In this section we will cover several psuedo methodologies that are primarily in the form of guidelines to the designers and coders involved in the use of Ada for real applications.

One category of guidelines that most methodologies above do not directly cover is designing for Reusability. The discussion that follows will focus on creating reusable components instead of the use of reusable components. We do this because it appears that the use of reusable components is a management problem and not a technical problem. The technical aspects of creating a reusable component is far more consistent with the nature of this section, which is to provide the practitioner with guidance in the design and coding of an Ada application.

Ada features such as packages and generics provide us with the flexibility required to create highly resuable components at a variety of levels — not simply at the algorithm level, but also at the system level. None of this can be achieved if we do not approach the design and coding process armed with the techniques needed to achieve reusability. Examples of reuseable components are:

- Math Libraries

- Statistical Libraries

- Graphics Packages - implementing standards such as GKS, CORE.

- General/Generic implementation of a Data Structure - an abstract data type implementation of a Stack, Queue, FIFO, Tree, Graph, etc.

- Table Driven Subsytem - generalized state machines, parsers, etc.

- User Interface

- Operating System Services

- Classical Algorithm Implementations - quicksort for one

The remainder of this discussion is deferred until the later discussion of the demonstration methodolgy where a summary of the recommendations for reusability found in the literature is provided. These recommendations should be used not as absolute rules, but as guidance to help you develop designs and implementations of those designs which have a high probability of being reused. As we hope you will agree, reuseable components do not just fall out of the development process; they require a concerted effort on the part of the developers, users and management in order to make them happen.

Design/Coding Style Guidance

Another area where guidance is readily available in the application of Ada is in the style guidelines for design and coding. The primary reason for considering style at all is that a consistent style, when used by the writer and understood by the reader, provides a common ground on which the two can communicate. The importance of communication cannot be overly emphasized since both in design and in coding we are required to communicate our results to others as well as to ourselves. The use of a uniform set of style conventions thus helps eliminate possible confusion between the individuals involved in any form of communication. One other use of style guidelines is to aid in making the structure of a program or design explicit. For example, the use of indentation to indicate the nesting of program statements gives us a feel for the structure of the program even before we read the code in detail. Since structure is important in regulating the amount of complexity we must handle at any point in time, style guidelines aid in making structure explicit. They are vital in establishing a concise understanding of the design or code under consideration.

Style guidelines will vary from those which are vague suggestions of how closely the design should map to the requirements of the real world system to detailed suggestions as to how many spaces to indent the statements nested in the **then** part of an **if** statement. All levels of style guidelines are needed when dealing with designs and programs of any significant size. The important thing to note is that style guidelines need not be specified as industry standards. They just have to be specified and understood by those using them. In light of this statement we will approach style guidelines in a slightly different manner. First we will identify those areas of design and coding in which style guidelines should be established. Then we will provide one or more suggestions for a guideline in that area. The suggestions in the demonstration methodology section are a compilation of guidelines found in the literature.

In this section we will not make a distinction between the guidelines for design and those for coding since most of us using Ada will use it as a PDL in design and finally as the implementation language. The fact that the same language is used in both phases is one of the reasons for not making the distinction between the guidelines on the basis of phase. The place where understanding is most required is at the design level. We should be doing everything possible during design to make the designs as comprehensible as possible.

Table 7-7 summarizes the degree to which each of the methodologies support the software engineering principles indentified above. The assessment is given here to show that very few of the existing Ada oriented methodologies proposed today will provide full coverage of the principles above. It should be apparent that no single methodology will satisfy your needs and you must to some extent mix and match elements of the methodologies proposed in order to tailor it to your organizational and personal needs.

TABLE 7-7   PRINCIPLES SUPPORTED BY THE ADA ORIENTED
            DESIGN METHODOLOGIES

METHODOLOGY	PRINCIPLES SUPPORTED	DEGREE OF SUPPORT
Object Oriented Design	Structuring	High
	Abstraction	High
	Modularity	High
	Hiding	Moderate
	Separation of Concerns	Moderate
Jackson System Design	Structuring	High
	Abstraction	Moderate
	Modularity	Moderate
	Hiding	Low
	Separation of Concerns	Low

System Design In Ada	Structuring	High
	Abstraction	High
	Modularity	High
	Hiding	High
	Separation of Concerns	Moderate
Program Design Language	Structuring	High
	Abstraction	Moderate
	Modularity	Moderate
Design/Coding Guidelines	Structuring	High
	Abstraction	Moderate

A Demonstration Methodology

To test the concept of mixing and matching various methodologies together to form a more complete methodology, we would like to describe aspects of several of the methodologies as if they were going to be used together. This demonstration methodology will be made up of:

- The **Process** of

    — Jackson Structured Development
    — Object Oriented Design.

- The **Representation** from

    — System Design with Ada Representation.
    — A Full Syntax Ada Program Design Language

- The **Guidance** from

    — Object Oriented Design Quality Procedures
    — Designing for Reusability Guidelines
    — Design/Coding Style Guidelines

The rationale for describing the three aspects of a methodology by using a demonstration methodology is to show that one can indeed combine portions of various methodologies together. But more importantly, one must get a methodology that addresses one's real needs. In order to keep within the scope of this book, we have been somewhat arbitrary about the methodologies combined and have been far from complete. This demonstration methodology is oriented towards the design of small to medium applications that have little or no realtime or other hard constraints on them. Even with this restricted view we believe you will find the specific aspects that were addressed useful.

The Process

This demonstration methodology starts out with the use of the Jackson System Development process guided by its associated guidance to structure the overall system into major program units (tasks and packages primarily). When this is completed, each of the processes and functions are designed using the Object Oriented Design methodology. The remainder of this discussion focuses on the process, representation, and guidance used after this initial design step.

Object Oriented Design is built on a three step process which includes:

1. Definition of the Problem to be Solved.

    — Review the relevant structure diagrams.
    — Summarize the problem to be solved in a single sentence.
    — Organize and clarify any given information about the problem.

2. Development of an informal "Strategy" for the Problem Domain.

    — State in a single paragraph "a solution" to the problem above.

3. Formalization of the Strategy.

    — Evolve the informal strategy to an Ada structural design.

The last step is the essence of Object Oriented Design while the first, although necessary, really just sets the context in which we can apply the third step. Since it appears that Object Oriented Design is most useful on a small to medium scale application, the first step would have typically been done using another methodology such as Jackson System Development.

The second step is where the methodology starts to give a great deal of guidance as to the manner in which one should develop this informal strategy or approach to the solution to the problem. You are encouraged to express the solution in a precise manner, but to avoid the use of computer terminology and rely on the terminology of the real world environment that you are dealing with. This approach would not work well if it were not for the capabilities to express real world concepts directly.

Once we have an informal strategy, we can apply the last step of the process. Here we have four major substeps to go through which are summarized in tables 7-8 through 7-11.

TABLE 7-8 IDENTIFY THE OBJECTS AND THEIR ATTRIBUTES

- The objects are the nouns, pronouns, and noun clauses in the single paragraph description of the solution found in the informal strategy.

- Their attributes are the qualifying adjectives in the informal strategy.

- From the identified objects above, separate those that are unique instances of an object from those that represent a class of objects. Those that represent classes of objects will later be implemented as Ada types; the instances will be implemented as Ada objects.

- Associate a legal Ada name with each object or class of objects that will be used from then on to refer to them.

TABLE 7-9   IDENTIFY THE OPERATIONS OF INTEREST

- The operations are the verbs, verb phrases, and predicates contained in the informal strategy.

- Each of the operations is then associated with one and only one of the objects or class of objects identified above.

- For each of the operations determine the information needed to perform the operation. This will eventually be used to determine the interface specificiation for the Ada program unit that will implement the operation.

- Associate a legal Ada name with each operation that will be used from then on to refer to it.

- From the informal strategy, identify the modifiers of the operations, the adverbs and adverbial phrases, these represent the attributes of the operations.

- Group the operations and attributes of the operations with the object and object classes they operate on. These groups will eventually help define the package structure of the solution.

TABLE 7-10 DEFINE THE INTERFACES

- Determine which of the four Ada program unit types (task, subprogram, package, or generic) will be used to implement each operation. Object Oriented Design gives some guidance as to how this should be done.

- Additional packages may be introduced at this time to group logically related program units together.

- Formally describe the interfaces among the objects, types, and operations. This description may be textual or graphical. Both representations will be covered in the representation section below.

- Supplement the objects, types, and operations above that will help with the eventual implementation.

- Use the graphical notation to build a "roadmap" that indicates the dependencies between the various interfaces identified, calling/caller, compilation order, etc.

TABLE 7-11   DECIDE ON THE IMPLEMENTATION

- Implement the operation interfaces.

- Use stepwise refinement of the higher level program units to identify other program units.

- Apply the whole methodology to any significant program unit or "new problem" that would be identified in the stepwise refinement substep above.

Structured Walkthroughs will be used throughout the process to assess the quality of the products, to detect errors as early as possible, and keep the whole design/implementation team aware of the evolving design.

The Design Representations

Two design representations are required to support the process described above: a graphical notation and a program design language. The graphical notation is used to express the structural aspects of the design while the program design language is used to detail the design and formally describe the interfaces and internal works of the operations that are identified in the process above. The design representations chosen for the demonstration methodology are:

- The System Design with Ada Notation

- Full Syntax Ada as A Program Design Language.

Below we will describe the two design representations in more detail.

The System Design with Ada Design Notation has been described as a "Pictorial System Description" technique in which the architectural design of the application or system is expressed as a set of pictures that reflect the structures that make up the architecture as well as the control and major dataflow between those structures. The notation allows currency of an application to be expressed as well as the sequential nature of the application. The notation used highlights the interfaces between the structures while suppressing the internal functions or data structures. Figure 7-1 summarizes the design notation as described in Buhr's book.

The architectural design of an application expressed in this notation is represented by a diagram that connects together the various structures to form a blueprint-like representation of the application. Figure 7-2 demonstrates the use of the design notation to express the architectural design of a simulation system.

The PDL used in the demonstration methodology will be full syntax Ada supplemented with a set of structured comments that will include forms that capture the following information :

- Program Unit Performance and Size Constraints

- Design Decisions

- Change History

- Identification Information - author, purpose, origination date, etc.

- Assertion - to aid in test generation

- Implementation Implications and Restrictions

The structured comments will be encoded as Ada comments with a general syntax that includes the comment delimiter followed by the name of special character sequences to identify the comment type. This will be followed by the text for that information.

The Guidance

From Object Oriented Design, our demonstration methodology will get part of the guidance needed to develop an application using the methodology. The

Main Procedure

Scenario

Count

Step Message

Request
Receive
Characters

Script

Step Message

Request
Transmit
Messages

Step Message

Step Message

Request
Receive
Messages

Scenario Definitions

Step

Types

Message

Request
Compose
Message Task

Step Message

Compose
Message

Length

Obtain Message
Template

Compose Message
Field

Validate Message
Sequence

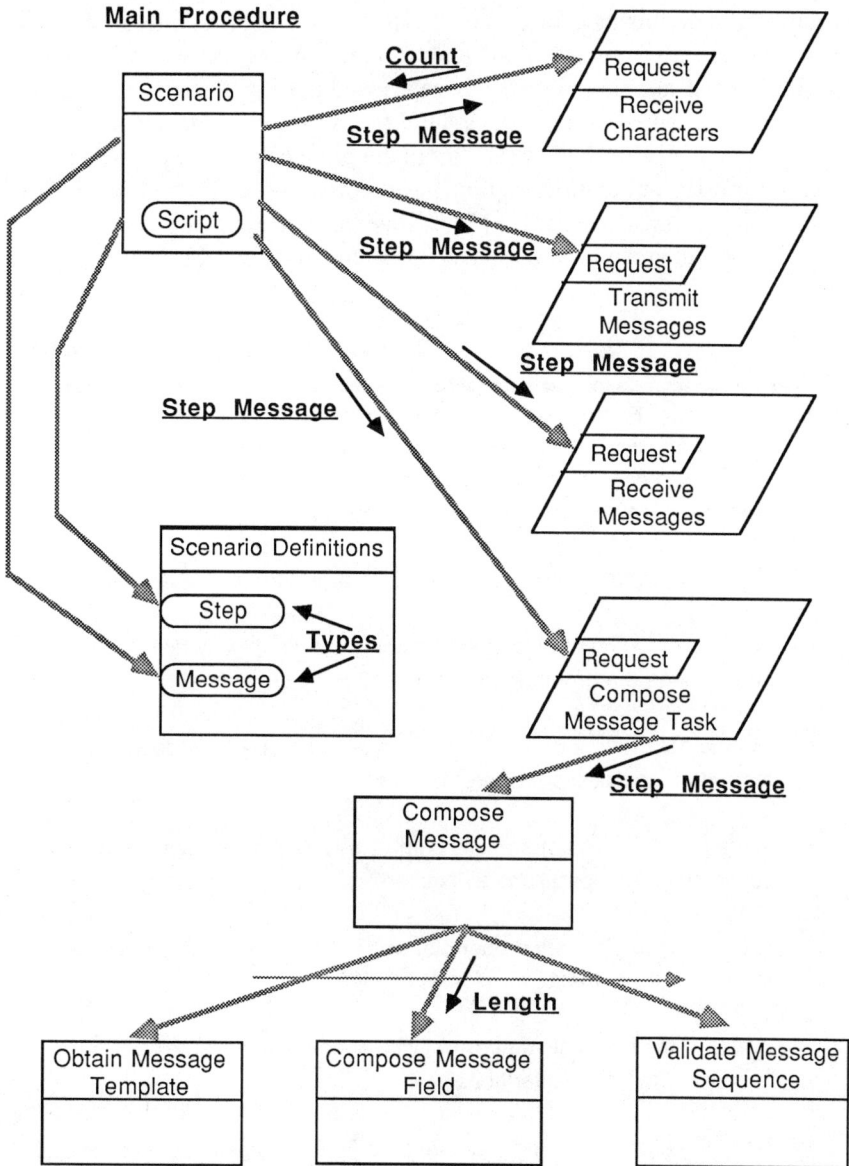

Figure 7-2   **Sample Usage of Notation**

specific form of guidance focuses on the assessment of the quality of the outputs of the steps and substeps that make up the process above. The guidance for starting and stopping the process steps is included in the detailed description of the individual process steps. Often, this type of guidance is given in the form of a checklist that one applies to the products that are produced during each substep of the process. For illustration purposes we will focus only on the guidance provided for the "Formalize the Strategy" step of the Object Oriented Design process. This guidance is summarized in table 7-12.

TABLE 7-12   FORMALIZE THE STRATEGY GUIDANCE

- Was the process of identifying the nouns and verbs in the informal strategy complete, accurate, and well documented?

- Are all names of objects and operations legal Ada identifiers?

- Was the grouping of objects vs. object types completely and correctly done? Does the grouping make sense?

- Did the assignment of operations to objects or types introduce redundant operations that are not required?

- Is the set of defined operations complete? Are the initialization, type conversion, . . . operations all defined?

- Are tasking implemented operations defined? If so, do they make sense for the nature of the application at hand?

- Are all of the informal strategy objects, operations, attributes, . . . accounted for in the interfaces?

- Does the allocation of program units to Ada packages make sense?

- Are any of the compilation dependencies that were identified cyclical or self-referring?

- Were any unnecessary detailed design level items identified in the interfaces that should be deferred to another step?

- During any iterations of the interface definition, were all deletions of interface items properly documented and justified?

- For any change to an interface, does it make sense and is the design decision and associated rationale properly documented?

- Does the graphical representation of the design seem uncluttered and readable?

- When going from one substep to the next were all interface items accounted for and properly translated or modified?

- Were the most straightforward acceptable algorithms and data structures used to implement the design?

- Were the designing for reusability and design/coding style guidelines below followed? Were there any identifiable violations?

Designing for Reusability Guidelines

The following guidance is intended to assist the designer in insuring that the resulting designs will achieve a high degree of reusability. The specific guidelines are included in table 7-13 [30, 71].

TABLE 7-13 DESIGNING OF REUSABILITY GUIDANCE

- Develop a model for each reusable component that communicates what it is and how to apply it. The model should serve as the primary vehicle for evaluating the suitabliity of the component. The approach used to document the model should communicate all the information needed to assess the usefulness of the component. For the demonstration methodology, these models would consist of a set of graphical models and a PDL description of the design using the representations above.

- All reusable components must have a single well behaved and well defined interface.

- A reusable component may have hidden efficiency impacts or costs that must be highlighted in order to allow for proper evaluation by the users of the components. These hidden costs could include one or more of the following:

  — Extra parameters needed to make the component general and flexible.
  — Code used to check for potential errors that may never occur in the use being considered for the component.
  — Extra procedure calls to mask some levels of details from the component interface.
  — Extra subprograms provided to support other uses.

- Use generic parameters to allow the compiler to optimize the component to the requirements of a particular application.

- When using Ada packages to achieve reuse (by creating an abstraction or abstract interface) remember to include operations for:

  — Creation - bring the abstraction into existence
  — Termination - orderly disposal of an abstraction and related entities
  — Conversion between type
  — State Inquiry - access information relative to the status of an abstraction (needed primarily when state determining information is stored inside one or more of the program units that make up the abstraction.)
  — State Change - modify the state defining information
  — Input/Output representation

- Full support for an abstraction should be through a single package specification, not through several.

- Implement the bodies of subprograms declared in a package specification as subunits in order to allow for flexibility of changing and conditional linking of unused subprograms (if that is supported by the environment).

- For each assumption that a component depends upon to operate correctly, implement an exception that is raised when that assumption is violated.

- For all of the above exceptions, provide at the component interface a function that will return an indication if an exception would be raised under existing conditions. This is provided to allow the user of the component to determine the manner in which exceptional conditions will be handled.

- Raise an exception if it is "cheap" for the user to retry and/or fix the problem. If it is not "cheap" have the user provide a procedure that can be used in the component as part of the exception handler.

- When additional information about the situation that caused an exception is available, provide a subprogram that returns that information to the user of the component.

- Documentation for a reusable component must include the following information above and beyond the information normally generated in the development of software:

  — Functional Summary
  — Sizing Information
  — Timing Information
  — Known Limitations
  — User Modification/Customization Procedures
  — List of Potential Reuses
  — Error Handling
  — Examples of Use

Design/Coding Style Guidelines

The following guidance is intended to assist the designer in insuring that the resulting designs will achieve a high degree of readability and will meet the maintainability goals for the software. The specific guidelines are included in table 7-14 [4, 6, 26, 46, 61, 76].

TABLE 7-14   DESIGN AND CODING STYLE GUIDELINES

- Ada PDL and code should read "naturally." Statements within a program should read well in English, assuming that you "add on the fly" a few small pronouns, verbs, etc.

  — all identifiers should be made up of a sequence of pronounceable syllables or words rather than just a sequence of characters
  — selection of any element of style must be from the need to serve the reader, not the writer.

- All program units should exhibit strong cohesion and weak coupling.

  — use hiding principle as one criteria to determine what is visible in a program unit specification

- Select program unit, type names and object names from the real world application name space whenever possible.

- Whenever possible avoid the declaration of a common database. Instead, distribute the "database" to the principle users and provide access routines to the other users.

- When using low level features, isolate them within a limited number of packages. Use the package as the mechanism to map the physical nature of the low level features to the logical nature to be used within the program.

- Use Ada features in a uniform manner throughout the design. It should be obvious to the reader of a PDL or Source Code description what the possible uses of an Ada feature are. Use features as indicated in table 7 -15.

- Use uniform naming conventions for Ada features. Naming conventions should be considered a design issue since it is there that the name space for any program will be determined. Table 7-16 suggests some possible naming conventions.

- Use indentation, alignment, and grouping to explicitly show the structure of the program. Indentation should be considered at design time since it shows the structure of the program. Structure is a major concern at this time.

— Use a consistent indentation style that expresses the structure of the design and code.
— Localize logically related entities into well indicated groups
— Align common elements of a list of entities
   {align the colons of all declarations in a group}
   {align the "is"s in a list of program unit declarations}
   {align "begin," "exception," and "end" in a program unit}

• Use a block comment structure for each program unit that indicates its purpose, its normal effects, and exceptions raised.

• Use a block comment structure for each independent compilation unit that indicates current version, change history, and compilation history if not part of a source code control system already in use.

• Use capitalization to aid the reader in distinquishing between various entity classes.

— Use lower case letters for all Ada reserved words
— Identifiers are written in mixed upper and lower case
— All upper case is reserved for abbreviations and single letter identifiers.

• Global objects should be passed as parameters if the subprogram is going to modify it.

• Global objects which are only read by a subprogram need not be passed as a parameter. The subprogram should indicate such usage with a comment.

• Use identifiers to describe the type, object, or program units instead of relying on comments to do it.

• Use comments (on the same line comments) at the "end" associated with a loop statement to indicate the conditions that causes the loop to complete.

TABLE 7-15 CONVENTIONS FOR USING ADA FEATURES

- **Subprogram** as:
    - — Main program units
    - — Definitions of functional control
    - — Definition of operators on a data type

- **Packages** as:
    - — Named collections of type and program unit declarations
    - — Structuring tool for related program units
    - — Abstract data type implementations

- **Tasks** to implement:
    - — Concurrent actions within an application
    - — Access controls on shared resources
    - — Interrupt handlers
    - — Object managers as in Object Oriented Programming

- **Generic program units** to:
    - — Factor the common properties of a class of program units

- **Exceptions** for:
    - — Detecting and recovering from error conditions

- **Fixed point data types** to implement:
    - — Objects that in the real world have finite resolution units

---

TABLE 7-16   SUGGESTED NAMING CONVENTIONS

- All identifiers made up of more than a single word should use underscore characters to separate the words.

- Procedures should be named with verb phrases or imperative clauses to indicate action

- Functions should be named with noun phrases since they denote values when they appear in expressions.

- Functions that return Boolean values should be named in a manner that indicates the value of the true condition that is returned.
  {Output_Is_Ready, Completed, End_of_File}

- Task entries should be named with verb phrases or imperative clauses to indicate action

- Packages should be named with noun phrases to the object or group nature of the package.

- Tasks should be named with noun phrases that indicate the services that they provide. This can often be done by adding an "er" to a verb phrase that indicates the action performed by a task.
  {a task that "schedules an action" - Scheduler}

- Types should be named as common noun phrases.

- The structure of a type or the fact that it is a type should be indicated with a suffix (_Type or _Array or _Pointer or _Record).

- Derive access type names from the names of the objects they designate.
  {if the designated type is List_Entry_Type, then name the access type List_Entry_Pointer_Type}

- Objects should be named as proper noun phrases.

- Corresponding components in different records should use the same component name.

Wrapup

Hopefully, the demonstration methodology will be useable as a model for those aspects one must consider when designing with Ada. As stated before, the intent was not to provide a complete methodology. In the real world it is difficult to conceive of the complete process, representation, and guidance that one would need to address significant applications in Ada. The best we can do is to build upon the works of others to develop a methodology that is adequate for our purposes.

With the application of any new technology, there are many issues one must consider in order to make effective and efficient use of that technology. In the remainder of this chapter we will try to identify some of the issues that one should be aware of as one applies Ada. These issues are posed as questions and are organized into topic areas that include:

- Design Issues

- Testing Issues

- Runtime Support Environment Issues

- Other Language Interfaces Issues

- Product Management Issues

- Project Management Issues

To address the full range of issues involved in the application of Ada, a practitioner must selectively address these issues. For specific approaches to the issues, you are referred to the indicated references associated with each topic area. Tables 7-17 through 7-21 summarize these design issues that should be considered.

TABLE 7-17   DESIGN ISSUES TO CONSIDER

- What effect does runtime efficiency have on architectural designs or vice versa?

- How do the traditional approaches requiring deterministic performance, fit in with Ada's asynchronous tasking implementation?

- How does an application detect and recover from possible deadlock conditions that can arise in an Ada implementation that uses tasking?

- How do you get exact timing out of the delay statement?

- How do you distribute realtime program across machines?

- How do you use exceptions effectively?

References: [17, 27, 28, 41, 43, 51, 78]

TABLE 7-18   TESTING ISSUES TO CONSIDER

- Does the environment support remote target debugging, source level debugging, timing analysis, and performance analysis techniques?

- How does one debug and test applications that make use of tasking?

References: [11, 47, 75, 77]

TABLE 7-19   RUNTIME SUPPORT ENVIRONMENT ISSUES TO CONSIDER

- Since early Ada implementations focused on functionality and not efficiency, how do I select a Runtime environment that meets my application needs?

- Does the implementation support distributed applications?

References: [72, 73]

TABLE 7-20   OTHER LANGUAGE INTERFACES ISSUES TO CONSIDER

- Are interfaces to other languages available and efficient as well as supported by the full environment?

- How can I mix AI and Ada?

•   What is the role of automatic conversion to/from Ada and other
    languages?

    References: [32]

TABLE 7-21   PRODUCT/PROJECT MANAGEMENT ISSUES TO CONSIDER

•   How well does the configuration management approach of the
    environment fit such features of Ada as separate compilation, program
    libraries, evolution products, program families,etc?

•   How does Ada influence the approach to software QA?

•   Will the limited performance of compilers and environments impact the
    overall resource needs and project schedules? If so, by how much?

•   Do conflicts exist between the various software development standards
    and use of Ada?

•   How can I encourage reusability?

    References: [38, 39]

---

8. OTHER USES OF ADA AND FUTURE DIRECTIONS

Due to its expressive power, Ada is being used for purposes beyond those for which it was originally intended. Just look at the almost universal acceptance within the industry of Ada as a Program Design Language even for applications which will not be coded in Ada. The range of these other uses varies from Hardware Description to Database Definition. These other uses take three forms:

- Supplementing Ada with specialized features using the package concept of Ada. This form has been used to extend Ada into new application domains.

- Adding features to Ada with extensions to its syntax and semantics. This form results in a new language which is often preprocessed to yield Ada as the executable language.

- Using selective Ada features and concepts for a new language.

In this chapter we will give an example of each of these forms that is currently in use or being considered for use and where Ada is going in the future.

Ada as a General Purpose Simulation Language

Several uses of Ada as a simulation language have been suggested and demonstrated just as they have been for languages like Pascal [1, 9, 10]. Ada is suited for this kind of application, since it supports concurrent processing in accordance with a well defined model. This makes Ada a good candidate for use as a discrete event simulation language providing similar capabilities as languages like SIMSCRIPT II.5.

The features needed to support the use of Ada as a simulation languge can be provided with a set of packages that provide special capabilities. Ada features are used directly for the general purpose processing and program structuring aspects of the simulation language. For a wide range of simulation applications, we can get away with only defining a limited number of packages that allow us to express such concepts or data structures as:

- Simulation Time
- Events
- Event Maintenance
- Queues
- Queue Ordering Disciplines

Figure 8-1 illustrates one possible package specification that implements some of the concepts and data structures above. The package specification consists of definitions for event features including some type and operation declarations, as well as random number generation procedures. The features provided by this package were derived from simulation languages such as SLAM and SIMSCRIPT II.5. This package alone is not sufficient to implement a complete simulation language. One also needs a mechanism for expressing simulation time as well as an overall program structure which manages event scheduling and causes the proper tasking interaction to support event scheduling.

The features that are built into Ada such as generics, tasking, and packaging as well as the software engineering concepts, directly supported by the language, make the development of a simulation at least as easy as with specialized simulation languages. In addition, the availability of Ada oriented support environments and design methodologies for the use of Ada, actually extends the modeler's capabilities to develop and maintain simulations.

```
package Event_Features is
   -- provides the user with an event oriented simulation view

   -- definition of the concept of simulation time
```

```
type Time is delta 0.000001 range   0.0 .. 360_000_000.0;
```

-- definition of time durations

```
type Milliseconds is delta 0.000001  range 0.0 .. 360_000_000.0;
type Seconds is delta 0.000000001 range 0.0 .. 360_000.0;
```

-- operations on objects of type time and durations of time

```
function "+" ( X : Seconds; Y : Time)           return Time;
function "+" ( X : Milliseconds; Y : Time)      return Time;
function "+" ( X : Time; Y : Seconds)           return Time;
function "+" ( X : Time; Y : Milliseconds)      return Time;

function "-" ( X : Seconds; Y : Time)           return Time;
function "-" ( X : Milliseconds; Y : Time)      return Time;
function "-" ( X : Time; Y : Seconds)           return Time;
function "-" ( X : Time; Y : Milliseconds)      return Time;

function "*" ( X : Seconds; Y : Time)           return Time;
function "*" ( X : Milliseconds; Y : Time)      return Time;
function "*" ( X : Time; Y : Seconds)           return Time;
function "*" ( X : Time; Y : Milliseconds)      return Time;
```

-- time and time duration unit conversions

```
function To_Seconds ( X : Milliseconds )        return Seconds;
function To_Seconds ( X : Float )               return Seconds;

function To_Milliseconds ( X : Seconds )        return Milliseconds;
function To_Milliseconds ( X : Float )          return Milliseconds;

function To_Float ( X : Seconds )               return Float;
function To_Float ( X : Milliseconds )          return Float;
```

```
Current_Time : Time := 0.0; -- value of time at any instant
End_Time     : Time;   -- simulation end time
```

-- event oriented declarations and operations

```
subtype Event_Name  is String ;    -- a name for an event
type Event_Notice is private;
```

```
procedure Schedule_Now ( Notice : in Event_Notice);
procedure Schedule_At    ( Notice : in Event_Notice; Instant : in
                                                             Time);

procedure Schedule_Delay  ( Notice : in Event_Notice;
                                      Increment : in Milliseconds );
procedure Schedule_Delay  ( Notice : in Event_Notice;
                                      Increment : in Seconds );

procedure Schedule_Before ( Notice : in Event_Notice;
                                      Name   : in Event_Name );
procedure Schedule_After  ( Notice : in Event_Notice;
                                      Name   : in Event_Name );
procedure Cancel          (Name   : in Event_Name);

function Scheduled (Name : Event_Name)    return Boolean;

function Event_Time (Name : Event_Name) return Time;

procedure  Start_Simulation;

Current_Event : Event_Notice;  -- a copy of the currently active event

-- psuedo random number generators

function U_Random ( Stream  : Integer := 0 ) return Float;
function Normal     ( Stream  : Integer := 0;
                                Mu, Sigma : Float ) return Float;

-- declarations shown here are to illustrate the concept of an Ada
-- package which provides simulation services
-- and as such is not complete.

private
    -- complete declaration of event notice (out of the scope of example)
    type Event_Notice ................................. ; -- TBD
end Event_Features;
```

Figure 8-1   **Package Specification for Simulation Language Features**

Ada as a Database Oriented Language

Many large scale systems in use today require not only the use of a general purpose programming language capability, but also a fully functional database management system. To support this kind of application, several groups, including Computer Corporation of America, have been engaged in research concerning the major issues associated with providing database management capabilities for Ada applications. This research has focused on both an interactive query language as well as an Ada application language. In the Computer Corporation of America research, the application language is called Adaplex. This language adds to Ada, at the declaration and statement level, the data definition and manipulation capabilities of an interactive query language [42].

The approach taken with Adaplex was to add to Ada a database sublanguage which would allow the application developer to freely intermix the full capabilities of the two languages in a highly integrated manner,thereby creating an overall language environment that is easy to use and maintain. To support this approach, the developer must have access to a set of tools that will preprocess this new language, Adaplex, to separate the database transactions from the Ada program source, yet still support the interface between the two. Figure 8-2 illustrates this process.

Adaplex has added two categories of features to Ada, which are called schema declarations and transaction statements. In one sense, this can be viewed as extending the Ada typing features and statement types supported by Ada, thereby creating a new language. Figure 8-3 identifies the features added and shows the relationship between features. The database declaration con-structs support the specification of:

- Data Objects within the Database

- Data Types of those Objects

- Consistency/Integrity requirements imposed on updates of those Objects

The atomic transaction statements allow application developers to specify a set of compound operations that must be performed in an indivisible manner.

A database in Adaplex has similar interface characteristics as an Ada package, but has been added as a separate structural unit. Within the various

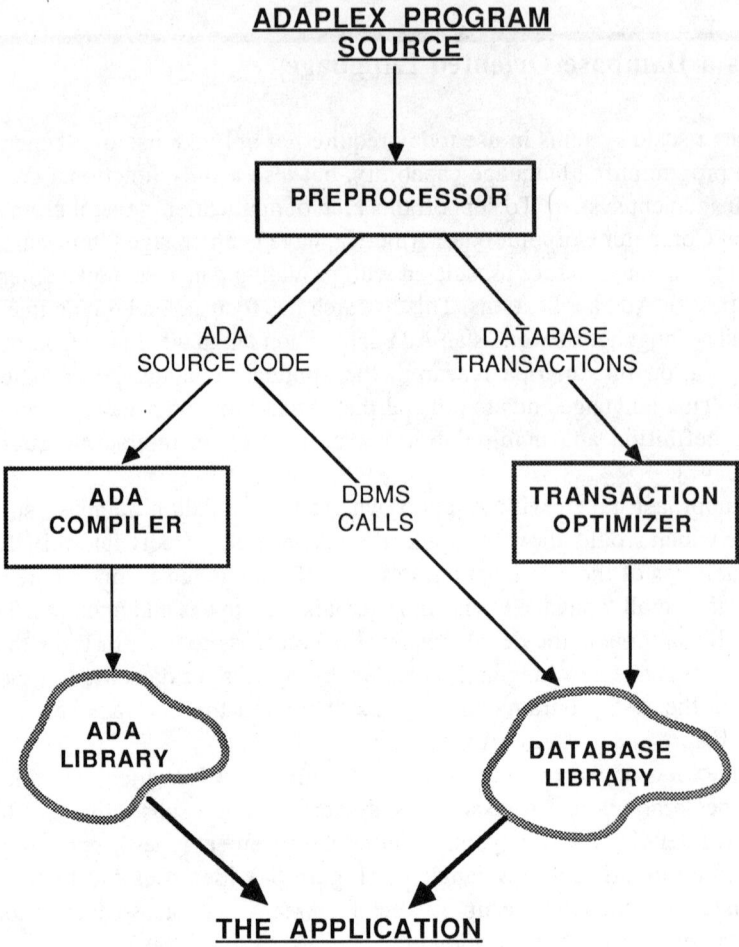

**ADAPLEX PROGRAM
SOURCE**

PREPROCESSOR

ADA
SOURCE CODE

DATABASE
TRANSACTIONS

**ADA
COMPILER**

DBMS
CALLS

**TRANSACTION
OPTIMIZER**

**ADA
LIBRARY**

**DATABASE
LIBRARY**

THE APPLICATION

Figure 8-2   **Adaplex Approach To Integrating Databases
Into An Ada Program**

ADAPLEX FEATURES

ADA FEATURES

- Program Units
- Data Types
- General Purpose Statements
- Separate Compilation

DATABASE DECLARATIONS	ATOMIC TRANSACTION STATEMENTS
• Entity Type • Set Type • Consistency Rules • Integrity Declaration • Database Specification	• For Each • Create • Destroy • Move • Set Include • Set Exclude • Quantified Relation

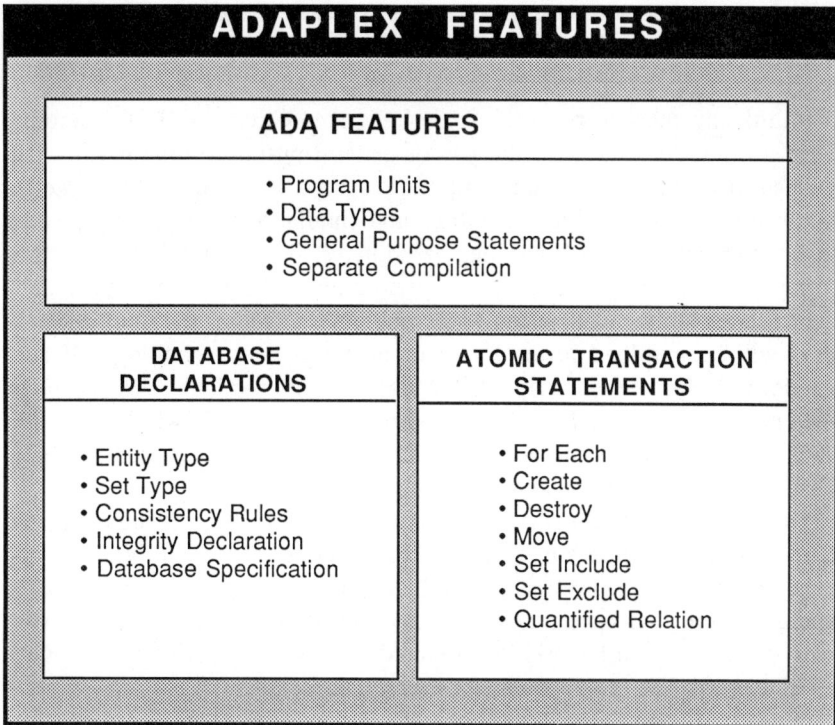

Figure 8-3   **Database Features Added To Ada With Adaplex**

program units that make up the Ada application, we can freely use the various statement types and expressions that use attributes associated with entities in the database.

This use of Ada falls into the second category defined above. In order to support this, the Ada development environment must supplement the normal Ada development tools with database oriented preprocessors and tools.

Ada as a Hardware Description Language

With the advent of Very Large Scale Integrated Circuits (VLSI), there has been a renewed interest in the use of general purpose programming languages to describe hardware designs. The need for a single language for hardware description, documentation, and simulations is no more apparent than in the DoD. The DoD has long been interested in the application of VLSI to its systems, due to the increased performance, increased reliability, and decreased cost that VLSI offers. The problem for DoD is that multiple vendors will be involved in the application of this new technology. If each vendor uses his own description language for his particular VLSI device, then many of the gains DoD expects to receive from VLSI will be lost. One such expected gain is the ability to mix and match devices from different vendors to achieve the desired system characteristics.

In 1980, the DoD launched what is called the Very High Speed Integrated Circuits (VHSIC) program. This program addresses the unique VLSI device needs of the DoD, as well as the tools required to support the development and use of the devices in real systems. As part of VHSIC program, an effort was started to define a VHSIC oriented Hardware Description Language (VHDL) [40]. The requirements for the VHDL include:

- The language must support the design, documentation, and efficient simulation of hardware from the system design level to the gate level.

- It must be independent of the underlying hardware implementation technologies, design methodologies and support environment.

- It must be extendable to various hardware technologies, methodologies, and support environments.

- The language must use Ada constructs wherever possible.

This VHDL has been partially implemented and is currently under evaluation and review. This implementation includes not only the language definition (based on Ada), but a set of tools including analyzers, simulators, and a design library manager. The IEEE is considering the use of VHDL as part of the standard for automatic-test program generation that it is currently developing.

In VHDL, extended Ada features are used to support various categories of abstractions. The data typing features, subprograms, and packages are supported as well as object declaration and the elementary control constructs. The following have been added to the set of Ada features to address the unique needs of describing, documenting, and simulating VHSIC level devices and systems:

Design Entities — having an interface and two bodies that implement the functional, structural, and timing aspects of a hardware device, subsystem, or system.

Component Instance — a declaration that allows a parameterized instance of a design entity to be constructed.

Generate Statement — provides a macro expansion capability that allows regular structures to be created from more elementary structures; a component.

Physical Types — data types that express the value of a variable as well as the units used to measure it.

Signals — used to represent buses or dataflows in hardware which can be driven from multiple sources and retain their values over time.

Attributes — a property of an object that is user declared and assigned to a class of objects.

Assertions — statements which specify conditions that are expected to be true during the execution of a design by one or more of the tools. Violations of assertions are reported to the user during simulation.

VHDL Provided Packages — packages that contain types, subtypes and standard operations to directly support hardware concepts such as One's and Two's complement number systems, voltage, capacitance, etc.

In addition to extending Ada features as indicated above, some subsetting of Ada was also used to reduce the overall size of VHDL. Figure 8-4 illustrates the use of VHDL to describe part of a simple four bit adder structure.

```
with Adder_Resources;          -- some useful conversion routines
entity Four_Bit_Adder (        A, B : in Bit_Vector ( 3 .. 0 );
                               Cin   : in Bit;
                               Cout : out Bit;
                               Sum : in Bit_Vector ( 3 .. 0 ) ) is

-- special parameters

generic

      (Delay : Time := 36ns);

assertion
      Delay  > 3ns;
      Sum'Fanout <= Max_Fanout;

end Four_Bit_Adder;

-- structural decomposition

architectural body Pure_Structure of Four_Bit_Adder is

   signal C : Bit_Vector ( 3 .. 0 );

   component Full_Adder ( Cin, I1, I2 : in Bit;  Cout, Res : out Bit );

begin

   for I in  3 .. 0 generate
    if I = 0 generate
       Full_Adder ( Cin, A(I), B(I), C(I), Sum(I));
    end generate;
    if I > 0 generate
       Full_Adder (C(I - 1), A(I), B(I), C(I), Sum(I));
    end generate;
   end generate;

      Cout := C(3);

end Pure_Structure;
```

Figure 8-4   **Use of VHDL – A Four Bit Adder**

VHDL is one example of how a well defined language like Ada can be used as the basis for a specialized language.

The three examples of other uses of Ada are only representative of the potential uses that we will see Ada being applied to in the future. In one sense, Ada is being viewed by researchers as a base technology ready to be extended or molded to address new classes of problems.

Future Directions

If there were one question that is most appropriate to ask at this point, it would have to be:

"Is Ada the solution to the Software Crisis?"

Given this question, the answer would have to be:

"No, Ada is not the solution to the Software Crisis!"

The only solution to the Software Crisis will come from the efforts of the practitioners in this field. It will be only you, the practitioners, who will resolve this crisis if it can ever be resolved. Ada plays a role potentially in the solution, but only when it is used properly.

If you look at the the efforts over the last few years some would say Ada has actually been part of the Software Crisis, because its development did not or perhaps could not benefit from the software engineering concepts on which the whole Ada Effort was built. It is only now that we are in a position to attack the Software Crisis with the full Ada Effort. But again, it must be emphasized that it is the practitioner and his or her ability to apply the results of the Ada Effort that is our only hope of satisfactorily resolving the Software Crisis (see figure 8-5). The purpose of this book was to provide the practitioners with an insight into the Ada Effort, and to allow them to develop their abilities to apply the results of the Ada Effort.

What we have presented in this book is an overview of an effort that is ongoing and expanding in our industry. The future of the Ada Effort may well be charted by the DoD planners, but universal industry acceptance is the key to the sustained growth and evolution of the effort. Acceptance will only come by having an informed group of practitioners, and by the continuous involvement of all segments of our industry.

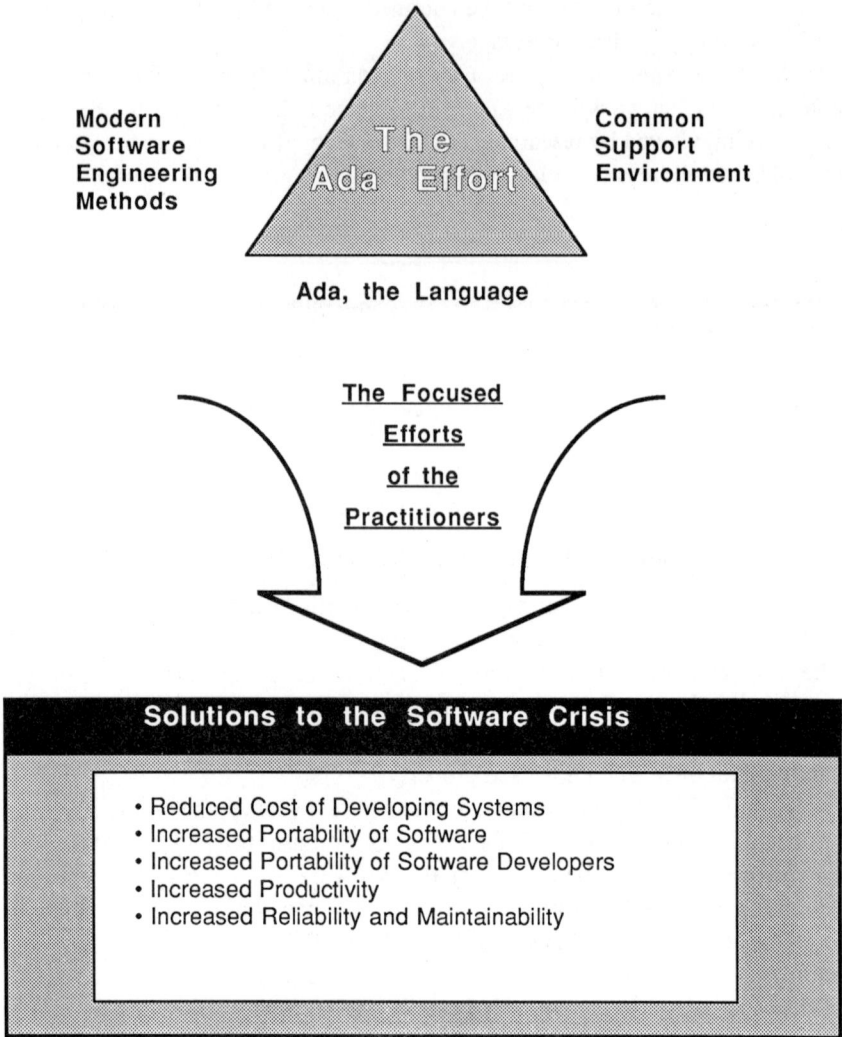

Figure 8-5   **The Role Of The Ada Effort In The Solution Of The Software Crisis**

If we were to look into our crystal ball, we would see some of the following events occurring in the future relative to the Ada Effort [62]:

- The real use of Ada within DoD on a widespread basis will begin in 1987.

- Ada component stores, sometimes called package stores, will begin to appear in 1987. These stores will supply the industry with off-the-shelf highly reusable packages and programs.

- The 1988 version of the Language Reference Manual will nail down some of the ambiguous elements of the language definition, but no features will be added or deleted from the language.

- Applications that readily use Ada, AI oriented languages, and advanced database techniques, in an integrated manner, will start to appear in 1989.

- Specialized very high performance Ada oriented development environments will be in common use by 1990, thus getting around the limitations of current environments.

- Ada will be generally available and useable in distributed systems by 1991.

- A complete Ada oriented design methodology and support environment for large scale development of embedded systems will be in general use by 1995.

Only time will tell if this is the direction in which the Ada Effort is heading.

APPENDIX A: ADA AS A LANGUAGE — FULL OVERVIEW

This appendix provides a fairly complete overview of the programming language Ada. The specific features and concepts covered here are summarized in table A-1.

TABLE A-1 SUMMARY OF FEATURES COVERED

- General Structure of Program Units
- Lexical Elements and Style
- Data Typing
- Object Declarations
- Program Unit Declarations - Subprograms, Packages, Tasks, and Generics
- Other Declarations - Exceptions and Renaming
- Expressions
- Statements
- Exception Handler
- Sample Program Units - All forms
- Predefined Program Units
- Support for Large Scale Development
- Ada's Execution Model
- Dynamics of Error Handling
- Tasking

Some Ada features such as Input and Output have not been covered due to the somewhat unique nature of these features and the scope of this book. For further coverage of I/O and other language features I refer you to the selected reading list provided at the back of this book.

The Static Framework of Ada

The static framework of Ada addresses the syntax and semantics of the language without consideration for the execution time implication of the semantics. This static framework focuses on overall program structure as well as a program's developmental structure. Within this framework, program structure represents the Ada features that are combined together in order to create a program. This program, once compiled, linked, and loaded on a target machine, will be executed. Developmental structure represents the set of features that support the orderly building of a program. This support allows for such activities as separate compilation and incremental development of a program's constituent parts.

Figure A-1 identifies the major pieces that can make up the structure of an Ada program. Also shown are several usage oriented relationships between the pieces. All Ada programs follow this basic structure and differ only in the size and number of application library units as well as the number of language and/or environment defined library units accessed to make up the program. The structural parts identified in figure A-1 are referred to as Program Units. Each program unit may be further divided into pieces that support concepts such as separate compilation. This will be discussed later in this appendix.

General Structure of Program Units

In Ada, all program units have the same logical structure, although some variation in the physical realization may exist between individual program units. Every program unit can be viewed as having the following basic form that consists of a:

- **Specification** - which describes what the program unit does to those that will make use of the program unit.

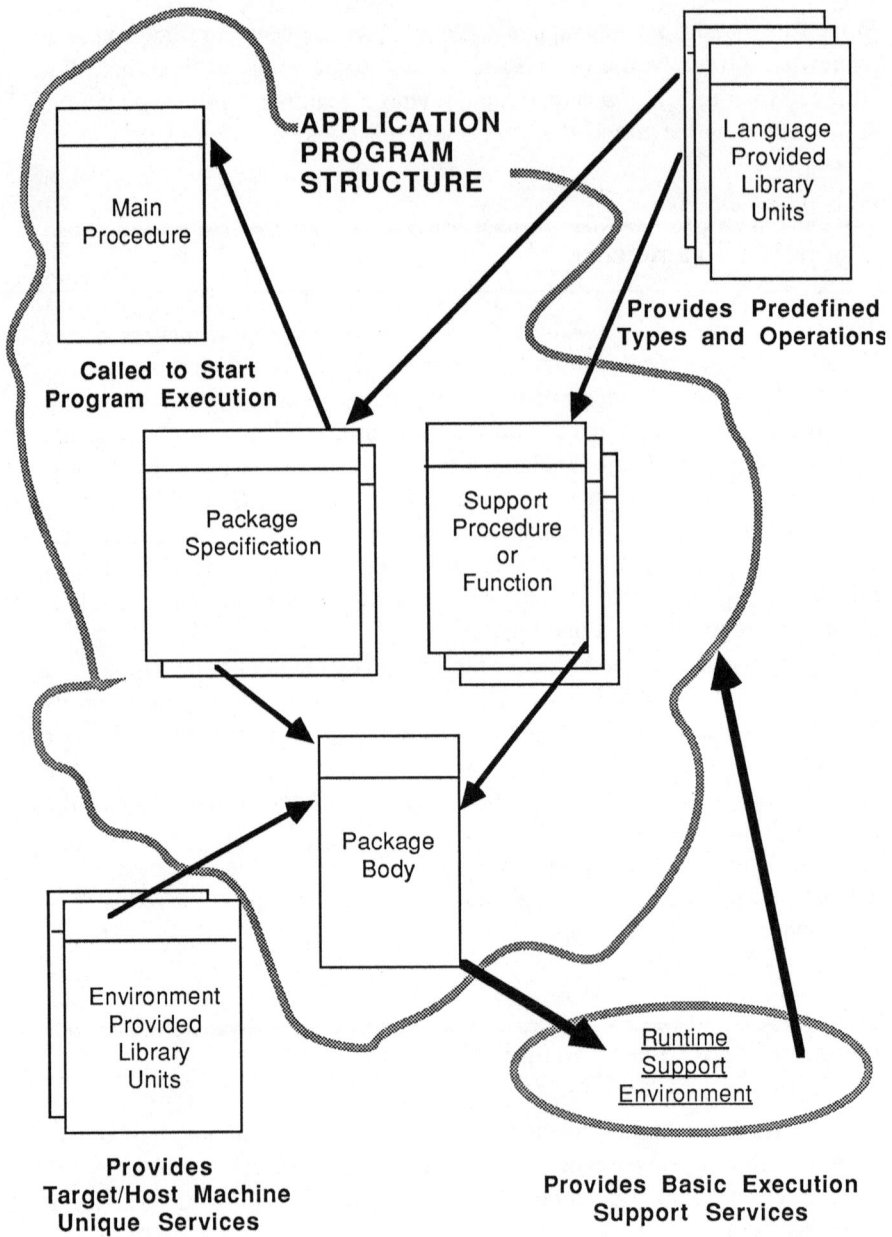

APPLICATION PROGRAM STRUCTURE

Main Procedure

Called to Start Program Execution

Language Provided Library Units

Provides Predefined Types and Operations

Package Specification

Support Procedure or Function

Package Body

Environment Provided Library Units

Provides Target/Host Machine Unique Services

Runtime Support Environment

Provides Basic Execution Support Services

Figure A - 1   **Structure of An Ada Program**

- **Body** - which details how the program unit will implement the required operations, algorithms or structures specified or implied by the specification.

The intent of the separation of the specification and the body is to increase the reliability and maintainability of programs which effectively use Ada program units. The reliability of a program is increased because a common class of errors — interface errors — can easily be detected at compilation time and not at system test time, as typically happens when using assembly lan-guage. The maintainability of a program is increased because changes in the implementation details can be restricted to the body of the program unit without affecting the user of the program unit. This is because the user can only take advantage of that which is provided in the specification for the program unit, not the body. Table A-2 summarizes the principle features and uses of the various program units. Figure A-2 illustrates the form of the program units supported by Ada.

Also illustrated in figure A-2 is the basic internal structuring of Ada program units. This structure in general consists of a declarative region and executable region. Optionally, some program units will have a private part and/or a exception handler region.

TABLE A-2 PROGRAM UNIT FEATURES AND USES

PROGRAM UNIT	FEATURE	USE

Subprogram	• Basic Executable Program Structures
	• Can have separate specification
	    (interface) and body (implementation)
		• Main Programs
		• Definition of an
		    Algorithm
		• Operators

-Procedure	• Defines a Sequence of Actions • Invoked by a procedure call	
-Function	• Defines a computation that returns a value • Invoke from within an expression	

Package	• Basic Structuring Unit of Ada	• Grouping Related Program Units
	• Textually Separate Specification and Body	• Named Collection of Declarations
	• ControlsVisibility/Access to Data, Types, and Operations	• Abstract Data Types
Task	• Runs "concurrently" with other tasks	• Concurrent Actions/Processes
	• Implements parallel threads of control	• Controlling Access to Shared Resources
	• Has mechanisms to support synchronization and data passing	• Interrupt Handlers
		• Buffers/Queues/FIFOs
Generic	• Parameterized Template of other program units	• Reusable Components
		• Libraries

Procedures

PROCEDURE SPECIFICATION

procedure PUSH (E : **in** ELEMENT_TYPE; S : **in out** STACK);
-- a subprogram declaration specifies the services that are provided

PROCEDURE BODY

procedure PUSH (E : **in** ELEMENT_TYPE; S : **in out** STACK) **is**
begin   -- begins the executable part
  if S.INDEX = S.SIZE then
    raise STACK_OVERFLOW;
  else
    S.INDEX := S.INDEX + 1;
    S. SPACE (S.INDEX) := E;

```
    end if;
exception  -- optional region for exception handlers
    when CONSTRAINT_ERROR => raise;
end PUSH;
```

Functions

FUNCTION SPECIFICATION

```
function DOT_PRODUCT (LEFT, RIGHT : VECTOR) return REAL;
```

FUNCTION BODY

```
function DOT_PRODUCT (LEFT, RIGHT : VECTOR) return REAL is
 SUM : REAL := 0.0;  -- declarative region
begin
 CHECK (LEFT'FIRST = RIGHT'FIRST and LEFT'LAST = RIGHT'LAST);
 for J in LEFT'RANGE loop
    SUM := SUM + LEFT (J)*RIGHT (J);
 end loop;
 return SUM;
exception  -- optional region for exception handlers
    when CONSTRAINT_ERROR => raise;
end DOT_PRODUCT;
```

Packages

PACKAGE SPECIFICATION

```
package KEY_MANAGER is
    type KEY is private;   -- declarative region
    NULL_KEY : constant KEY;
    procedure GET_KEY (K : out KEY);
    function "<" (X, Y : KEY) return BOOLEAN;
private                          -- private part only required for private
                                 -- type declarations
    type KEY is new NATURAL;
    NULL_KEY : constant KEY := 0;
end KEY_MANAGER;
```

PACKAGE BODY

```
package body KEY_MANAGER is
    LAST_KEY : KEY := 0;
    procedure GET_KEY (K : out KEY) is
    begin
        LAST_KEY := LAST_KEY + 1;
        K := LAST_KEY;
    end GET_KEY;

    function "<" (X,Y : KEY) return BOOLEAN is
    begin
        return INTEGER (X) < INTEGER (Y);
    end "<";
begin    -- optional executable region
    null; -- executed when body is elaborated
exception   -- optional region for exception handlers for executable region
    when CONSTRAINT_ERROR => raise;
end KEY_MANAGER;
```

Tasks

TASK SPECIFICATION

```
task PROTECTED_ARRAY is
    entry READ (N : in INDEX ; V : out ITEM);
    entry WRITE (N : in INDEX ; E : in ITEM);
end PROTECTED_ARRAY ;
```

TASK BODY

```
task body PROTECTED_ARRAY is
    TABLE : array (INDEX) of ITEM := (INDEX => NULL_ITEM);
begin
    loop
        select
                accept READ (N : in INDEX; V : out ITEM) do
                V := TABLE (N);
                end READ;
        or
```

```
            accept WRITE (N : in INDEX; E : in ITEM) do
               TABLE (N) := E;
            end WRITE;
         end select;
      end loop;
exception -- optional region for exception handlers
   when CONSTRAINT_ERROR => raise;
end PROTECTED_ARRAY;
```

Generic Subprogram

GENERIC PROCEDURE SPECIFICATION

— *can have generic functions also*

```
generic
   type ELEM is private;
procedure EXCHANGE (U, V : in out ELEM);
```

GENERIC PROCEDURE BODY

```
procedure EXCHANGE (U, V : in out ELEM) is
   T : ELEM; -- the generic formal type
begin
   T := U;
   U := V;
   V := T;
exception -- optional region for exception handlers
   when CONSTRAINT_ERROR => raise;
end EXCHANGE;
```

GENERIC PROCEDURE INSTANTIATION

```
procedure SWAP is new EXCHANGE (ELEM => INTEGER);
procedure SWAP is new EXCHANGE (CHARACTER);
-- creates useable copies of the generic templates parameterized for
-- various data types
```

Generic Package

GENERIC PACKAGE SPECIFICATION

```
generic
    SIZE : POSITIVE;
    type ITEM is private;
package STACK is
    procedure PUSH (E : in ITEM);
    procedure POP (E : out ITEM);
    OVERFLOW, UNDERFLOW : exception;
end STACK;
```

GENERIC PACKAGE BODY

```
package body STACK is

    type TABLE is array (POSITIVE range <>) of ITEM;
    SPACE : TABLE (1 .. SIZE);
    INDEX : NATURAL := 0;

    procedure PUSH (E : in ITEM) is
    begin
        if INDEX >= SIZE then
                raise OVERFLOW;
        end if;
        INDEX := INDEX + 1;
        SPACE (INDEX) := E;
    end PUSH;

    procedure POP ( E : out ITEM) is
    begin
        if INDEX = 0 then
                raise UNDERFLOW;
        end if;
        E := SPACE (INDEX) ;
        INDEX := INDEX - 1;
    end POP;
```

```
begin    -- optional executable region executed when body is elaborated
   null;
exception  -- optional region for exception handlers for executable region
   when CONSTRAINT_ERROR => raise;
end STACK;
```

GENERIC PACKAGE INSTANTIATION

```
package STACK_INT is new STACK (SIZE => 200, ITEM => INTEGER);
package STACK_BOOL is new STACK (100, BOOLEAN);
```

Figure A -2   **Basic Ada Program Unit Forms**

Lexical Elements

In any language, the text that makes up a program can be considered to be just a sequence of lexical elements which in turn are represented as a sequence of graphic characters of some character set. Ada has a well defined lexical structure as its base. In addition, it has a textual structure. Both types of structure were defined to improve the human readability of the language as well as to improve the machine translatability. The concern for the structure of Ada builds on the desire of the language designers to allow the textual structure of the program to convey, in an intuitive manner, the logical structure of the program.

All Ada programs can be viewed as simply a sequence of characters formed into lines which are placed on pages. The arrangement on the pages is determined mainly by the need of the human to be able to read the program text, and from that reading to understand the meaning of the program. To aid in this human understanding, Ada program text is built on a set of lexical elements that share the common characteristics identified in table A-3. The set of lexical elements of which all Ada programs are built are summarized in table A-4. This table identifies the various elements and provides an overview of their basic characteristics. Table A-5 identifies the reserved words of Ada that are used in combination to form the structure for program units, statements, object declarations, etc. Provided after these tables are a set of examples that illustrate the uses and forms of the various lexical elements that make up the language.

TABLE A-3 COMMON CHARACTERISTICS OF ALL LEXICAL ELEMENTS

CATEGORY	CHARACTERISTICS
Character Set	• program text may only include ASCII graphic characters and format effectors (horizontal and vertical tabulation, line feed, carriage return and form feed)
	• full character set (graphic and control characters) can be used through predefined **type** CHARACTER and constants declared in **package** ASCII
Format	• lexical elements must fit on a single line
	• character sequence for end of a line is not defined as part of the language (implementation dependent)
	• no continuation marks required to continue program text across multiple line, provided no single lexical element is split between lines
	• spaces, tabs and blank lines can be used freely to enhance readability

---

TABLE A-4   CHARACTERISTICS OF ADA LEXICAL ELEMENTS

LEXICAL ELEMENT	CHARACTERISTICS
Delimiters	• used as separators and operators
	• are formed as a single or multiple special characters

- single character delimiters include:
  & ' ( ) * + , - . / : ; < = > |

- compound delimters include:
  => .. ** := /= >= <= << >> <>

Identifiers
- used as names of entities within program text
- must start with a letter; subsequent characters can be letters, digits and underscores
- underscores can only appear between two letters or digits or between a letter and a digit
- upper and lower case letters are considered the same
- can be as long as a line
- include user defined names and reserved words

Integer Literals
- represents a numeric literal with no decimal(radix) point
- data type is *universal_integer*
- allowed values are <u>positive numbers or zero</u>
- can be represented in any radix from 2 to 16
- can have a <u>positive integer</u> exponent
- must start with a digit (underscores allowed between digits)

Real Literals
- represents a numeric literal with a decimal(radix) point
- data type is *universal_real*
- allowed values are <u>positive numbers or zero</u>
- can be represented in any radix from 2 to 16
- can have a <u>negative or positive</u> exponent
- must start with a digit (underscores allowed between digits)

Character Literals
- represents one of the 95 graphic characters (ASCII)
- data type is a character type
- formed by enclosing a single character between two single apostrophe characters

String Literals
- represents a sequence of zero or more characters

- formed by enclosing zero or more graphic characters of the ASCII character set between quote characters
- must fit on a single line
- quotes can be included in string literal by double quoting

Comments
- are used to enlighten the reader and have no program effect
- start with two adjacent hypens and extends to the end of the line

---

TABLE A-5 ADA RESERVED WORDS

<u>abort</u>	begin	case	declare	else	for
abs	body	constant	<u>delay</u>	elsif	function
accept			delta	end	
access			<u>digits</u>	entry	
all			do	exception	
and				exit	
array					
at					
generic	if	limited	mod	<u>new</u>	of
goto	<u>in</u>	loop		not	or
	is			<u>null</u>	others
					<u>out</u>
package	raise	select	task	use	when
pragma	range	separate	<u>terminate</u>		while
private	record	subtype	then		with
procedure	rem		type		
	renames				
	return				
	<u>reverse</u>				
xor					

Notes: - *reserved words cannot be used as user defined identifiers*

— *the underlined words indicate the reserved words often used as user defined names in programs written in other languages which are illegal to use in an Ada program.*

Examples A-1: Identifiers

```
Math_Library        -- a package name
Sine                -- a function name
Distance            -- a variable name
x                   -- another variable name Index
Index               -- a loop parameter
```

```
A_Very_Long_Identifier_That_Means_Nothing_At_All_3000_X
```

```
INDEX               -- same loop parameter as above (no distinction made
                    -- between upper and lower case letters)
iNdEx               -- same loop parameter as above
```

Examples A-2: Integer Literals

```
4095                -- a value of 4,095
4_095               -- same value
2600                -- a value of 2,600
26E2                -- same value
260E01              -- same value
10#2600#            -- same value using based literal notation

2#1111_1111#        -- base 2 notation for 255
16#FF#              -- base 16 notation for 255
16#0000FF#          -- base 16 notation for 255

16#E#E01            -- base 16 notation for 224 with exponent
                    -- (base 16** E)
2#1110_0000#        -- base 2 notation for 224
```

Examples A-3: Real Literals

4095.0	-- a real value of 4,095.0
4_095.00000	-- same value
2600.0	-- a value of 2,600.0
26.0E2	-- same value
260000.0E-02	-- same value
10#2600.0#	-- same value using based literal notation
2#1111_1111.0#	-- base 2 notation for 255.0
16#FF.0#	-- base 16 notation for 255.0
16#F.F#E01	-- base 16 notation for 255.0 with exponent
	(base 16 ** E)

Examples A-4: Character Literals

'A'	-- upper case letter A
'a'	-- lower case letter a (not the same as 'A')
' '	-- the space character

Examples A-5: String Literals

" A short string "

""   -- the null string
" A string with a "" in it"

"A"   -- is a string literal not the character literal 'A'

" this string has special characters in it $, %, + "

When used together, these lexical elements form specific statements, declarations and program units. If they are written consistently, they will have a textual structure associated with them. This basic structure, as will be illustrated in examples in this appendix, is comb-like, allowing for easy discrimination of one program structure from another [48]. The advantage of a common textual structuring, is that it aids in the process of learning the language, as well as reducing the first time coding errors we all seem to generate over and over again.

Some pitfalls and hints in the use of the lexical features of Ada include:

- The use of reserved words as user defined identifiers (i.e., names of subprograms, etc.) is illegal. Some of the reserved words are likely to cause you trouble so review the list in table A-5 if you are not sure.

- Select identifiers on the basis of improving the readability of a program. Don't use short cryptic names that can only be understood by the designers or implementor.

- Use the free format nature of Ada to explicitly show the structure of the data and the program by means of indentation and spacing.

Declarative Part

All program units in Ada have a declarative part which defines a textual region in which various forms of declarations can be made. In Ada a declaration is defined as follows:

"A declaration associates an identifier (or some other notation) with an entity."

In this definition, the identifier serves as a name by which the entity is referred to. An entity is any one of the following language items:

- Procedure Specification or Body
- Function Specification or Body
- Package Specification or Body
- Task Specification or Body

- Type Declaration
- Object Declaration
- Use Clause
- Generic Declaration or Instantiation
- Representation Clause
- Exception Declaration

The declarative part of the various program units is shown in the following examples.

Examples A-6: Declarative Regions

— In general, declarative regions start with the "**is**" of a program unit body and ends with the "**begin**". A region can contain Basic and Later Declarative Items. Basic Items must appear before Later Items.

— For package specifications, the declarative region starts at the "**is**" and ends with the "**end**".

```
--    Basic Declarative Items include:
--    types, objects, program unit declarations, and renaming declarations
--    representation clauses, use clauses, and exception declarations

--    Later Declarative Items include:
--    program unit bodies and declarations
--    use clauses
```

```
package KEY_MANAGER is
     type KEY is private;                -- Basic Declarative Items Only
     NULL_KEY : constant KEY; --
          -- a deferred constant
     procedure GET_KEY (K : out KEY);
     function "<" (X, Y : KEY) return BOOLEAN;
private
     type KEY is new NATURAL;  -- Complete Type Declarations
     NULL_KEY : constant KEY := 0;  -- for private types only
end KEY_MANAGER;
```

```ada
package TABLE_MANAGER is
     type ITEM is                          -- Only consists of Basic
        record                             -- Declarative Items
            ORDER_NUM : INTEGER;
            ITEM_CODE : INTEGER;
            QUANTITY  : INTEGER;
            ITEM_TYPE  : CHARACTER;
        end record;

     NULL_ITEM : constant ITEM :=
        (ORDER_NUM | ITEM_CODE | QUANTITY => 0, ITEM_TYPE => ' ');

     procedure INSERT (NEW_ITEM : in ITEM);
     procedure RETRIEVE (FIRST_ITEM : out ITEM);

     TABLE_FULL : exception ;
end TABLE_MANAGER;

package body TABLE_MANAGER is
     SIZE : constant := 2000;              -- order of Basic Items is not
                                           -- important
     subtype INDEX is INTEGER range 0 .. SIZE;
     type INTERNAL_ITEM is
        record
            CONTENT                : ITEM;
            SUCC                   : INDEX;
            PRED                   : INDEX;
        end record;

     TABLE : array (INDEX) of INTERNAL_ITEM;
     FIRST_BUSY_ITEM : INDEX := 0;
     FIRST_FREE_ITEM : INDEX := 1;

     -- ... notation is used to indicate that text has been omitted to simplify
     -- the presentation, there is no ... operator or statement type in Ada
     -- although some times it would be useful.

        -- Beginning of Later Declarative Items

     function FREE_LIST_EMPTY return BOOLEAN is ... end;
```

```
        function BUSY_LIST_EMPTY return BOOLEAN is ... end;
        procedure EXCHANGE (FROM : in INDEX; TO : in INDEX) is ... end;
        procedure INITIALIZE_TABLE is ... end;

        -- a procedure with no declarative region
        procedure INSERT (NEW_ITEM : in ITEM) is
        begin
            if FREE_LIST_EMPTY then
                raise TABLE_FULL;
            end if;
            -- remaining code for insert
        end INSERT;

        procedure RETREIVE (FIRST_ITEM : out ITEM) is ... end;

    begin
        -- initilization of the table linkages

        INITIALIZE_TABLE;  -- executable part of a package body
                        -- executed only during elaboration of
                        -- the package
    end TABLE_MANAGER;
```

— Block statements allow you to introduce local declarations in the executable portion of the program. They also have a declarative region that starts with a "**declare**" and ends with the "**begin.**"

```
    SWAP:
        declare
            TEMP : INTEGER;  -- declarations allowed here
        begin
            TEMP := V;
            V := U;
            U := TEMP;
        end SWAP;
```

Data Oriented Declarations

Within Ada, all objects (i.e., variables and constants in other languages) are declared, usually explicitly and sometimes implicitly. These declarations associate the object with a name that is used elsewhere in the program to refer to the object as well as associating a data type with the object. The data type characterizes the set of values that the object may assume. It further characterizes the objects by defining the allowed operations on the object itself as well as all other objects of that data type.

Data Typing

The rationale for associating a data type with an object comes from over 20 years of programming language development. The stated rationale for Ada data typing facilities is the support of sound Software Engineering principles and goals such as:

Factor the Properties of Data - knowledge about common properties of an object to be used in a program should be collected in one place and referred to by a name (i.e., a type name)

Enhance the Maintainability of a Program - changes in the common properties of a set of objects can be affected by a change at a single point in the program. This eliminates the potential requirement to change the program at every occurrence of an object with those common properties.

Separate the Abstract Properties of Objects from their Physical Representation - since only the abstract nature of an object is needed in order to operate on it.

Hide Implementation Details - the details of how an object is represented should, in most cases, be hidden from the users of the object.

Increase Program Reliability - objects that have distinct properties should be clearly distinquished from other objects. Mixing of objects with distinct properties should be detected and not allowed by the compiler or translator.

The Ada typing facilities described below address these goals in a uniform and consistent manner.

Ada supports a wide range of data types as illustrated in table A-6. This table identifies the various data types supported, as well as the hierarchy of properties that objects of each data type can assume. The language allows the user to define his own data types using the syntax shown in table A-7. As with any language, the user is also provided with a number of language defined types that can be used in normal program development. These are summarized in table A-8. Table A-8 also indicates the properties of objects of each predefined data type and the place in which the data type was defined.

TABLE A-6 OVERVIEW OF ADA DATA TYPES

DATA TYPES
- characterize a set of values
- characterize the set of allowed operations on those values

  SCALAR TYPES
- set of allowed values has no component structures (i.e., the atoms of the language)
- have a defined ordering
- have an allowed contiguous range of values

    DISCRETE TYPES
- represent values in a finite number of discrete positions

      ENUMERATION TYPES
- represent an ordered set of distinct values specified by listing them

      CHARACTER TYPES
- represent enumeration type in which one of its allowed values is a character literal

INTEGER TYPES { A NUMERIC TYPE }
- represent a set of consecutive integers over a limited range of values
- are represented exactly on the underlying machine

REAL TYPES
- approximately represent continuous real world numeric values within a specified accuracy

FLOATING POINT TYPES { A NUMERIC TYPE }
- have error bounds that vary with the magnitude of the value being represented

FIXED POINT TYPES { A NUMERIC TYPE }
- have error bounds that are constant for all values represented

COMPOSITE TYPES
- have a component structure consisting of other data types whose value is determined by the values of its components

ARRAY TYPES
- represent indexed collection of similar components

RECORD TYPES
- represent collection of named components of potentially different types

ACCESS TYPES
- have values that designate objects of another type

PRIVATE TYPES
- have values whose underlying representation is hidden from the user of the type

TASK TYPES
- have values that designate tasks

TABLE A-7 DATA TYPE SYNTAX

type identifier [discriminant_part] **is** type_definition

Notation used:
    -- { } repeat zero, one or times
    -- [ ] optional
    -- ::= defines
    -- | or

• SCALAR TYPES
    DISCRETE TYPES
        ENUMERATION TYPES
            type *type*_name **is** (enum_lit {, enum_lit});
            enum_lit ::= identifier | character_literal

        CHARACTER TYPES
            -- same as enumeration type
            -- must have at least one character_literal in definition

        INTEGER TYPES
            type *type*_name **is range** *lower*_bound_expr ..
                                *upper*_bound_expr;

        REAL TYPES

            FLOATING POINT TYPES
                type *type*_name **is digits** number_of_digits
                    [**range** *lower*_bound_expr..*upper*_bound_expr];

            FIXED POINT TYPES
                type *type*_name **is delta** accuracy_expr
                    range *lower*_bound_expr .. *upper*_bound_expr;

• COMPOSITE TYPES
    ARRAY TYPES
        -- constrained array types
        type *type*_name **is array** (discrete_range {, discrete_range}) **of**
                        component_subtype;
        discrete_range ::= discrete_subtype | range
        discrete_subtype ::= type_mark [**range** Lower_Bound ..
                          Upper_Bound]

        -- unconstrained array types

type *type*_name **is array** (type_mark **range <>** {, type_mark
range <>}) **of** component_subtype;

<u>RECORD TYPES</u>

type *type*_name [(discr_spec {; discr_spec})] **is**
record
    component_list
end record;

discr_spec ::= identifier {, identifier} : type_mark [:= expression]

component_list ::= component_decl {component_decl} |
                {component_decl} variant_part |**null;**

component_decl ::= identifier {, identifier} : component_subtype
                        [:= expression];

variant_part ::=
  case discr_name **is**
    when choice {| choice} => component_list
    {**when** choice {| choice} => component_list}
  end case;

choice := simple_expression | discrete_range | **others** |
                  component_simple_name

• <u>ACCESS TYPES</u>

type *type*_name **is access** designated_subtype;

• <u>PRIVATE TYPES</u>

type *type*_name [(discr_spec {; discr_spec})] **is [limited] private;**

• <u>TASK TYPES</u>

-- see tasking sections for allowed definition

When one defines a data type, one is not only specifying a set of values, but one is also defining the set of allowed operations on objects of that type. Table A-9 identifies the language provided operations as well as attributes that characterize a data type or object of a data type. The examples that follow the tables illustrate the flexibility in data typing provided by Ada.

TABLE A-8 LANGUAGE PROVIDED DATA TYPES (TYPES/SUBTYPES)

TYPE DECLARATION	DECLARED IN	DEFINITION/USAGE
ENUMERATION		
type BOOLEAN **is** (FALSE, TRUE);	STANDARD	• predefined type used in logical and conditional expressions
type CHARACTER **is**	STANDARD ASCII characters	• predefined type that represents
(nul, soh, stx, etx, eot, enq, ack, bel, bs, ht, lf, vt, ff, cr, so, si, dle, dc1, dc2, dc3, dc4, nak, syn, etb, can, em, sub, esc, fs, gs, rs, us, ' ', '!', '"', '#', '$', '%', '&', ''', '(', ')', '*', '+', ',', '-', '.', '/', '0', '1', '2', '3', '4', '5', '6', '7', '8', '9', ':', ';', '<', '=', '>', '?', '@', 'A', 'B', 'C', 'D', 'E', 'F', 'G', 'H', 'I', 'J', 'K', 'L', 'M', 'N', 'O', 'P', 'Q', 'R', 'S', 'T', 'U', 'V', 'W', 'X', 'Y', 'Z', '[', '\', ']', '^', '_',		

```
'', 'a', 'b', 'c', 'd', 'e', 'f', 'g',
'h', 'i', 'j', 'k', 'l', 'm', 'n', 'o',
'p', 'q', 'r', 's', 't', 'u', 'v', 'w',
'x', 'y', 'z', '{', '|', '}', '~', del);
```

type NAME is
(*I_D_List_of_Configuration_Names*);

SYSTEM   • list of allowed system names supported by this implementation

type FILE_MODE is (IN_FILE, OUT_FILE);

SEQUENTIAL_IO   • allowed modes for internal files indicate direction of data flow

type FILE_MODE is
(IN_FILE, INOUT_FILE, OUT_FILE);

TEXT_IO
DIRECT_IO

type TYPE_SET is
(LOWER_CASE, UPPER_CASE);

TEXT_IO   • indicates manner in which enumeration literals will be displayed

INTEGER TYPES

universal_integer

no declaration   • an anonymous type used in the reference manual to specify the type for integer literals, etc.

type INTEGER is range
I_D_Lower .. I_D_Upper,

STANDARD   • a predefined type for general use

subtype NATURAL is INTEGER range 0 .. INTEGER'LAST;	STANDARD	• a predefined subtype for general use
subtype POSITIVE is INTEGER range 1 .. INTEGER'LAST;	STANDARD	• a predefined subtype for general use
subtype PRIORITY is INTEGER range I_D_Lower .. I_D_Upper;	SYSTEM	• indicates the priority of a task or main subprogram used by runtime system for scheduling
type COUNT is range 0 .. I_D_Upper;	DIRECT_IO	• indicates a position in a file used to located individual elements of a file
subtype POSITIVE_COUNT is COUNT range 1 .. COUNT'LAST;	TEXT_IO DIRECT_IO	
subtype FIELD is INTEGER range 0 .. I_D_Upper;	TEXT_IO	
subtype NUMBER_BASE is INTEGER range 2 .. 16;	TEXT_IO	• used to indicate the number of character positions to be used in an I/O operation • indicates the number base to be used when outputing numerics
subtype YEAR_NUMBER is INTEGER range 1901 .. 2099;	CALENDAR	• represents years
subtype MONTH_NUMBER is INTEGER range 1 .. 12;	CALENDAR	• represents months
subtype DAY_NUMBER is INTEGER range 1 .. 31;	CALENDAR	• represents days of a month

REAL TYPES

universal_reall	no declaration	• an anonymous type used in the reference manual to specify the type for real literals, etc.

FLOATING POINT

type FLOAT **is digits** *I_D_Digits* **range** *I_D_Lower* .. *I_D_Upper*;	STANDARD	• predefined type for general use

FIXED POINT

universal_fixed	no declaration	• an anonymous type used in the reference manual to specify the type of the result of fixed point multiply and divide operations.
type DURATION **is delta** *I_D_Delta* **range** *I_D_Lower* .. *I_D_Upper*;	STANDARD	• represents time measured in seconds used with delay statements
subtype DAY_DURATION **is** DURATION **range** 0.0 .. 86_400.0;	CALENDAR	• represents the time of the start of a day to the current time

ARRAY

type STRING **is array** (INTEGER **range** <>)   STANDARD   predefined type for general use
   of CHARACTER;

RECORD

A set of machine instruction format   MACHINE_CODE   • optional set of types that define the allowed
   record declarations;   instruction formats for the machine
                                                           associated with a particular implementation

ACCESS

none defined

PRIVATE

type TIME **is private**;   CALENDAR   • represents values of real time (wall clock
                                                           time)

type FILE_TYPE **is limited private**;   SEQUENTIAL_IO   • represents internal files
                                              DIRECT_IO
                                              TEXT_IO

none defined

IMPLEMENTATION DEPENDENT

type ADDRESS **is** *Implementation_Dependent* ; SYSTEM
- represents machines addresses used in address clauses
- maybe represented as a record or array type depending on machine

A set of device type declarations; LOW_LEVEL_IO
- represent the allowed device types that an implementation provides a low level interface for

A set of device data type declarations; LOW_LEVEL_IO
- represents the data type set over the low level interfaces defined above

Note: I_D_ - short for Implementation_Dependent

TABLE A-9 OPERATIONS AND ATTRIBUTES

<u>BASIC OPERATIONS</u>

Assignment	**:=**
Allocator	**new**
Membership Test	**in**
	not in
Short-Circuit Control	**and then**
	or else
Selected Component	name_1.name_2
Indexed Component	name(exp_1)
	name(exp_1{, exp_#})
Slice	name(exp_1 .. exp_2)
Qualification	type'(expression)
Array Aggregate	(exp_1{, exp_#})
	(INDEX => exp_1 {, INDEX => exp_2})
Record Aggregate	(exp_1{, exp_#})
	(COMP => exp_1 {, COMP => exp_2})

<u>OPERATORS</u>

Logical	**and or xor**
Relational	**= /= < <= > >=**
Binary Adding	**+ - &**
Unary Adding	**+ -**
Multiplying	*** / mod rem**
Highest Precedence	**** abs not**

<u>USEFUL ATTRIBUTES</u>
(form Name'Attribute)

First	'FIRST	• lower bound of a discrete type
		• lower bound of first index of an array type or object
	'FIRST(N)	• lower bound of N-th index of an array type or object
Last	'LAST	• upper bound of a discrete type
		• upper bound of first index of an array type or object
	'LAST(N)	• upper bound of N-th index of an array type or object
Length	'LENGTH	• length of first index of array type or object

	'LENGTH(N)	• length of N-th index of array type or object
Pos	'POS(X)	• numeric position of X in the type declaration
Pred	'PRED(X)	• predecessor to X for this type
Range	'RANGE	• first index range for an array type or object
	'RANGE(N)	• N-th index range for an array type or object
Succ	'SUCC(X)	• successor to X for this type
Val	'VAL(X)	• value in position X of type declaration

OTHER ATTRIBUTES

Aft, Fore, Image, Last_Bit, Mantissa, Position, Value, Width
Address, Base, Constrained, Size, Storage_Size
Delta, Digits, Emax, Epsilon, Large, Safe_Emax,
Safe_Large, Safe_Small, Small
Callable, Count, Storage_Size, Terminated
Machine_Emax, Machine_Emin, Machine_Mantissa, Machine_Overflows
Machine_Radix, Machine_Rounds

---

exp_# - an expression whose value is of a discrete type
comp - component name

Examples A-7 Data Type Declarations

— All type declarations have the form, **type** Name **is** Type_Definition

-- sample type definitions

(WHITE, RED, YELLOW, GREEN, BLUE, BROWN, BLACK)
                              -- enumeration

range 1 .. 72   -- integer

array (1 .. 10) **of** INTEGER   -- array

-- Full Type declarations
type COLOR **is** (WHITE, RED, YELLOW, GREEN, BLUE, BROWN,
                                        BLACK);

```
type COLUMN is range 1 .. 72;

type TABLE is array (1 .. 10) of INTEGER;

A, B : array (1 .. 10) of BOOLEAN; -- an anonymous array type
                    -- declaration, actually two, one for A and another for B
```

Examples A-8   Integer Types

—For an Integer type (actually all numeric types) the compiler is going to select the best manner to represent it within the program that meets the range constraints specified

```
type PAGE_NUMBER is range 1 .. 2_000;

type LINE_SIZE   is range 1 .. MAX_LINE_SIZE;
 -- bounds must be a static expression but need not always be an integer
     --literal

type INDEX is range MIN_INDEX .. MAX_DELTA * K;

type COUNTER is range 0 .. 16#FFF#;
```

Examples A-9 Enumeration Types

— Enumeration types allow you to more accurately model the real world nature of data by allowing you to explicitly list the values that an object of the defined type can assume.

```
type DAY  is (MON, TUE, WED, THU, FRI, SAT, SUN);

type SUIT  is (CLUBS, DIAMONDS, HEARTS, SPADES);
```

```
type GENDER is (Male, Female);
   -- enumeration literals follow the rules for character literals and
   -- identifiers
   -- they are case insensitive

type LEVEL  is (LOW, MEDIUM, URGENT);

type COLOR  is (WHITE, RED, YELLOW, GREEN, BLUE, BROWN,
                                              BLACK);

type LIGHT  is (RED, AMBER, GREEN);

type MASK  is (FIX, DEC, EXP, SIGNIF);

type CODE  is (FIX, CLA, DEC, TNZ, SUB);
   -- enumeration literal need only be unique within a single type
   -- declaration not between declarations
```

— Character types are defined as enumeration types in which at least one enumeration literal is a character literal.

```
type ROMAN_DIGIT is ('I', 'V', 'X', 'L', 'C', 'D', 'M');

type HEXA_F   is ('A', 'B', 'C', 'D', 'E', 'F');

type MIXED     is ('A', 'B', '*', B, NONE, '?', '%');
        -- this is a character type; also
        -- 'B' is a character literal and B is an identifier they;  are different
        -- values
```

Examples A-10 Floating Point Types

— The rules by which a compiler selects a representation for a Floating Point type are defined in section 3.5.7 of the Ada Language Reference Manual.

```
type COEFFICIENT is digits 10 range -1.0 .. 1.0;
```

```
type REAL is digits 8;        -- range constraint is not required
                              -- this type is used in many of the examples that
                              -- follow, so remember it

type MASS is digits 7 range 0.0 .. 1.0E35;

type SALES_TYPE is digits 9 range 0.00 .. 1_000_000.00;
              -- an implementation is not required to support
              --  all possible floating point
              -- types. Digits 9 or higher may not be provided in some
              -- implementations.
```

Examples A - 11 Fixed point types

— The rules by which a compiler selects a representation for a Fixed Point type are defined in section 3.5.9 of the Ada Language Reference Manual.

```
type VOLT is delta 0.125 range 0.0 .. 255.0;
                                      -- range constraint is required

WORD_LENGTH : constant := 16;
DEL : constant := 1.0/2**(WORD_LENGTH - 1);
type FRACTION is delta DEL range -1.0 .. 1.0 - DEL;
                -- models the numeric characteristics of a two's
                -- complement 16 bit fraction

type Current_Type is delta 0.025 range 0.0 .. 100.0;

type Voltage_Type is delta 0.1 range -12.0 .. 24.0;

type Speed_Type is delta 0.1 range 0.0 .. 2700.0;

type Direction_Type is delta 0.001 range 0.0 .. 359.9;
                -- the range does not need to be specified to the same
                -- accuarcy as the delta

type Latitude_Type is delta 0.01 range -180.0 .. 180.0;
```

type Longitude_Type **is delta** 0.01 **range** -90.0 .. 90.0;

— Fixed Point types are very useful for modeling real world data that have units associated with them or in representing measurements using instruments with finite accuracies.

Examples A-12 Array Types

— An Array Type allows you to model real world collections of objects with the only restriction being that all component objects must be of the same data type.

— Ada supports any number of dimensions and either Integer or Enumeration type indexes.

```
-- Type declarations w/constrained array definitions
-- index bound defined in the type

type TABLE  is array (1 .. 10) of INTEGER;

type SCHEDULE is array (DAY) of BOOLEAN;
    -- DAY is an enumeration type (see above for type declaration)
    -- the index has 7 values: MON, TUE, WED, THU, FRI, SAT, SUN

type LINE  is array (1 .. MAX_LINE_SIZE) of CHARACTER;

type MATRIX  is array (DAY range MON .. WED,
                         INTEGER range -10 .. 10) of REAL;
```

— Unconstrained Array Types allow you to defer the specification of the index array bounds until an object of this type is declared.

```
-- Type declarations w/unconstrained array definitions
-- index bound defined in object declaration

type VECTOR  is array (INTEGER range <>) of REAL;
        -- <> notation is read as box, as in "a box to be filled in later"

type MATRIX   is array (INTEGER range <>, INTEGER range <>) of
                                                            REAL;
        -- all indices must be unconstrained, if one is

type BIT_VECTOR is array (INTEGER range <>) of BOOLEAN;

type ROMAN    is array (INTEGER range <>) of ROMAN_DIGIT;

type SEQUENCE is array (INTEGER range <>) of INTEGER;
```

— Array Components can be of any data type.

```
type DIRECTORY _UNIT_RECORD is
    record
            NAME : NAME_TYPE;
            TELEPHONE_NUMBER : TELEPHONE_NUMBER_TYPE;
    end record;

type DATABASE_TYPE is array (INDEX) of
                            DIRECTORY_UNIT_RECORD;
        -- an array type with a record component type
```

Examples A-13 Record Types

— A Record Type allows you to model real world collections of objects whose component values are not the same data type.

```
type DATE is -- models a day on a calendar, like 23 Jan 1986
    record
    DAY    : INTEGER range 1 .. 31;
                -- components are ordered as well as named
    MONTH       : MONTH_NAME;
    YEAR  : INTEGER range 0 .. 4000;
```

```
  end record;

type COMPLEX is
  record
    RE : REAL := 0.0;
          -- default intial values are assigned to each object of this type
    IM : REAL := 0.0;
  end record;
```

— Records with discriminants allow you to modify the structure of individual record objects while still keeping all of the properties and operations of the record type common for all objects of that type.

```
  -- record types with discriminants

type BUFFER (SIZE : BUFFER_SIZE := 100) is
                          -- discriminants are components of
  record                  -- the type
    POS  : BUFFER_SIZE := 0;
    VALUE : STRING (1 .. SIZE);
                      -- size of this string can vary based on the value for
                      -- the discriminant SIZE.
  end record;

type SQUARE (SIDE : INTEGER) is
          -- models a square matrix whose dimensions
  record                  -- will always be equal
    MAT : MATRIX(1 .. SIDE, 1 .. SIDE);
  end record;

type DOUBLE_SQUARE (NUMBER : INTEGER) is
  record
    LEFT : SQUARE (NUMBER);
          -- components of a record can be other records
    RIGHT : SQUARE (NUMBER); -- even records with discriminants
  end record;
```

```
type ITEM (NUMBER : POSITIVE) is
 record
   CONTENT : INTEGER;
   -- no component depends on the discriminant
 end record;
   -- this record type has two components NUMBER and CONTENT

type VAR_LINE (LENGTH : INTEGER) is
 record
   IMAGE : STRING (1 .. LENGTH);
 end record;
```

— There are no restrictions on the size, type, or number of components that a record type may have.

```
-- A large scale record data type, some component types

type Military_Craft_Type is (F_104, F_15, F_14, C_5A, FB_111, B_1B);

type Country_Type is (USA, FRANCE, GERMANY, USSR, POLAND,
                                             JAPAN, ITALY);

type Aircraft_ID_Type is (CIVILIAN, MILITARY, FOE, UNKNOWN);

type Threat_Level_Type is (LOW, MODERATE, HIGH);

type Aircraft_Status_Type (Kind : Aircraft_ID_Type := UNKNOWN) is
 record -- default value is not always needed
   Speed : Speed_Type;
   Heading : Direction_Type;
   Latitude : Latitude_Type;
   Longitude : Longitude_Type;
   case Kind is              -- the variant part structure is determined
                            -- by the value of Kind for the object
       when CIVILIAN => -- no additional components
           null;
       when MILITARY =>      -- two additional components
           Classification : Military_Craft_Type;
           Source : Country_Type;
```

```
            when FOE | UNKNOWN => -- one additional component
                    Threat : Threat_Level_Type;
        end case;
    end record;
```

— Record Types can be components of other types including other record types or array types.

```
    type INDEX is range 1 .. 3000;          -- an INTEGER type

    type NAME_TYPE is
        record
                FIRST               : STRING (1 .. 10);
                MIDDLE_INITIAL      : STRING (1 .. 1);
                LAST                : STRING (1 .. 20);
        end record;

    type TELEPHONE_NUMBER_TYPE is range 1000 .. 4999;

    type DIRECTORY_UNIT_RECORD is
                        -- records are logical data structures
        record                          -- which have different
                NAME : NAME_TYPE;       -- types of things in them
                TELEPHONE_NUMBER : TELEPHONE_NUMBER_TYPE;
        end record;

    type DATABASE_TYPE is array (INDEX) of
                                DIRECTORY_UNIT_RECORD;
                -- an array type
```

Examples A-14 Record Types with Variant Parts

— A special form of record type that allows the structure (i.e., the number and types) of the components to be varied based on the value of the discriminant.

```
type DEVICE is (PRINTER, DISK, DRUM);

type STATE is (OPEN, CLOSED);

type PERIPHERAL (UNIT : DEVICE :=DISK) is
  record
    STATUS            : STATE := CLOSED;
    case UNIT is
     when PRINTER =>
         LINE_COUNT      : INTEGER range 1 .. PAGE_SIZE;
     when others =>
         CYLINDER    : CYLINDER_INDEX;
         TRACK            : TRACK_NUMBER;
    end case;
  end record;
               -- all objects of this type have a UNIT and STATUS component, as
               -- well as a LINE_COUNT
               -- component if UNIT = PRINTER, or CYLINDER and TRACK if
               -- UNIT has any other value
               -- (i.e., DISK or DRUM)

type FIGURE_TYPE ( KIND : SHAPE := POINT ) is
 record
   POSITION : COORDINATES;
   -- all record objects have a component KIND and POSITION
   case KIND is
    when LINE =>
        LENGTH : FLOAT;
    when RECTANGLE =>
        HEIGHT, WIDTH : FLOAT := 0.0;
    when CIRCLE =>
        RADIUS : FLOAT;
    when others =>
        null; -- no variant component
   end  case;
 end  record;
```

Examples A-15 Access Types

— Access Types designate other objects. An object of an Access Type "points to" the object it designates. Thus it acts as an address for that object.

— Access Types have a very restricted set of allowed operations.

```
type FRAME is access MATRIX;
        -- objects of type FRAME point to objects of type MATRIX

type BUFFER_NAME is access BUFFER;

        -- incomplete type declarations
        -- used for implementing recursive type

type CELL; -- incomplete type declaration
type LINK is access CELL;
type CELL is -- models a doubly linked list cell structure
  record
    VALUE  : INTEGER;
    SUCC   : LINK;      -- access type component
    PRED   : LINK;
  end record;

        -- mutually dependant access types

type PERSON (SEX : GENDER);           -- incomplete type declaration
type CAR;                             -- incomplete type declaration
type PERSON_NAME is access PERSON;
type CAR_NAME  is access CAR;

type CAR is
  record
    NUMBER : INTEGER;
    OWNER : PERSON_NAME;
  end record;
```

```
type PERSON (SEX : GENDER) is
 record
   NAME  : STRING (1 .. 20);
   BIRTH : DATE;
   AGE   : INTEGER range 0 .. 130;
   VEHICLE : CAR_NAME;
   case SEX is
    when Male  => WIFE  : PERSON_NAME (SEX => Female);
    when Female => HUSBAND : PERSON_NAME (SEX => Male);
    end case;
  end record;
```

— Access Types allow you to dynamically create and destroy objects.

Examples A-16 Private Types

— A Private Type is conceptually a data type that hides the details of the
definition of the type from the user of the type.

```
type KEY is private;
```

```
type FILE_NAME is limited private;
```

```
NULL_KEY : constant KEY;
            -- a deferred constant, initail value provided in private
            -- part of the package that the type is declared in
```

— A Private Type can only be declared in a limited number of places, usually
in a package specification in which a private part exists. That private part
defines the full details of the type.

```
package KEY_MANAGER is
   type KEY is private;
   NULL_KEY : constant KEY;
   procedure GET_KEY (K : out KEY);
   function "<" (X, Y : KEY) return BOOLEAN;
```

```
private
        -- full type declarations, fills in implementation of private types
        -- and deferred constants
    type KEY is new NATURAL;
    NULL_KEY : constant KEY := 0;
end KEY_MANAGER;
```

— A Private type has a very restricted set of allowed operations (assignment, membership tests, selected components for the selection of any discriminant, qualification, explicit conversions), but you can further restrict the allowed operations by making a private type limited (you will not be able to assign to an object of a **limited** type).

```
package I_O_PACKAGE is
    type FILE_NAME is limited private;
    procedure OPEN (F : in out FILE_NAME);
    procedure CLOSE (F : in out FILE_NAME);
    procedure READ (F : in out FILE_NAME; ITEM : out INTEGER);
    procedure WRITE (F : in out FILE_NAME; ITEM : in INTEGER);
private
    type FILE_NAME is
        record
                INTERNAL_NAME : INTEGER := 0;
        end record;
end I_O_PACKAGE;
```

Examples A-17 Task Type Declarations

— An object of a task type has the characteristics of a limited data type as well as those of a program unit that potentially can run concurrently with other tasks.

```
task type RESOURCE is
    entry SEIZE;  -- entries define the interaction points between tasks
    entry RELEASE;
end RESOURCE;

task type KEYBOARD_DRIVER is
    entry READ (C : out CHARACTER);
                            -- parameters can be passed at these entry
                            -- points between tasks.
    entry WRITE (C : in CHARACTER);
end KEYBOARD_DRIVER;

task type SHARED_COUNT is
    entry INCREASE_COUNT (BY : in POSITIVE);
        entry GET_COUNT (SUM_SO_FAR : out POSITIVE);
    entry CLEAR_COUNT;
end KEYBOARD_DRIVER;
```

Two additional facilities provided with Ada allow the creation of data types that inherit the properties of existing data types. One facility constrains the values an object can assume, but does not introduce a new type. The other facility introduces a new distinct data type. These facilities are subtyping and derived typing respectively. Figures A-3 and A-4 characterize these facilities. These figures are followed by examples of subtypes and derived type declarations.

Examples A-18   Subtype and Derived Type Declarations

— A subtype declaration adds a restriction or constraint to a data type without introducing a new distinct data type.

— Objects of a subtype can be mixed with objects of its base type or another subtype of its base type. Such mixing does not require any type conversions.

Base_Type

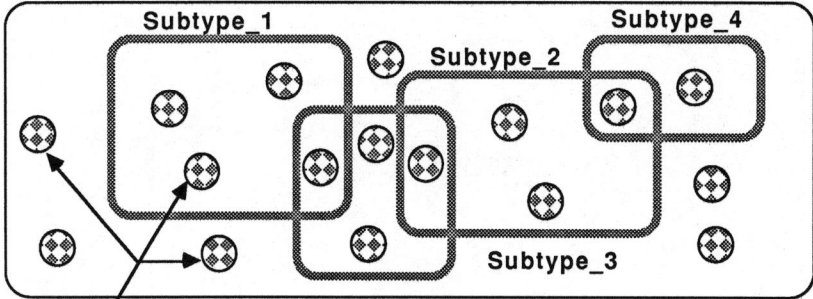

Possible Object Values

SUBTYPE DECLARATION - GENERAL FORM

subtype *Subtype_Name* is *Base_Type_Name* [*Constraint*];

Does not Create a Distinct Data Type

Restricts the allowed values that objects of the subtype may assume

BASIC DATA TYPE	CONSTRAINT
INTEGER	range Lower_Bound .. UpperBound
ENUMERATION	range Lower_Bound.. UpperBound
FLOATING POINT	digits Number_of_Digits
	[range Lower_Bound .. UpperBound
FIXED POINT	delta Accuracy_Definition
	[range Lower_Bound .. UpperBound]
UNCONSTRAINED ARRAY	(Discrete_Range, {Discrete_Range})
RECORD WITH DISCRIMINANT	(Discriminant_Expression,
	{Discriminant_Expression})
ALL TYPES	no constraint - subtype has all values
	of the Base_type

Figure A-3 **Subtyping**

Base_Type

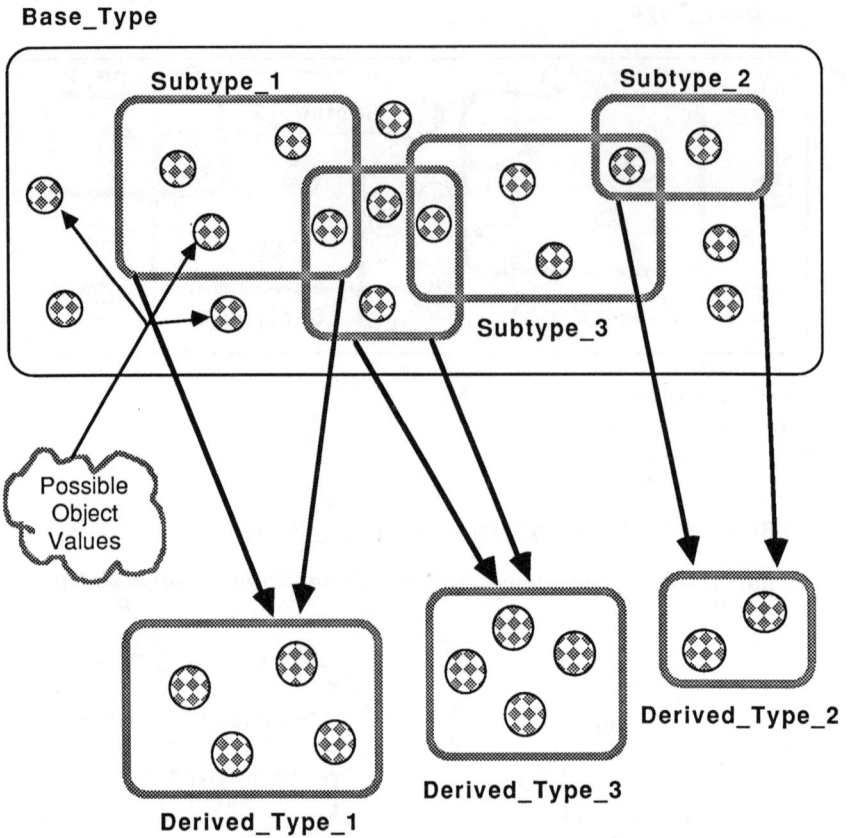

Subtype_1

Subtype_2

Possible
Object
Values

Subtype_3

Derived_Type_2

Derived_Type_3

Derived_Type_1

DERIVED TYPE DECLARATION - GENERAL FORM

type Derived_Type_Name is new Base_Type_Name [Constraint];

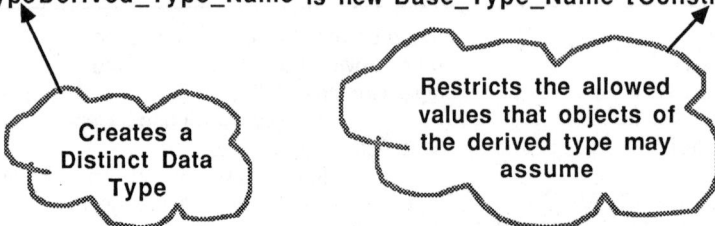

Creates a
Distinct Data
Type

Restricts the allowed
values that objects of
the derived type may
assume

Figure A-4   **Derived Data Typing**

subtype SMALL_INT **is** INTEGER **range** -10 .. 10;

subtype COLUMN_PTR **is** LINE_SIZE **range** 1 .. 10;

subtype BUFFER_SIZE **is** INTEGER **range** 0 .. MAX;
   -- the constraint can be dynamic - can change at runtime

subtype UP_TO_K **is** COLUMN **range** 1 .. K;

subtype INT **is** INTEGER; -- creates a new name for a type

subtype WEEKDAY **is** DAY **range** MON .. FRI;

subtype MAJOR **is** SUIT **range** HEARTS .. SPADES;

subtype RAINBOW **is** COLOR **range** RED .. BLUE;

subtype RED_BLUE **is** RAINBOW;

subtype SHORT_COEFF **is** COEFFICIENT **digits** 5;

subtype PROBABILITY **is** REAL **range** 0.0 .. 1.0;
   -- if REAL is a subtype of say FLOAT then PROBABILITY is a
   -- subtype of FLOAT, we have
   -- further constrained the type

subtype ROUGH_VOLTAGE **is** VOLT **delta** 1.0;

— Constraints on array types apply to the index ranges for unconstrained types only.

subtype SQUARE **is** MATRIX (1 .. 10, 1 .. 10);

subtype DOZEN **is** SEQUENCE (1 .. 12);

— Record subtype provides constraints through the discriminants.

```
subtype MALES is PERSON (SEX => Male);

type PERIPHERAL (UNIT : DEVICE :=DISK) is
  record
    STATUS             : STATE := CLOSED;
    case UNIT is
      when PRINTER =>
          LINE_COUNT       : INTEGER range 1 .. PAGE_SIZE;
      when others =>
          CYLINDER   : CYLINDER_INDEX;
          TRACK            : TRACK_NUMBER;
    end case;
  end record;

subtype DRUM_UNIT is PERIPHERAL (DRUM);

subtype PRINTERS is PERIPHERAL (PRINTER);
```

— Like a subtype, a derived type adds a constraint on a data type, but introduces a unique and distinct data type.

```
type LOCAL_COORDINATE is new COORDINATE;
    -- the use of new is almost intuitive, we are creating a "new" data type

type MIDWEEK is new DAY range TUE .. THU;

type COUNTER is new POSITIVE;

type SPECIAL_KEY is new KEY_MANAGER.KEY;
    -- the derived subprograms have the following specifications:

    -- procedure GET_KEY (K : out SPECIAL_KEY);
    -- function "<" (X,Y : SPECIAL_KEY) return BOOLEAN;
```

The data typing features of Ada are the most extensive of any of the modern well-known languages. As such, one should keep the points made in table A-10 in mind when using the data typing features.

TABLE A-10   DATA TYPE HINTS

- Data typing can be used to correct a large class of errors that typically would not be detected until testing or integration.

- Data types can be used as a mechanism for documenting the real world constraints on data and they allow one to directly model the real world characteristics of data .

- Real types can be used to model real world data, which have required accuracy constraints on them.

- In most cases, it is illegal to perform an operation on objects of different data types. So carefully pick your user defined data types or provide functions that allow you to convert between user defined data types.

- Attributes, in general, can be considered as functions that return values which characterize a data type or an object. Attributes can be very useful when one is trying to write programs with a high degree of abstraction or information hiding. Use attributes whenever you need a characteristic of an object or a data type. Do not use the value of the characteristic directly.

- Avoid overuse of the predefined types. User defined types allow more flexibility to model the real nature and constraints on the data you are trying to model.

- Remember that array indexes can be enumeration types as well as integer types.

Object Declarations

As stated above, Ada uses the term object when referring to the variables and constants used within a program. This more general terminology allowed the designers of Ada to provide a more uniform implementation of the data abstraction portion of the language. Objects can be viewed as containers which hold data that are manipulated by a program. These containers hold more information than the simple value of the object. They also contain the following properties when used within a program:

An Identifier — the name we use to refer to the object

A Data Type — the data type that constrains the form and allowed values that the object may assume

A Set of Allowed Operations — the operations that are allowed on the object. Really part of the concept of a data type but can be viewed as a characteristic of an object. These operations include both the set of predefined operations and those provided by the user.

An Object Specific Constraint — a constraint on the values which an object can assume that is above and beyond those that were imposed in the type declaration.

An Initial Value — the value an object will assume when it comes into existence

A Set of Attributes — can be viewed as a set of functions which allows the program to gain access to the properties of an object or its data type

As software developers, this more generalized view of data allows us to express the data portion of our application in a manner that minimizes the gap between the real world application and the resultant code. We get a fairly complete characterization of a piece of data, simply by declaring the objects that represent our application data using Ada features.

The various object types that can be declared in Ada are illustrated below through examples: constants, named numbers (i.e., a mechanism that associates a symbolic name with a number), and variable declarations are shown. Ada also has several other situations in which objects are declared. These objects include formal parameters of program units and a **for** loop index.

Examples A-19   Object Declarations

— Objects can be variables or constants.

```
-- Variable Declarations
COUNT, SUM   : INTEGER;

SIZE             : INTEGER range 0 .. 10_000 := 0;
    -- you can further constrain an object in an object declaration

SORTED        : BOOLEAN := FALSE;

COLOR_TABLE: array (1 .. 10) of BOOLEAN := (others => TRUE);
    -- variables can be initailized in their declarations
```

—— Constants are assigned a value in their declarations.

—— The value is determined when the constant declaration is elaborated. Constants can be treated as having dynamic values. The value once assigned during elaboration cannot be changed until the object is elaborated again.

```
LIMIT            : constant INTEGER := 10_000;

LOW_LIMIT    : constant INTEGER := LIMIT/10;

TOLERANCE   : constant REAL := DISPERSION (1.15);   -- a function call
```

— Named numbers are constants of numerics that are of a universal type which allows them to be used in expressions with other objects without type conversions.

```
PI            : constant := 3.14159_26536;

TWO_PI        : constant := 2.0*PI;

MAX           : constant := 500;

POWER_16   : constant := 2**16;

ONE, UN, EINS : constant := 1;
```

— Multiple object can be declared in a single declaration.

```
JOHN, PAUL : PERSON_NAME := new PERSON (SEX=> Male);
- - is equivalent to the two single object declarations in the order given
JOHN  : PERSON_NAME := new PERSON (SEX => Male);
PAUL : PERSON_NAME := new PERSON (SEX => Male);
```

— Object declarations with constrained array definitions; the index constraints are part of the declaration.

```
GRID  : array (1 .. 80, 1 .. 100) of BOOLEAN;

MIX   : array (COLOR range RED .. GREEN) of BOOLEAN;

PAGE : array (1 .. 50) of LINE;
```

— Array object declarations must include an index constraint for unconstrained array types.

```
BOARD          : MATRIX (1 .. 8,  1 .. 8);

RECTANGLE   : MATRIX (1 .. 20, 1 .. 20);

INVERSE      : MATRIX (1 .. N,  1 .. N);   -- N need not be static

FILTER        : BIT_VECTOR (0 .. 31);

STARS          : STRING (1 .. 120) := (1 .. 120 =>'*');

               -- Bounds are determined by the initialization value's bounds
QUESTION    : constant STRING := "HOW MANY CHARACTERS?";

ASK_TWICE  : constant STRING := QUESTION & QUESTION;

NINETY_SIX  : constant ROMAN := "XCVI";
```

— Array declaration with a constrained array subtype.

```
MY_SCHEDULE : SCHEDULE;
               -- all arrays of type SCHEDULE have same bo· ids
```

— Array aggregates can be used as initial values.

```
A : TABLE := (7, 9, 5, 1, 3, 2, 4, 8, 6, 0);        -- A(1)=7, A(10)=0

B : TABLE := TABLE'(2 | 4 | 10 =>1, others => 0);       -- B(1)= 0, B(10)=1

C : constant MATRIX := (1 .. 5 => (1 .. 8 => 0.0));

D : BIT_VECTOR (M .. N) := (M .. N => TRUE);

E : BIT_VECTOR (M .. N) := (others =>TRUE);

F : STRING (1 .. 1) := (1 => 'F'); -- a one component aggregate; same as "F"
```

— Record variables

```
TOMORROW, YESTERDAY : DATE;
```

```
A, B, C                  : COMPLEX;
-- both components of A, B, and C are implicitly initialized to zero

-- discriminant constraints

LARGE    : BUFFER (200); -- constrained, always 200 characters (explicit)

MESSAGE : BUFFER; -- unconstrained, initially 100 characters (default)

BASIS    : SQUARE (5); -- constrained, always 5 by 5

ILLEGAL  : SQUARE; -- illegal, a SQUARE must be constrained
                   -- type declaration did not specify default value for the
                   -- discriminant

-- record type with a component that is an array

type VAR_LINE (LENGTH : INTEGER) is
   record
             IMAGE : STRING (1 .. LENGTH);
   end record;

NULL_LINE : VAR_LINE (0);    -- a zero length string (null string)
LONG_LINE : VAR_LINE (132);

-- constrained record variables

WRITER  : PERIPHERAL (UNIT => PRINTER);

ARCHIVE : DISK_UNIT;

-- Access type objects

HEAD   : LINK := new CELL'(0, null, null);

NEXT   : LINK := HEAD.SUCC;

MY_CAR, YOUR_CAR, NEXT_CAR : CAR_NAME;
             -- implicitly initialized with null value
```

— A loop index is implicitly declared in the suffix to the loop. Its type is determined by the type of the index range specified.

```
for J in BUFFER'RANGE loop       -- legal even with null range
  if BUFFER(J) /= SPACE then
            PUT(BUFFER(J));
  end if;
end loop;

for J in 15 .. 35 loop
            SUM := SUM + LEFT (J) * RIGHT (J);
end loop;
```

Before leaving our discussion of data type and object declarations, an additional topic should be covered. When dealing with embedded computer system applications, we are often required to interface with other systems or to the underlying hardware on the machine that will be running our application. In these situations, we must have the ability to map the characteristics of our program level objects to the requirements and/or constraints of the underlying machine. We may need to force an object to reside at a particular memory location or to map its values to specific bit positions within a single memory location. Ada provides this capability with a set of representation specifications which are associated with those objects or data types one needs to have low level control over. Table A-11 identifies the syntax and characterizes the representation specification features of the language. The examples that follow illustrate the use of representation specifications.

TABLE A-11   CHARACTERISTICS OF REPRESENTATION CLAUSES

TYPE REPRESENTATION CLAUSES -- specify how a type is to be mapped to the underlying target machine.

LENGTH CLAUSES   -- specifies values for type attributes

```
for type_name'SIZE use static_integer_expression;
for access_type_name'STORAGE_SIZE use simple_integer_expression;
for task_type_name'STORAGE_SIZE use simple_integer_expression;
for fixed_point_type'SMALL use static_real_expression;
```

ENUMERATION CLAUSES -- specifies integer values that
                         -- represents each literal in an
                         -- enumeration type

```
for enum_type_name use (list_of_coresponding_universal_integers);
```

RECORD CLAUSES   -- specifies record alignment in
                          -- storage units as well as component
                          -- word and bit position alignments

```
for record_type_name use
        record [at mod static_integer_type_expression;]
                {component_name at static_integer_type_expression
                        range static_integer_type_range;}
        end record;
```

<u>**ADDRESS CLAUSES**</u>   -- specify the address in the under-
                          -- lying machine an entity will start at

OBJECT ADDRESS CLAUSES

```
for object_name use at simple_address_type_expression;
        -- specifies address of variable or constant
```

PROGRAM UNIT ADDRESS CLAUSES

```
for subprogram_name use at simple_address_type_expression;
        -- specifies address of machine code for subprogram body
```

```
for package_name use at simple_address_type_expression;
        -- specifies address of machine code for package body
```

```
for task_unit_name use at simple_address_type_expression;
        -- specifies address of machine code for task body
```

for single_entry_name **use at** simple_address_type_expression;
specifies interrupt address to be associated with this entry

Examples A-20 Representation Clauses

— Length clauses specify the number of bit positions that a data type should be represented as.

```
-- assumed declarations
type MEDIUM is range 0 .. 65000;

type SHORT    is delta  0.01 range -100.0 .. 100.0;

type DEGREE   is delta  0.1  range -360.0 .. 360.0

BYTE : constant := 8;
PAGE : constant := 2000;

-- length clauses:

for COLOR'SIZE    use 1 * BYTE;
                            -- type'SIZE is the size attribute of the type

for MEDIUM'SIZE  use 2 * BYTE;

for SHORT'SIZE    use 15;
```

— You can force the length of objects of a Real type (fixed or floating point).

```
for DEGREE'SMALL use 360.0/2**(SYSTEM.STORAGE_UNIT - 1);
```

— You can specify the amount of storage allocated to all objects that will be designated by an access type or to each object of a task type.

```
for CAR_NAME'STORAGE_SIZE use   -- approximately 2000 cars
    2000 * ((CAR'SIZE/SYSTEM.STORAGE_UNIT)+1);

for KEYBOARD_DRIVER'STORAGE_SIZE use 1 * PAGE;
```

— Enumeration representation clauses force the mapping of enumeration literal to specific values that will be used by the compiler when generating code.

```
type MIX_CODE is (ADD, SUB, MUL, LDA, STA, STZ);

for MIX_CODE use
    (ADD => 1, SUB => 2, MUL => 3, LDA => 8, STA => 24, STZ => 33);
    -- values must be ordered smaller to larger
```

— Record representation clauses affect the layout of record objects in memory.

```
WORD : constant := 4;  -- storage unit is byte, 4 bytes per word

type STATE    is (A, M, W, P);

type MODE     is (FIX, DEC, EXP, SIGNIF);

type BYTE_MASK     is array (0 .. 7) of BOOLEAN;

type STATE_MASK    is array (STATE) of BOOLEAN;

type MODE_MASK     is array (MODE) of BOOLEAN;

type PROGRAM_STATUS_WORD is
    record
            SYSTEM_MASK            : BYTE_MASK;
            PROTECTION_KEY         : INTEGER range 0 .. 3;
            MACHINE_STATE          : STATE_MASK;
            INTERRUPT_CAUSE        : INTERRUPTION_CODE;
            ILC                    : INTEGER range 0 .. 3;
            CC                     : INTEGER range 0 .. 3;
```

```
            PROGRAM_MASK : MODE_MASK;
            INST_ADDRESS        : ADDRESS;
    end record;
```

-- will map objects of this type to word boundaries in memory and individual
   --bits within those words

```
for PROGRAM_STATUS_WORD use
    record at mod 8;
            SYSTEM_MASK          : at 0*WORD range 0 .. 7;
            PROTECTION_KEY       : at 0*WORD range 10 .. 11;
            MACHINE_STATE        : at 0*WORD range 12 .. 15;
            INTERRUPT_CAUSE      : at 0*WORD range 16 .. 31;
            ILC              : at 1*WORD range 0 .. 1;
            CC               : at 1*WORD range 2 .. 3;
            PROGRAM_MASK : at 1*WORD range 4 .. 7;
            INST_ADDRESS   : at 1*WORD range 8 .. 31;
    end record;
```

```
for PROGRAM_STATUS_WORD'SIZE use 8*SYSTEM.STORAGE_UNIT;
```

— Representation specifications can be used to change the representation of a
type.

-- PACKED_DESCRIPTOR and DESCRIPTOR are two different types
-- with identical characteristics, apart from their representation

```
type DESCRIPTOR is
    record
            -- components of a descriptor
    end record;
```

```
type PACKED_DESCRIPTOR is new DESCRIPTOR;
```

```
for PACKED_DESCRIPTOR use
    record
            -- component clauses for some or for all components
    end record;
```

```
D : DESCRIPTOR;
P : PACKED_DESCRIPTOR;

P := PACKED_DESCRIPTOR(D);        -- pack D
D := DESCRIPTOR(P);           -- unpack P
```

Some hints associated with the use of object declarations include:

- An object can be thought of as a container that holds data. Each individual container has a property called a type that characterizes the data values and operations allowed on those values that the container can assume.

- Declare numeric values used in a program as named numbers. This avoids unnecessary type conversions in the executable portion of the program.

- Remember that in an object declaration you can further constrain the values that a particular object can assume without introducing a new type or subtype.

Program Unit Declarations

In Ada, the real work associated with a program is performed by the various program unit types supported by the language. To make use of a program unit, the unit must be declared in some manner consistent with the rules of the language. In this section, we are going to focus on the simplest form of these declarations, those that appear inside of another program unit. The other forms or options for program unit declarations will be covered in the developmental structure section of this appendix. Program unit declarations serve several purposes:

- Associating a name with the unit.

- Specifying the interface to the services provided by the program unit.

- Indirectly specifying the service provided by the program unit. This specification is indirect since the service is only identifiable by the name given to the program unit and the parameters specified.

The syntax and characteristics of the various forms of program unit declarations is illustrated with the examples below.

Examples A-21 Subprogram Declarations

— Procedures can have any number of formal parameters.

— You can restrict how a parameter can be used inside the procedure by indicating the mode of the parameter.

```
procedure TRANSVERSE_TREE;

procedure INCREMENT (X : in out  INTEGER);
    -- X can be read and written to in the body for the procedure

procedure RIGHT_INDENT (MARGIN : out LINE_SIZE);
    -- MARGIN can only be written to inside the procedure

procedure SWITCH (FROM, TO : in out LINK);

procedure STEP (NUMBER : in INTEGER);
    -- NUMBER can only be read in the body of the procedure
```

— Parameters of functions are always of in mode, meaning that the formal parameters can be only read inside the body of the function.

```
function RANDOM return PROBABILITY;
    -- the type after the return, PROBABILITY, indicates the data type that is
    -- returned after successful execution of a function.

function MIN_CELL (X : LINK) return CELL;

function NEXT_FRAME (K : POSITIVE) return FRAME;

function DOT_PRODUCT (LEFT,RIGHT: VECTOR) return REAL;

function "*" (LEFT, RIGHT : MATRIX) return MATRIX;
```

— Default values on "in" mode formal parameters allow you to specify optional parameters, ones which do not need to be assigned a value during a call.

```
procedure PRINT_HEADER (     PAGES      : in NATURAL;
                     HEADER : in LINE := (1 .. LINE'LAST=>' ');
                     CENTER     : in BOOLEAN:= TRUE);

procedure ACTIVATE     (      PROCESS: in PROCESS_NAME;
                     AFTER     : in PROCESS_NAME :=
                                          NO_PROCESS;
                     WAIT  : in DURATION := 0.0;
                     PRIOR      : in BOOLEAN := FALSE);

procedure PAIR (LEFT, RIGHT : PERSON_NAME := new PERSON);
```

— Formal parameters can be of any data type, provided the mode selected is consistent with the allowed operations for the data type (e.g., a limited type cannot be assigned to).

Examples A-22   Package Specifications and Declarations

— Package specifications define the interface to the user of the package.

— Typically a package can be viewed as providing a set of services to the users of the package.

```
package PLOTTING_DATA is -- only object declarations include here
  PEN_UP : BOOLEAN;
  CONVERSION_FACTOR, X_OFFSET, Y_OFFSET,
  X_MIN, Y_MIN, X_MAX, Y_MAX         : REAL;
  X_VALUE                   : array (1 .. 500) of REAL;
  Y_VALUE                   : array (1 .. 500) of REAL;
      -- these arrays are of different types.

end PLOTTING_DATA;

package WORK_DATA is -- provides types and objects
  type DAY is (MON, TUE, WED, THU, FRI, SAT, SUN);
  type HOURS_SPENT is delta 0.25 range 0.0 .. 24.0;
  type TIME_TABLE is array (DAY) of HOURS_SPENT;

  WORK_HOURS    : TIME_TABLE;
  NORMAL_HOURS: constant TIME_TABLE :=
            (MON .. THU => 8.25, FRI => 7.0, SAT | SUN => 0.0);
end WORK_DATA;
```

— Packages can be used to provide the definitions of abstract data types as illustrated below. Abstract data types allow us to "extend" Ada to be a more application oriented language without having to change the definition of the language as it appears in the Language Reference Manual.

```
package RATIONAL_NUMBERS is
            -- provides types and operations on those types
  type RATIONAL is
      record
            NUMERATOR   : INTEGER;
            DENOMINATOR : POSITIVE;
      end record;

  function EQUAL (X,Y : RATIONAL) return BOOLEAN;
```

```
function "/"   (X,Y : INTEGER)    return RATIONAL;
function "+"  (X,Y : RATIONAL) return RATIONAL;
function "-"  (X,Y : RATIONAL) return RATIONAL;
function "*"  (X,Y : RATIONAL) return RATIONAL;
function "/"  (X,Y : RATIONAL) return RATIONAL;

-- the functions define operations that include the conversion from/to
-- existing types as well as the operations between objects
-- of the type itself.

end RATIONAL_NUMBERS;
```

Examples A-23   Task Specifications

— Task specifications define the interface between a task or task type and other tasks.

— The interface looks to the user tasks like a set of procedures that are called entries.

```
task type RESOURCE is
    entry SEIZE;   -- the users interface to the task
    entry RELEASE;
end RESOURCE;

task type KEYBOARD_DRIVER is
    entry READ (C : out CHARACTER);
    entry WRITE(C : in CHARACTER);
end KEYBOARD_DRIVER;
```

— A single task declaration is equivalent to declaring a task type (with no name), then declaring only one task object of that type.

```
-- Examples of specification for a single task
task PRODUCER_CONSUMER is
    entry READ  (V : out ITEM);
    entry WRITE (E : in ITEM);
end PRODUCER_CONSUMER ;

task PROTECTED_ARRAY is
    -- INDEX and ITEM are global types
    entry READ  (N : in INDEX ; V : out ITEM);
    entry WRITE (N : in INDEX ; E : in ITEM);
end PROTECTED_ARRAY;

task BUFFER is
    entry READ  (C  : out CHARACTER);
    entry WRITE ( C : in CHARACTER);
end BUFFER ;
```

— A family of entries allows you to define a collection of entries, all of which have the same interface to other tasks. Each of the entries is distinct.

```
task CONTROLLER is
    entry REQUEST (LEVEL) (D : ITEM);   -- a family of entries
end CONTROLLER;

task USER;                             -- has no entries
```

— Declaring tasks as task objects allows you to include them in data structures, which have the characteristics of both a data object and a program unit.

—The task object features of Ada allow you to define a set of tasks, all of which have the same interface and program control structure but execute as independent units.

```
CONTROL  : RESOURCE;

TELETYPE : KEYBOARD_DRIVER;
```

POOL   : **array** (1 .. 10) **of** KEYBOARD_DRIVER;

type KEYBOARD **is access** KEYBOARD_DRIVER;

TERMINAL : KEYBOARD := **new** KEYBOARD_DRIVER;

Other Declarations

Other information that can appear in any declarative regions within an Ada program unit includes:

- Exceptions - exception declarations allow you to identify and name error or exceptional conditions that can exist within your program and that will be detected and possibly handled to support fault tolerant programming.

- Pragmas - pragmas typically appear where declarations appear but are not declarations as such. They are used to convey information to the compiler and to give it guidance. Table A-12 summarizes the language defined pragmas.

- Renaming - allows the creation of another name that refers to an existing program entity.

Examples of these other declarations are provided after the table.

TABLE A-12   LANGUAGE DEFINED PRAGMAS

FORM	PARAMETER	CHARACTERISTICS
CONTROLLED	(access_type_name)	• specifies that automatic storage reclamation must be performed for objects designated by this access type.

ELABORATE	(library_unit_names)	• specifies that the listed library unit bodies must be elaborate before the compilation unit that this pragma is associated with.
INLINE	(subprogram_names)	• specifies that the listed subprogram bodies should be expanded inline at each call.
INTERFACE	(language, subprogram)	• specifies that the subprogram is coded in another language and will be supplied as object coded.
LIST	(ON | OFF)	• specifies the region of a compilation unit in which a listing is to be generated for.
MEMORY_SIZE	(numeric_literal)	• specifies the value to be used for the named number SYSTEM.MEMORY_SIZE which defines the number of storage units in the target machine configuration.
OPTIMIZE	(TIME | SPACE)	• specifies whether time or space is to be used as the optimization criterion.
PACK	(composite_type_name)	• specifies that storage minimization should be the main criterion for selecting the representation of the type.
PAGE		• specifies that the program text that follows should start on a new page of the listing.
PRIORITY	(static_expression)	• specifies the priority of a task type or main subprogram as the value of the static expression (which must be of the predefined subtype PRIORITY).

SHARED	(variable_name)	• specifies that every read or update of the variable is a synchronization point for that variable. An implementation must restrict the objects for which this pragma is allowed to objects in which reading and updating can be performed as indivisible operations.
STORAGE_SIZE	(numeric_literal)	• specifies the value to be used for the named number SYSTEM.STORAGE_SIZE which defines the number of bits per storage unit in the target machine configuration.
SUPPRESS	(see text)	• takes as arguments the name of a check and optionally the name of an object, type(subtype), subprogram, task unit, or a generic unit. • specifies that permission to omit the check for the entity indicated.
SYSTEM_NAME	(enumeration_literal)	• specifies the value to be used for the constant SYSTEM.SYSTEM_NAME which defines one of the possible target configurations to generate code for.

Examples A-24   Other Declarations

—User defined error conditions can be defined with Exception Declarations.

    SINGULAR : **exception**;

```
ERROR      : exception;

OVERFLOW, UNDERFLOW : exception;
```

— Pragmas may have restrictions placed on them by an implementation.

```
pragma SUPPRESS (RANGE_CHECK);

pragma SUPPRESS (INDEX_CHECK, ON => TABLE);
```

— Renaming declarations allows us to create an alias for various entities, primarily used to enhance readability by shortening identifiers or eliminating overloaded identifiers.

```
declare
    L : PERSON renames LEFTMOST_PERSON;
begin
    L.AGE := L.AGE + 1;
end;
```

```
FULL : exception renames TABLE_MANAGER.TABLE_FULL;
```

```
package TM renames TABLE_MANAGER;
```

```
function REAL_PLUS (LEFT, RIGHT : REAL) return REAL renames "+";
```

```
function INT_PLUS (LEFT, RIGHT : INTEGER) return INTEGER
                                              renames "+";
```

```
function ROUGE return COLOR renames RED;
```

```
function ROT return COLOR renames RED;
```

```
function ROSSO return COLOR renames ROUGE;
```

```
function NEXT (X : COLOR) return COLOR  renames COLOR'SUCC;
```

```
function "*" (X,Y : VECTOR) return REAL renames DOT_PRODUCT;
```

```
function MINIMUM (L : LINK := HEAD ) return CELL  renames
                                              MIN_CELL;
```

Executable Part of Program Units

The executable part of a program unit is the place where the real work of an application program takes place. This is where we would implement the algorithms and control structures that constitute the logic of our programs. The executable part of a program unit consists of two major pieces, a sequence of statements optionally followed by an exception handling section. Within both sections we execute various types of statements that may be made up of expressions. The following sections detail the characteristics of the various expression forms, statement types, and exception handlers.

Expressions

Expressions in Ada provide the basic mechanism for the computation of a value. As such, an expression can be viewed as a computation that, when executed, will return a result of some data type which is determined by the rules of the language and the form of the expression itself. Ada expressions serve a wide range of uses within a program, including:

- Conditions for control statements

- Actual parameters passed to program units

- Values in which objects are assigned

In general, expressions define the computation of a value and have a result data type determined by the constituent parts of the expression and the operators applied.

The following examples illustrate the forms and uses of expressions in Ada.

Examples A-25   Names

— Names are used within an expression to refer to the value of an object or the value returned by a function.

PI   -- simple name of a number

LIMIT   -- simple name of a constant

COUNT   -- simple name of a scalar variable

BOARD   -- simple name of an array variable

MATRIX   -- simple name of a type

RANDOM   -- simple name of a function

ERROR   -- simple name of an exception

— Indexed components, in general, refer to the components or subcomponents of data objects that are of an array type.

MY_SCHEDULE (SAT)   -- a component of a one-dimensional array

PAGE (10)   -- a component of a one-dimensional array, yields a line

BOARD (M, J + 1)   -- a component of a two-dimensional array

PAGE (10)(20)   -- a component of a component,
                     -- yields a character on line 10

NEXT_FRAME (L)(M, N)   -- a component of a function call who returns an
                       --array type

— Array slices allow you to refer to a contiguous set of components of a one dimensional array object as if it were the array object itself.

STARS (1 .. 15)   -- a slice of 15 characters

PAGE (10 .. 10 + SIZE)   -- a slice of SIZE +1 components

PAGE (L)(A .. B)   -- a slice of the array PAGE(L)

STARS (1 .. 0)   -- a null slice

MY_SCHEDULE (WEEKDAY)   -- bounds given by subtype's range

STARS (5 .. 15)(K)   -- a component of a slice, provided that K is in 5 .. 15

— Selected components, in general, refer to the components or subcomponents of data objects that are of a record type.

TOMORROW.MONTH -- a record component

NEXT_CAR.OWNER -- a record component

NEXT_CAR.OWNER.AGE   -- a record component of a record component

WRITER.UNIT   -- a record component (a discriminant)

MIN_CELL(H).VALUE -- a record component of the result
                   -- of the function call MIN_CELL(H)

— A form of selected component uses ".all" to indicate that we want access to the full record object designated by an access type object, not just one of its components.

NEXT_CAR.all   -- the object designated by
                  -- the access variable NEXT_CAR

NEXT_CAR.NUMBER -- the ID component

NEXT_CAR.OWNER -- the owner of the car

—Expanded names allow you to refer to objects and operations that are within packages or program units.

TABLE_MANAGER.INSERT   -- a procedure of the visible part of the
                                                  -- package

KEY_MANAGER."<"   -- an operator of the visible part of the package

DOT_PRODUCT.SUM   -- a variable declared in a procedure body

BUFFER.POOL   -- a variable declared in a task unit

BUFFER.READ   -- an entry of a task unit

SWAP.TEMP   -- a variable declared in a block statement

STANDARD.BOOLEAN   -- the name of a predefined type

—Attributes, in most cases, can be treated as functions that return a value of a language defined type.

COLOR'FIRST   -- minimum value of the enumeration type COLOR

RAINBOW'BASE'FIRST   -- same as COLOR'FIRST
              -- subtype'BASE yields the name of the base type of RAINBOW

REAL'DIGITS   -- precision of the type REAL

BOARD'LAST (2)   -- upper bound of the second dimension of BOARD

BOARD'RANGE (1)   -- index range of the first dimension of BOARD

POOL (K)'TERMINATED   -- TRUE if POOL(K) is terminated

DATE'SIZE   -- number of bits for records of type DATE

MESSAGE'ADDRESS   -- address of the record type MESSAGE

Examples A-26   Basic Operations

— An operation is an elementary action associated with one or more types.

— When evaluated, an operation returns a value of a single type defined solely by the operation and the data type involved in the operation.

```
3.14159_26536       -- a real literal

1_345               -- an integer literal

CLUBS               -- an enumeration literal

'A'                 -- a character literal

"SOME TEXT"         -- a string literal
```

—Aggregates allow you to assign full values to record and array objects.

```
-- Record aggregate with positional associations

(4, JULY, 1776)

--Record aggregates with named associations

(DAY => 4, MONTH => JULY, YEAR => 1776)
(MONTH => JULY, DAY => 4, YEAR => 1776)

(DISK, CLOSED, TRACK =>5, CYLINDER => 12)
(UNIT => DISK,  STATUS => CLOSED, CYLINDER > 9, TRACK =>1)

-- Component association with several choices

(VALUE => 0, SUCC | PRED => new CELL'(0, null, null))
            -- The allocator is evaluated twice : SUCC and PRED designate
            -- different cells
```

-- Array aggregates with positional associations

(7, 9, 5, 1, 3, 2, 4, 8, 6, 0)

-- Array aggregates with named associations

(1 .. 5 => (1 .. 8 => 0.0))   -- two-dimensional

(1 .. N => **new** CELL)   -- N new cells, in particular for N = 0

TABLE'(2 | 4 | 10 => 1, **others** => 0)

SCHEDULE'(MON .. FRI => TRUE, **others** => FALSE)
SCHEDULE'(WED | SUN => FALSE, **others** => TRUE)
   -- qualified expressions

   -- Two-dimensional array aggregates
   -- Three aggregates for the same value of type MATRIX :

((1.1, 1.2, 1.3),
 (2.1, 2.2, 2.3))

(1 => (1.1, 1.2, 1.3),
 2 => (2.1, 2.2, 2.3))

(1 => (1 => 1.1,
       2 => 1.2,
       3 => 1.3),
 2 => (1 => 2.1,
       2 => 2.2,
       3 => 2.3))

— Aggregates as initial values

A : TABLE := (7, 9, 5, 1, 3, 2, 4, 8, 6, 0);   -- A(1)=7, A(10)=0

B : TABLE := TABLE'(2 | 4 | 10 =>1, **others** => 0); -- B(1)= 0, B(10)=1

```
C : constant MATRIX := (1 .. 5 => (1 .. 8 => 0.0));
                                    -- C'FIRST(1)=1, C'LAST(2)=8

D : BIT_VECTOR(M .. N) := (M .. N => TRUE);

E : BIT_VECTOR(M .. N) := (others =>TRUE);

F : STRING(1 .. 1) := (1 => 'F');
        -- a one component aggregate; same as "F"
```

Examples A-27   Expressions

— Primaries

4.0	-- real literal
PI	-- named number
(1 .. 10 => 0)	-- array aggregate
SUM	-- variable
INTEGER'LAST	-- attribute
SINE (X)	-- function call
COLOR' (BLUE)	-- qualified expression
REAL (M*N)	-- conversion
(LINE_COUNT + 10)	-- parenthesized expression

— Various forms of expressions

VOLUME	-- primary
not DESTROYED	-- factor
2*LINE_COUNT	-- term
-4.0	-- simple expression
-4.0 + A	-- simple expression
B**2 - 4.0*A*C	-- simple expression
PASSWORD (1 .. 3) = "BWV"	-- relation
COUNT **in** SMALL_INT	-- relation
COUNT **not in** SMALL_INT	-- relation
INDEX = 0 **or** ITEM_HIT	-- expression
(COLD **and** SUNNY) **or** WARM	-- expression
A**(B**C)	-- expression

— Operators and expression evaluation

not SUNNY **or** WARM	-- same as (not SUNNY) or WARM
x > 4.0 **and** y > 0.0	-- same as (X > 4.0) and (Y > 0.0)
-4.0*A**2	-- same as -(4.0 * (A**2))
abs (1 + A) + B	-- same as (abs(1 + A)) + B
Y**(-3)	-- parentheses are necessary -- 3 is an integer literal and - is an operator
A / B * C	-- same as (A/B)*C

A + (B + C)   -- evaluate B + C before adding it to A

— Logical operators

SUNNY **or** WARM

FILTER (1 .. 10) **and** FILTER (15 .. 24)

— Short-circuit control forms

NEXT_CAR.OWNER /= **null and then** NEXT_CAR.OWNER.AGE > 25
    -- the part of expression after the "and then" is not evaluated if the first
    -- part is evaluated as false

N = 0 **or else** A(N) = HIT_VALUE
    -- the part of expression after the "or else" is not evaluated if the first part
    -- is evaluated as true

— Relational operators

X /= Y

    -- relational operations on strings is in acordance with the order that the
    -- character set is defined
"" < "A" **and** "A" < "AA"   -- TRUE

"AA" < "B" **and** "A" < "A "   -- TRUE

MY_CAR = **null**   -- true if MY_CAR has been set to null
MY_CAR = YOUR_CAR   -- true if both share the same car
MY_CAR.**all** = YOUR_CAR.**all**   -- true if both cars are identical

N **not in** 1 .. 10   -- range membership test

TODAY **in** MON .. FRI   -- range membership test

TODAY **in** WEEKDAY   -- subtype membership test

ARCHIVE **in** DISK_UNIT   -- subtype membership test

— Binary adding operators

Z + 0.1   -- Z must be of a real type

"A" & "BCD"   -- catenation of two string literals, result is "ABCD"

'A' & "BCD"   -- catenation of a character literal and a string literal

'A' & 'B'   -- catenation of two character literals

— Multiplying operators

```
I   : INTEGER := 1;
J   : INTEGER := 2;
K   : INTEGER := 3;

X   : REAL digits 6 := 1.0;
Y   : REAL digits 6 := 2.0;

F   : FRACTION delta 0.0001 := 0.1;
G   : FRACTION delta 0.0001 := 0.1;
```

Expression	Value	Result type
I*J	2	same as I and J, that is, INTEGER
K/J	1	same as K and J, that is, INTEGER
K **mod** J	1	same as K and J, that is, INTEGER
X/Y	0.5	same as X and Y, that is, REAL
F/2	0.05	same as F that is, FRACTION
3*F	0.3	same as F that is, FRACTION

F*G	0.01	universal_fixed, type conversion needed
FRACTION (F*G)	0.01	FRACTION, as stated in the conversion
REAL (J) * Y	4.0	REAL,the type of both operands after conversion of J

— Qualified expressions

type MASK **is** (FIX, DEC, EXP, SIGNIF);

type CODE **is** (FIX, CLA, DEC, TNZ, SUB);

PRINT (MASK'(DEC));   -- DEC is of type MASK

PRINT (CODE'(DEC));   -- DEC is of type CODE

for J **in** CODE'(FIX) .. CODE'(DEC) **loop** ...   -- qualification needed for
                                                          -- FIX or DEC
for J **in** CODE **range** FIX .. DEC **loop** ..   -- qualification unnecessary
for J **in** CODE'(FIX) .. DEC **loop** ...   -- qualification unnecessary for DEC

DOZEN'(1 | 3 | 5 | 7 =>2, **others** => 0)

— Allocators

new CELL'(0, **null, null**)   -- initialized explicitly

new CELL'(VALUE=>0, SUCC=>**null**, PRED=>**null**)   -
                  -- initialized explicitly

new CELL   -- not initialized

new MATRIX (1 .. 10, 1 .. 20)   -- only the bounds are given

new MATRIX'(1 .. 10 => (1 .. 20 => 0.0))   -- initialized explicitly

new BUFFER (100)   -- only discriminant given

```
new BUFFER'(SIZE => 80, POS => 0, VALUE => (1 .. 80 =>'A'))
     -- initialized explicitly
```

— Universal expressions

```
1 + 1                              -- 2

abs (-10)*3                        -- 30
KILO  : constant : = 1000;
MEGA : constant : = KILO*KILO;          -- 1_000_000

LONG  : constant := FLOAT'DIGITS*2;

HALF_PI : constant := PI/2;
DEG_TO RAD   : constant := HALF_PI/90;
RAD_TO_DEG  : constant := 1.0/DEG_TO_RAD;
```

— Expressions used to initialize objects

```
JOHN  : PERSON_NAME          := new PERSON(SEX => FEMALE);

LOW_LIMIT : constant INTEGER   := LIMIT/10;

TOLERANCE  : constant REAL    := DISPERSION(1.15);

PI : constant                := 3.14159_26536;

TWO_PI  : constant           := 2.0*PI;

DEL : constant               := 1.0/2**(WORD_LENGTH - 1);

STARS   : STRING (1 .. 120)     := (1 .. 120 =>'*');

QUESTION  : constant STRING   := "HOW MANY CHARACTERS?";
          --QUESTION string size determined by length of the string literal
```

```
ASK_TWICE : constant STRING     := QUESTION & QUESTION;

NINETY_SIX : constant ROMAN     := "XCVI";
```

Examples A-28   Type Conversions

— Language provided conversions are available for numeric types, subtypes, and derived types.

— Explicit conversions implemented as functions whose name is the result type name and parameter is the object to be converted.

```
-- Numeric type conversion

REAL (2*J)      -- value is converted to floating point

INTEGER (1.6) -- value is 2

INTEGER (-0.4) -- value is 0

-- Conversion between derived types

type A_FORM is new B_FORM;
X : A_FORM;
Y : B_FORM;

X := A_FORM (Y);
Y := A_FORM (X);    -- the reverse conversion

-- Conversions between array types

type SEQUENCE is array (INTEGER range <>) of INTEGER;

subtype DOZEN is SEQUENCE (1 .. 12);
```

LEDGER : **array** (1 .. 100) **of** INTEGER;

```
SEQUENCE (LEDGER)                -- bounds are those of LEDGER
SEQUENCE (LEDGER (31 .. 42))     -- bounds are 31 and 42
DOZEN  (LEDGER(31 .. 42))        -- bounds are those of DOZEN
```

— Implicit conversions are language defined and require no special function call.

X : INTEGER := 2;

```
X + 1 + 2        -- implicit conversion of each integer literal
1 + 2 + X        -- implicit conversion of each integer literal
X + (1 + 2)      -- implicit conversion of each integer literal
2 = (1 + 1)      -- no implicit conversion: the type is universal_integer
```

A'LENGTH = B'LENGTH
```
                 -- no implicit conversion: the type is universal_integer
```

C : **constant** := 3+2;
```
                 -- no implicit conversion: the type is universal_integer
```

X = 3 **and** 1 = 2 -- implicit conversion of 3, but not of 1 or 2

Statements

Statements in Ada are used to perform basic actions, real-time actions, and implement control logic. Table A-13 summarizes and characterizes the statement types supported by Ada. The richness of statement types supported by Ada is one of its strong points. The syntax for the various statement types is also provided in table A-13.

The examples which follow the table illustrate the flexibility of the various statement types.

TABLE A-13   ADA STATEMENT TYPES-
CHARACTERISTICS AND SYNTAX

BASIC ACTION STATEMENTS

ASSIGNMENT - provides a new value to a variable

      variable_name := expression;

NULL - states explicitly that no action is to be performed

   null;

BLOCK - introduces a new frame that can include a declarative part, an executable part, and an exception handler.

```
[Block_Name:]
[declare
      declarations]
begin
      statements
[exception
      exception handler
      {exception handler}]
end [Block_Name];
```

FLOW OF CONTROL STATEMENTS

IF - allows selection of a sequence of statements based on the value of a Boolean expression

```
if condition then
      statements
{elsif condition then
      statements}
[else
      statements]
end if;
```

CASE - selects a sequence of statements from several mutually exclusive alternatives based on the value of a discrete expression.

```
case expression is
  when choice { | choice} =>
      statements
  {when choice { | choice} =>
      statements}
end case;
```

choice can be a single value or range of values of the discrete type for the expression or the word **others**

LOOP - controls the repeating of a sequence of statements zero or more times.

```
[loop_name:] -- infinite loop
   loop
      statements
   end loop [loop_name];
```

```
[loop_name:] -- for loop,
for loop_parameter in [reverse] discrete_range
   loop
      statements
   end loop [loop_name];
```

```
[loop_name:] -- while loop
while condition
   loop
      statements
   end loop [loop_name];
```

EXIT - can only be within a loop statement. Forces control to be transferred to the end of the loop.

```
   exit [loop_name] [when condition];
```

GOTO - an explicit transfer of control to a statement with a label.

```
   goto statement_label;
```

PROCEDURE CALL - initiates the execution of a procedure.

procedure_name [(list_of_actual_parameters)];

RETURN - indicates the termination point of a subprogram.

return;   -- in a procedure
return expression;   -- in a function

RAISE (Exception) - causes an exception to occur and control to be transferred to an exception handler.

raise exception_name;
raise; -- only within an exception handler
    -- re-raises the exception that causes transfer of control to the handler

TASKING ORIENTED STATEMENTS

ENTRY CALL - initiates a rendezvous with the name tasks at the name entry.

task_name.entry_name [(list_of_actual_parameters)];
task_name.entry_name [(entry_index)] [(list_of_actual_parameters)];
    -- used when a family of entries has be defined

ACCEPT - identifies the region of program text that will be executed during a rendezvous.

accept entry_name [(entry_index)] [(list_of_formal_parameters)] **do**
    statements -- executed during the rendezvous
end [entry_name];

ABORT - causes one or more tasks to become abnormal, thus preventing any further rendezvous with those tasks.

abort task_name {, task_name};

DELAY - suspends execution of a task for at least the duration of time specified.

delay expression;

SELECT - controls which of several rendezvous alternatives can be executed.

see figures A-8 through A-13

Low Level Statements

CODE - allows machine code insertion, under limited situations.

machine_code_type_mark' code_record_aggregate;

Examples A-29 Simple Statements

— Labels on statements are used with goto's.

<<HERE>> <<ICI>> <<AQUI>> <<HEIR>> Z := 10 + 44;
   -- Multiple labels may be associated with a single statement

<<AFTER>> X := 1;

—Assignment statements provide a new value to a variable.

VALUE   := MAX_VALUE - 1;   -- general form Variable := Expression;

SHADE   := BLUE;

NEXT_FRAME (F)(M, N) := 2.5;
               -- individual components can be assigned to

```
U := DOT_PRODUCT (V, W);

WRITER := (STATUS => OPEN, UNIT => PRINTER, LINE_COUNT => 60);
                -- full record assignment

NEXT_CAR.all := (72074, null);

-- Array assignments

A   : STRING (1 .. 31);
B   : STRING (3 .. 33);
            •

            •

            •

begin
    A := B;         -- same number of components
    A(1 .. 9)  := "tar sauce";
    A(4 .. 12):= A(1 .. 9);-- A(1 .. 12) = "tartar sauce"
end;
```

— The value to be assigned is checked at runtime to determine if it satisfies all of the constraints for that variable by its object and associated type/sub-type declarations.

```
-- Examples of constraint checks on assignments
I, J: INTEGER range 1 .. 10 := 6;
K  : INTEGER range 1 .. 20 := 11;
            •

            •

            •

begin
    I := J;         -- identical ranges
    K:= J;          -- compatiable ranges
    J := K;         -- will raise exception CONSTRAINT_ERROR, K>10
end;
```

Examples A-30 Control Statements

— "If" statements allow selection of a sequence of statements depending on the value of a BOOLEAN expression.

```
if  MONTH = DECEMBER and DAY = 31 then
    MONTH := JANUARY;
                    -- any number or form of statement may appear here
    DAY  := 1;
    YEAR       := YEAR + 1;
end if;

if LINE_TOO_SHORT then
    raise LAYOUT_ERROR;
elsif LINE_FULL then
    NEW_LINE;
    PUT(ITEM);
else
    PUT(ITEM);
end if;

if MY_CAR.OWNER.VEHICLE /= MY_CAR then
    REPORT ("Incorrect data");
end if;

-- same as above, except else part shown

if MY_CAR.OWNER.VEHICLE /= MY_CAR then
    REPORT ("Incorrect data");
else
    null;
end if;
```

— Case Statements allow the selection of a sequence of statements depending on the value of discrete type expression.

```ada
case SENSOR is
   when ELEVATION  => RECORD_ELEVATION (SENSOR_VALUE);
   when AZIMUTH    => RECORD_AZIMUTH (SENSOR_VALUE);
   when DISTANCE   => RECORD_DISTANCE (SENSOR_VALUE);
   when others        => null;
end case;

case TODAY is
   when MON   => COMPUTE_INITIAL BALANCE;
   when FRI    => COMPUTE_CLOSING_BALANCE;
   when TUE .. THU => GENERATE_REPORT (TODAY);
   when SAT .. SUN => null;
end case;

case BIN_NUMBER (COUNT) is
   when 1              => UPDATE_BIN (1);
   when 2              => UPDATE_BIN (2);
   when 3 | 4   => UPDATE_BIN (1);
                    -- either 3 or 4 will select these statements
                    UPDATE_BIN (2);
   when others => raise ERROR;
end case;
```

Examples A-31 Loop Statements

— Loop statements can be of a number of forms:

   - infinite loops
   - for loops
   - while loops

```ada
loop
   GET (CURRENT_CHARACTER);
   PUT (CURRENT_CHARACTER);
end loop;
```

```
while BID(N).PRICE < CUT_OFF.PRICE loop
   RECORD_BID (BID(N).PRICE);
   N := N +1;
end  loop;


for J in BUFFER'RANGE loop        -- legal even with null range
   if BUFFER(J) /= SPACE then
    PUT (BUFFER(J));
   end if;
end loop;


SUMMATION:          -- loops can be named to allow for exiting outer
                    -- loops from an inner loop.
   while NEXT /= HEAD loop
        SUM := SUM + NEXT.VALUE;
        NEXT := NEXT.SUCC;
   end loop SUMMATION;
```

— Other forms of loops can be implemented using exit statements.

```
loop
   GET (CURRENT_CHARACTER);
   exit when CURRENT_CHARACTER = '*';
end loop;


for N in 1 .. MAX_NUM_ITEMS loop
   GET_NEW_ITEM (NEW_ITEM);
   MERGE_ITEM (NEW_ITEM, STORAGE_FILE);
   exit when NEW_ITEM = TERMINAL_ITEM;
end loop;
```

```
MAIN_CYCLE:
  loop
  for K in reverse 27 .. 373 loop
        -- initial statements
        exit MAIN_CYCLE when FOUND;
        -- final statements
  end loop;
end loop MAIN_CYCLE;
```

Examples A-32 Miscellaneous Statements

— Block Statements allow you to introduce a new declarative region in the executable part of a program unit.

```
SWAP:
  declare
        TEMP : INTEGER;
  begin
        TEMP := V;  V := U;
        U := TEMP;
  end SWAP;


  declare
     TEMP : INTEGER;
  begin
     TEMP := TEMP + SOME_VERY_LARGE_INTEGER;
  exception
     when CONSTRAINT_ERROR =>
        TEMP := INTEGER'LAST;
           -- exception handler clamps the maximum value of TEMP
  end;
```

— Return Statements explicitly force the exiting of a procedure or function.

— Return statements in functions are required and will always have an expression associated with them. When executed, they will compute the value to be returned from the function call.

```
return;                          -- in a procedure

return KEY_VALUE(LAST_INDEX);        -- in a function

return X_VAL * Y_VAL;             -- in a function

return Z**2;                      -- in a function

return CONDITION_1 = CONDITION_2;   -- in a function
```

— Goto Statements are allowed but should be avoided.

```
<< COMPARE>>
 if A(I) < ELEMENT then
  if LEFT(I) /= 0 then
   I := LEFT(I);
    goto COMPARE;
  end if;
   -- some statements
 end if;
```

— Subprogram and task entry calls are treated as statements in Ada. They both have the same form and syntax.

```
TRAVERSE_TREE;

TABLE_MANAGER.INSERT (E);

PRINT_HEADER (128, TITLE, TRUE);

SWITCH (FROM => X, TO => NEXT);
```

```
PRINT_HEADER (128,HEADER => TITLE, CENTER => TRUE);

PRINT_HEADER (HEADER => TITLE, CENTER => TRUE, PAGES => 128);

DOT_PRODUCT (U,V);

CLOCK;
```

— Procedure Calls to a procedure with default parameters can omit any or all optional parameters.

```
procedure ACTIVATE (PROCESS: in PROCESS_NAME;
                AFTER: in PROCESS_NAME := NO_PROCESS;
                WAIT  : in DURATION := 0,0;
                PRIOR : in BOOLEAN := FALSE);

procedure PAIR (LEFT, RIGHT : PERSON_NAME := new PERSON);

-- possible calls

ACTIVATE (X);
ACTIVATE (X, AFTER => Y);
ACTIVATE (X, WAIT => 60.0, PRIOR => TRUE);
ACTIVATE (X, Y, 10.0, FALSE);

PAIR;
PAIR (LEFT => new PERSON, RIGHT => new PERSON);
```

— Entry calls have similar logical effects as procedure calls except that tasks involved are required to synchronize before they can pass parameters.

```
CONTROL.SEIZE;          -- an entry of the task CONTROL

POOL(K).WRITE;          -- an entry of the task POOL(K)

BUFFER.READ;            -- an entry of a task unit
```

```
CONTROL.RELEASE;

PRODUCER_CONSUMER.WRITE(E);

POOL(5).READ(NEXT_CHAR);

CONTROLLER.REQUEST(LOW)(SOME_ITEM);
```

— Raise Statements will generate the specified exception and cause exception processing to occur.

```
raise SINGULAR;

raise NUMERIC_ERROR;      -- explicitly raising a predefined exception

raise;          -- only within an exception handler,
                -- re-raises the exception that got you
                -- to the exception handler
```

Examples A-33   Tasking Oriented Statements

— Accept statements define the actions that will take place when another task calls the indicated entry. This assumes that both tasks are ready to rendez-vous.

```
accept SEIZE;

accept READ (V : out ITEM) do
    V := LOCAL_ITEM;   -- this assignment is performed when read is called
end READ;

accept REQUEST (LOW)(D : ITEM) do
    ...
end REQUEST;
```

— Delay Statements allow a task to suspend execution for a duration of time.

```ada
delay 3.0;      -- delay 3.0 seconds

declare
  use CALENDAR;
                -- INTERVAL is a global constant of type DURATION
  NEXT_TIME : TIME := CLOCK + INTERVAL;
begin
  loop
        delay NEXT_TIME  - CLOCK;
        -- some actions
        NEXT_TIME := NEXT_TIME + INTERVAL;
  end loop;
end;
```

— Select statements allow a task to be written so that multiple entry call can be accepted. It will select only a single alternative when   simultaneous entries are made.

```ada
select    -- if DRIVER_AWAKE_SIGNAL entry call is not made within 30
          -- seconds then stop the train
   accept DRIVER_AWAKE_SIGNAL;
or
   delay 30.0 * SECONDS;
   STOP_THE_TRAIN;
end select;

select
        accept READ (N : in INDEX; V : out ITEM) do
             V := TABLE (N);
        end READ;
or
        accept WRITE (N : in INDEX; E : in ITEM) do
             TABLE (N) := E;
        end WRITE;
   end select;
```

```
select
   when not IN_USE =>
   accept SEIZE do
        IN_USE := TRUE;
   end SEIZE;
or
   when IN_USE =>
   accept RELEASE do
        IN_USE := FALSE;
   end RELEASE;
or
   terminate;   -- allows the task to complete if the program unit in
                --which activated
                --this task completes
end select;


-- Examples of a task body with a select statement

task body RESOURCE is
   BUSY : BOOLEAN := FALSE;
begin
   loop
       select
               when not BUSY =>
               accept SEIZE do
                   BUSY := TRUE;
               end;   -- a guard that is evaluated as part of the
                      -- select statement which indicates the
                      -- alternatives to look for

       or
               accept RELEASE do
                   BUSY := FALSE;
               end;
       or
               terminate;
       end select;
   end loop;
end RESOURCE;
```

— Conditional entry calls look like selects but determine if an entry can be made or not.

```
procedure SPIN (R : RESOURCE) is
begin
  loop
      select
            R.SEIZE;
            return;
        else        -- can not immediately rendezvous
            null;  -- busy waiting
        end select;
    end loop;
end SPIN;

-- Timed entry calls
select
   CONTROLLER.REQUEST(MEDIUM)(SOME_ITEM);
or
   delay 45.0;
   -- controller too busy, try something else
end select;
```

— Abort statements allow other tasks to force the termination of the execution of a task or group of tasks in an uncontrolled manner.

```
abort USER, TERMINAL.all, POOL(3);
```

— Additional examples of tasking statements.

```
task BUFFER is
   entry READ(C :out CHARACTER);
   entry WRITE( C : in CHARACTER);
end;

task body BUFFER is
   POOL_SIZE : constant INTEGER := 100;
   POOL      : array (1 .. POOL_SIZE) of CHARACTER;
```

```
COUNT        : INTEGER range 0 .. POOL_SIZE := 0;
IN_INDEX, OUT_INDEX : INTEGER range 1 .. POOL_SIZE :=1;
begin
   loop
        select
                when COUNT < POOL_SIZE =>
                accept WRITE (C : in CHARACTER) do
                        POOL (IN_INDEX) := C;
                end;
                IN_INDEX := IN_INDEX mod POOL_SIZE + 1;
                COUNT := COUNT + 1;
        or
                when COUNT >0 =>
                accept READ (C : out CHARACTER) do
                    C:=POOL (OUT_INDEX) ;
                end;
                OUT_INDEX := OUT_INDEX mod POOL_SIZE + 1;
                COUNT := COUNT - 1;
        or
                terminate;
        end select;
   end loop;
end BUFFER;


-- somewhere in the tasks that use buffer appears the following

loop
   -- produce the next character CHAR
   BUFFER.WRITE(CHAR);
   exit when CHAR = ASCII.EOT;
end loop;


loop
   BUFFER.READ(CHAR);
   -- consume the next character CHAR
   exit when CHAR = ASCII.EOT;
end loop;
```

Exception Handlers

Ada provides a powerful mechanism for defining and dealing with the inevitable errors and exceptional conditions that can occur during program execution. This mechanism is provided through the declaration of, raising of, and handling of what are called exceptions. Some exceptions are predefined and others can be defined by the user. User defined exceptions allow the specification of error or exceptional conditions which are important to the application, thereby not totally relying on what the language designers defined as possible error or exceptional conditions.

In general, when we deal with exceptions we must be concerned with three issues:

1.   What to name an exceptional or error condition.

2.   How to call attention to an exceptional or error condition.

3.   How to handle an exceptional or error condition when it occurs.

Ada addresses all three of these issues in a flexible, yet straightforward, manner. The Ada features that support these issues include:

Predefined Exceptions - language defined error conditions for detecting data type violations, processing errors, etc.

User Defined Exceptions - exception declaration facility.

Raise Statement - ability to generate an exceptional condition that causes normal program execution to stop and control to be transferred to an exception handling sequence of statements.

Exception Propagation Rules - language rules that govern the manner in which exceptions can be propagated from one subprogram or task to another.

Exception Handler - a region in a program unit where the exception handling sequence of statements may appear.

Table A-14 summarizes some of the language defined exceptions. Included after the table are examples of the exception declaration, exception raising, and exception handling. The dynamic aspects of exceptions will be covered later in this appendix.

TABLE A - 14   LANGUAGE DEFINED EXCEPTIONS

EXCEPTION	RAISING CONDITIONS/SITUATIONS
Constraint_Error	• attempt to assign to an object an out of range value • actual parameter not in subtype of formal parameter • index value being out of bounds • logical operation on array objects of different lengths
Data_Error	• when I/O reads an element that is not of the correct type or within the allowed range of values
Device_Error	• when I/O hardware malfunctions
End_Error	• attempt to read past an end of file
Layout_Error	• attempt to set an I/O column number that exceeds the line length
Numeric_Error	• execution of a predefined numeric operation that cannot deliver the correct mathematical result — overflow for example
Program_Error	• attempt to exit a function with other than a return statement • calling a subprogram whose body has not been elaborated • other erroneous program behavior
Storage_Error	• insufficient memory to allocate new objects or activate new program units

Tasking_Error	• at an entry call to an abnormal task or completed task
	• when a task fails during activation

Examples A - 34   Exception Handlers

— The proper use of exceptions is a high level design issue since they dramatically affect the flow of control of a program.

```
begin
        ...               -- a sequence of statements

exception
    when SINGULAR | NUMERIC_ERROR =>
      PUT (" MATRIX IS SINGULAR ");
            -- executed if one of the two exceptions is generated in the
            -- execution of any of the statements above
    when others =>
      PUT (" FATAL ERROR ");
      raise ERROR;
            -- executed if any other exception is generated in the sequence of
            -- statements above.
end;
```

— Subprogram bodies, package bodies, task bodies, as well as block statements can have an exception handler associated with them.

```
procedure ENTER_COLOR (SELECTION : out COLOR) is
begin
    loop
    -- block statement is used to localize the exception handler so
            -- that the execution of the GET can be retried even when a
            -- DATA_ERROR exception has occurred
        begin
            PUT ("Color selected : ");  -- prompts user
            GET (SELECTION);            -- accepts color typed or
```

```
                                        -- raises exception
                    return;
                exception
                    when DATA_ERROR =>
                    PUT("Invalid color, try again.");
                    NEW_LINE(2);
                    -- completes execution of the block statement
                end;
            end loop;    -- repeats the block statement until a color accepted
        end ENTER_COLOR;
```

— Exception handlers in a package body are associated with the execution of the code in the package body after the **begin**. Remember that this code is only executed once when the package is elaborated. This exception handler is not associated with any of the program unit's bodies contained within the declarative part of the package body.

Program Unit Sampler

Up to this point, we have been covering the individual features of Ada by highlighting them through the use of tables, figures and fragmented examples. This section attempts to tie the individual features together by giving you a sampling of full program units that make use of the various features we have covered up to this point. For this section,we are using a set of randomly selected examples that illustrate the form and usage of various Ada features. Some of the program units provided in this sampler may be useful as models of code which you are developing. The main emphasis of this section is on providing illustrative examples, not necessarily production quality implementations of algorithms.

Examples A-35   Subprogram Sampler

— Subprograms can be viewed as implementing operations on abstract data types.

```ada
-- basic operation on objects of type STACK - a push

procedure PUSH (E : in ELEMENT_TYPE;  S : in out STACK) is
begin
  if S.INDEX = S.SIZE then
   raise STACK_OVERFLOW;
         -- used to indicate attempt to push on to a full stack
   else
    S.INDEX := S.INDEX + 1;
    S. SPACE (S.INDEX) := E;
   end if;
end PUSH;


-- a mathematical operator on objects of VECTOR type - dot product

function DOT_PRODUCT (LEFT, RIGHT  : VECTOR) return REAL is
  SUM  : REAL := 0.0;
begin
  CHECK (LEFT'FIRST = RIGHT'FIRST and LEFT'LAST = RIGHT'LAST);
   -- the use of attributes makes this code work for vectors of any length
  for J in LEFT'RANGE loop
  SUM := SUM + LEFT (J) * RIGHT (J);
  end loop;
   return SUM;
end DOT_PRODUCT;


-- a square root operator

    function SQRT (X : FLOAT) return FLOAT is
        EPSILON : constant := 0.000001;              -- local declarations
        ROOT : FLOAT := 1.0;
    begin   -- SQRT
        if X = 0.0 then
            return 0.0;
        else
            ROOT := (X/ROOT + ROOT) / 2.0;
            while abs (X/ROOT*2 - 1.0) >= EPSILON  loop
                ROOT := (X/ROOT + ROOT) / 2.0;
            end loop;
            return ROOT;
```

```
      end if;
   end SQRT;
```

— Overloading of operators can produce more readable code by allowing the use of an infix notation for operators.

```
function "+" (LEFT, RIGHT : MATRIX) return MATRIX;
function "+" (LEFT, RIGHT : VECTOR) return VECTOR;
   •
   •
   •
                    -- assuming that A, B, and C are of the type VECTOR
                    -- the three following assignments are equivalent
A := B + C;    -- overloading allows the use of infix notation
A := "+" (B, C);
A := "+" (LEFT => B, RIGHT => C);

function "*" (LEFT, RIGHT  :  VECTOR) return REAL is
   SUM  :  REAL := 0.0;  -- local declarations
begin
  CHECK (LEFT'FIRST = RIGHT'FIRST and LEFT'LAST = RIGHT'LAST);
    -- the use of attributes makes this code work for vectors of any length
  for J in LEFT'RANGE loop
    SUM := SUM + LEFT (J) * RIGHT (J);
  end loop;
  return SUM;
end "*";
   •
   •
   •
X := B * C;  -- X is REAL, B and C are VECTOR then the
                 -- operation is not an element by
                      -- element multiply but a dot product
```

— Procedures and functions can be declared within other program units and can access declarations from the enclosing unit.

```ada
with TEXT_IO; use TEXT_IO;
procedure DIALOGUE is
  type COLOR is (WHITE, RED, ORANGE, YELLOW, GREEN, BLUE,
                                               BROWN);

  -- define I/O on user defined types

  package COLOR_IO is new ENUMERATION_IO (ENUM => COLOR);
  package NUMBER_IO is new INTEGER_IO (INTEGER);
  use COLOR_IO, NUMBER_IO;

  INVENTORY : array (COLOR) of INTEGER := (20, 17, 43, 10, 28, 173,
                                                              87);
  CHOICE : COLOR;

  -- ENTER_COLOR has access to all the declarations above
          -- they are "global"
  procedure ENTER_COLOR (SELECTION : out COLOR) is
  begin
      loop
          begin
              PUT ("Color selected : "); -- prompts user
              GET (SELECTION  );         -- accepts color typed or
                                         -- raises exception
              return;
          exception
              when DATA_ERROR =>
              PUT("Invalid color, try again.");
              --user has typed new line
              NEW_LINE(2);
              -- completes execution of the block statement
          end;
      end loop;    -- repeats the block statement until color accepted
  end;
begin  -- statements of DIALOGUE;

  NUMBER_IO.DEFAULT_WIDTH := 5;

  loop
```

```
        ENTER_COLOR(CHOICE);
                -- user types a new color and a new line

        SET_COL(5);   PUT(CHOICE); PUT("Items available:");
        SET_COL(40); PUT(INVENTORY(CHOICE));    -- default width is 5
        NEW_LINE;
    end loop;
end DIALOGUE;
```

— Nested procedures and functions are only accessible within the program
unit that they are declared in. If you need to extend their accessibility, place
them in a package specification and control access through the use of a Context Clause.

```
with TEXT_IO, VECTOR_SERVICES; -- context clause
use VECTOR_SERVICES; -- control direct visibility
procedure COMPUTE_TRACKING_DATA is
    -- the types used here are declared in VECTOR_SERVICES
    LAST_POINT, CURRENT_POINT, NEXT_POINT : POINT_TYPE;
    TIME_ELAPSED, TIME_PROJECTED : TIME_TYPE;
    DISTANCE, VELOCITY : FLOAT;

    package TIME_IO is new TEXT_IO.FIXED_IO (TIME_TYPE);
    package FLT_IO is new TEXT_IO.FLOAT_IO (FLOAT);
            -- generic instantiations to provide access to
                --I/O operations on application
            -- specific data types TIME_TYPE and FLOAT

    procedure GET_POINT (P : out POINT_TYPE) is
    begin   -- GET_POINT usable only in the enclosing procedure
            TEXT_IO.PUT (" X = ");
            FLT_IO.GET (P(X));
            TEXT_IO.PUT (" Y = ");
            FLT_IO.GET (P(Y));
            TEXT_IO.NEW_LINE;
    end GET_POINT;

    procedure PUT_POINT (P : in POINT_TYPE) is
```

```ada
begin   -- PUT_POINT usable only in the enclosing procedure
    TEXT_IO.PUT ("(");
    FLT_IO.PUT (P(X));
    TEXT_IO.PUT (",");
    FLT_IO.PUT (P(Y));
    TEXT_IO.PUT (")");
end PUT_POINT;

begin     -- COMPUTE_TRACKING_DATA
-- Input last and current point and reading times
TEXT_IO.PUT ("Enter coordinates of last position: ");
GET_POINT (LAST_POINT);
TEXT_IO.PUT ("Enter coordinates of current position: ");
GET_POINT (CURRENT_POINT);

TEXT_IO.PUT ("Time (in seconds) between readings: ");
TIME_IO.GET (TIME_ELAPSED); TEXT_IO.NEW_LINE;
TEXT_IO.PUT ("Time (in seconds) until next reading: ");
TIME_IO.GET (TIME_PROJECTED); TEXT_IO.NEW_LINE;

-- Calculate distance, velocity, and new coordinates

DISTANCE := DISTANCE_BETWEEN (LAST_POINT,
                                         CURRENT_POINT);
CALCULATE_VELOCITY (LAST_POINT, CURRENT_POINT,
                    TIME_ELAPSED, VELOCITY);
NEXT_POINT := NEXT_POINT_AFTER (LAST_POINT,
    CURRENT_POINT, TIME_ELAPSED, TIME_PROJECTED);

-- Output calculation results
TEXT_IO.PUT ("Distance between points was");
FLT_IO.PUT (DISTANCE);
TEXT_IO.PUT_LINE ("units.");

TEXT_IO.PUT ("Velocity was");
FLT_IO.PUT (VELOCITY);
TEXT_IO.PUT("units per second.");

TEXT_IO.PUT ("After");
FLT_IO.PUT (TIME_PROJECTED);
```

```
        TEXT_IO.PUT ("seconds, the next point should be");
        PUT_POINT (NEXT_POINT);

    end COMPUTE_TRACKING_DATA;
```

Examples A-36   Package Sampler

— A package can be used to define an abstract data type. These abstract data types can be viewed as application specific extensions to Ada.

```
    -- a package that allows you to declare rational numbers
    -- (signed integer value)/(positive non-zero integer value)
    -- and perform elementary mathematical operations with them.

    package RATIONAL_NUMBERS is

        type RATIONAL is
            record
                    NUMERATOR   : INTEGER;
                    DENOMINATOR : POSITIVE;
            end record;

        -- operations on rational numbers

        function EQUAL (X,Y : RATIONAL) return BOOLEAN;
        function "/"   (X,Y : INTEGER)    return RATIONAL;
        function "+"   (X,Y : RATIONAL) return RATIONAL;
        function "-"   (X,Y : RATIONAL) return RATIONAL;
        function "*"   (X,Y : RATIONAL) return RATIONAL;
        function "/"   (X,Y : RATIONAL) return RATIONAL;
    end RATIONAL_NUMBERS;

    package body RATIONAL_NUMBERS is
        -- SAME_DENOMINATOR is used to implement other operators
            -- it is local
        procedure SAME_DENOMINATOR ( X, Y : in out RATIONAL) is
```

```ada
begin
        -- reduces X and Y to same denominator
        -- used only to implement other procedures and functions
        •
        •
        •
end SAME_DENOMINATOR;

function EQUAL (X, Y : RATIONAL) return BOOLEAN is
        U, V : RATIONAL;
begin
        U := X;
        V := Y;
        SAME_DENOMINATOR (U,V);
        return U.NUMERATOR = V.NUMERATOR;
end EQUAL;

function "/" (X, Y : INTEGER) return RATIONAL is
begin
        if Y >0 then
                return (NUMERATOR => X, DENOMINATOR => Y);
        else
                return (NUMERATOR => -X, DENOMINATOR => -Y);
        end if;
        -- multiple return statements may appear in a program unit
end "/";

function "+" (X,Y : RATIONAL) return RATIONAL is ... end "+";
function "-" (X,Y : RATIONAL) return RATIONAL is ... end "-";
function "*" (X,Y : RATIONAL) return RATIONAL is ... end "*";
function "/" (X,Y : RATIONAL) return RATIONAL is ... end "/";
end RATIONAL_NUMBERS;
```

— Private types allow you to hide the details of the implementation of a data type from the user. Access to the data type characteristics and values is controlled by the services provided in the package specification.

```ada
-- this package allows us to get a key and compare it with other keys
```

```
package KEY_MANAGER is
   type KEY is private;
   NULL_KEY : constant KEY;
   procedure GET_KEY(K : out KEY);
   function "<" (X, Y : KEY) return BOOLEAN;
private
   type KEY is new NATURAL;
   NULL_KEY : constant KEY := 0;
end  KEY_MANAGER;
```

— A package body can save state information within it, as normal variables. These variables will exist as long as the package is within scope.

```
package body KEY_MANAGER is
   LAST_KEY : KEY := NULL_KEY;
           -- a state variable that records what was the last key assigned.
   procedure GET_KEY  (K : out KEY) is
   begin
          LAST_KEY := LAST_KEY + 1;  -- LAST_KEY is global
          K := LAST_KEY;
   end GET_KEY;

   function "<" (X, Y : KEY) return BOOLEAN is
   begin
          return  INTEGER (X) < INTEGER (Y);
   end "<";
end KEY_MANAGER;
```

— Packages allow you to collect various declarations together. These declarations can be used by other program units through the use of a context clause.

```
package VECTOR_SERVICES is
   type COORDINATE_TYPE is (X, Y);
   type POINT_TYPE is array (COORDINATE_TYPE) of FLOAT;
   subtype TIME_TYPE is DURATION;
   function DISTANCE_BETWEEN (LAST_POINT,
                        THIS_POINT : POINT_TYPE) return FLOAT;
```

```ada
      procedure CALCULATE_VELOCITY (FROM, TO : in POINT_TYPE;
                              IN_TIME : in TIME_TYPE;
                              VELOCITY : out FLOAT);
      function NEXT_POINT_AFTER (LAST_POINT, THIS POINT :
                                           POINT_TYPE;
                       TIME_BETWEEN_LAST,
                       TIME_BETWEEN_NEXT   : TIME_TYPE)
             return POINT_TYPE;
   end VECTOR_SERVICES;

   package body VECTOR_SERVICES is
      function SQRT (X : FLOAT) return FLOAT is
             EPSILON : constant := 0.000001;              -- local declarations
             ROOT : FLOAT := 1.0;
      begin   -- SQRT
             if X = 0.0 then
                    return 0.0;
             else
                    ROOT := (X/ROOT + ROOT) / 2.0;
                    while abs (X/ROOT*2 - 1.0) >= EPSILON  loop
                           ROOT := (X/ROOT + ROOT) / 2.0;
                    end loop;
                    return ROOT;
             end if;
      end SQRT;

      procedure CALCULATE_VELOCITY (FROM, TO : in POINT_TYPE;
                           IN_TIME   : in TIME_TYPE;
                           VELOCITY : out FLOAT)  is

      begin    -- CALCULATE_VELOCITY
           VELOCITY := DISTANCE_BETWEEN(FROM,
                                           TO)/FLOAT(IN_TIME);
      end CALCULATE_VELOCITY;

      procedure CALCULATE_VELOCITY (FROM, TO : in POINT_TYPE;
                           IN_TIME : in TIME_TYPE;
                           VELOCITY : out FLOAT) is separate;
```

```
    function NEXT_POINT_AFTER(LAST_POINT, THIS_POINT :
                                                POINT_TYPE;
                        TIME_BETWEEN_LAST, TIME_BETWEEN_NEXT :
                                                TIME_TYPE)
                return POINT_TYPE is separate;

end VECTOR_SERVICES;
```

```
-- even though this is textually separate and can be submitted to the
    --compiler separately, it still has the same scope and visibility as if it
        --appeared within the package body.

separate (VECTOR_SERVICES)
function NEXT_POINT_AFTER
            (LAST_POINT, THIS_POINT : POINT_TYPE;
            TIME_BETWEEN_LAST, TIME_BETWEEN_NEXT : TIME_TYPE)
                    return POINT_TYPE is

    NEXT_POINT : POINT_TYPE;

begin   -- NEXT_POINT_AFTER

    if TIME_BETWEEN_LAST = 0 then
            return THIS_POINT;
    else
            NEXT_POINT(X) := LAST_POINT(X) +
                    FLOAT (TIME_BETWEEN_NEXT/TIME_BETWEEN_LAST)
                    * abs (THIS_POINT(X) - LAST_POINT(X));
            NEXT_POINT(Y) := LAST_POINT(Y) +
                    FLOAT (TIME_BETWEEN_NEXT/TIME_BETWEEN_LAST)
                    * abs (THIS_POINT(Y) - LAST_POINT(Y));
            return NEXT_POINT;
    end if;

end NEXT_POINT_AFTER;
```

— A Context Clause provides access to the services provided by the package.

```
-- using vector sevices
with TEXT_IO, VECTOR_SERVICES; -- context clause
use VECTOR_SERVICES;   -- makes the declarations in
                               -- VECTOR_SERVICES directly visible
procedure COMPUTE_TRACKING_DATA is
   LAST_POINT, CURRENT_POINT, NEXT_POINT : POINT_TYPE;
   TIME_ELAPSED, TIME_PROJECTED : TIME_TYPE;
   DISTANCE, VELOCITY : FLOAT;

   package TIME_IO is new TEXT_IO.FIXED_IO (TIME_TYPE);
   package FLT_IO is new TEXT_IO.FLOAT_IO (FLOAT);

   procedure GET_POINT (P : out POINT_TYPE) is
   begin   -- GET_POINT
         TEXT_IO.PUT (" X = ");
         FLT_IO.GET (P(X));
         TEXT_IO.PUT (" Y = ");
         FLT_IO.GET (P(Y));
         TEXT_IO.NEW_LINE;
   end GET_POINT;

   procedure PUT_POINT (P : in POINT_TYPE) is
   begin   -- PUT_POINT
         TEXT_IO.PUT ("(");
         FLT_IO.PUT (P(X));
         TEXT_IO.PUT (",");
         FLT_IO.PUT (P(Y));
         TEXT_IO.PUT (")");
   end PUT_POINT;

begin     -- COMPUTE_TRACKING_DATA
   -- Input last and current point and reading times
   TEXT_IO.PUT ("Enter coordinates of last position: ");
   GET_POINT (LAST_POINT);
   TEXT_IO.PUT ("Enter coordinates of current position: ");
   GET_POINT (CURRENT_POINT);
```

```
TEXT_IO.PUT ("Time (in seconds) between readings: ");
TIME_IO.GET (TIME_ELAPSED); TEXT_IO.NEW_LINE;
TEXT_IO.PUT ("Time (in seconds) until next reading: ");
TIME_IO.GET (TIME_PROJECTED); TEXT_IO.NEW_LINE;

-- Calculate distance, velocity, and new coordinates

DISTANCE := DISTANCE_BETWEEN (LAST_POINT,
                                    CURRENT_POINT);
CALCULATE_VELOCITY (LAST_POINT, CURRENT_POINT,
                    TIME_ELAPSED, VELOCITY);
NEXT_POINT := NEXT_POINT_AFTER (LAST_POINT,
                                    CURRENT_POINT,
                        TIME_ELAPSED, TIME_PROJECTED);

-- Output calculation results

TEXT_IO.PUT ("Distance between points was");
FLT_IO.PUT (DISTANCE);
TEXT_IO.PUT_LINE ("units.");

TEXT_IO.PUT ("Velocity was");
FLT_IO.PUT (VELOCITY);
TEXT_IO.PUT("units per second.");

TEXT_IO.PUT ("After");
FLT_IO.PUT (TIME_PROJECTED);
TEXT_IO.PUT ("seconds, the next point should be");
PUT_POINT (NEXT_POINT);

end COMPUTE_TRACKING_DATA;
```

Examples A - 37 Task Sampler

— Tasks can be used to implement buffers or protected data structures. Tasks of this form prevent problems associated within uncontrolled updates of a data structure by concurrent programs.

```
-- interface to other tasks looks like procedure call; one to read the array the
-- other to write to it

task PROTECTED_ARRAY is
    -- INDEX and ITEM are global types
    entry READ  (N : in INDEX ; V : out ITEM);
    entry WRITE (N : in INDEX ; E : in  ITEM);
end  PROTECTED_ARRAY ;

task body PROTECTED_ARRAY is
    TABLE : array (INDEX) of ITEM := (INDEX => NULL_ITEM);
    -- the array is declared local to the task so no other program unit can
        --access it other than through the entries provided in the
            --specification.
begin
    loop
            -- the select statement allows either a read or write to be
            -- serviced but the accept statements require that a complete
            -- read or write operation be performed on the array before
            -- any other operation can be performed.
        select
                accept READ (N : in INDEX; V : out ITEM) do
                    V := TABLE (N);
                end READ;
        or
                accept WRITE (N : in INDEX; E : in ITEM) do
                    TABLE (N) := E;
                end WRITE;
        end  select;
    end loop;
end PROTECTED_ARRAY;
```

— Tasks can be used to implement hardware interrupt handlers using an address clause.

```
task POWER_FAILURE is
    entry FAIL;
    for FAIL use at 16#FF10#;
```

```
    -- maps hardware trap address to an entry
    -- may not be supported on all implementations
end POWER_FAILURE;

task body POWER_FAILURE is
begin
    accept FAIL;
    SHUT_DOWN;
end POWER_FAILURE;
```

— Tasks can be used to implement semaphores.

```
task SEMAPHORE is
    entry SEIZE;
    entry RELEASE;
end SEMAPHORE;

task body SEMAPHORE is
    IN_USE : BOOLEAN := FALSE;
begin
  loop
  select
    when not IN_USE =>
    -- can only accept a SEIZE if the semaphore is not in use
        accept SEIZE do
          IN_USE := TRUE;
        end SEIZE;
    or
      -- can accept a RELEASE anytime
        accept RELEASE do
          IN_USE := FALSE;
        end RELEASE;
    or
      terminate;
          -- allow the task to complete if the program unit in which activated
                  --this task completes
    end select;
    end loop;
end SEMAPHORE;
```

— Tasks have the characteristics of a program unit, as well as a data object. A task object always has a task type.

```
-- a semaphore task type allows us to create any number of semaphores

task type SEMAPHORE is
    entry SEIZE;
    entry RELEASE;
end SEMAPHORE;

-- body will not change from above

task body SEMAPHORE is
   IN_USE : BOOLEAN := FALSE;
begin
   loop
   select
     when not IN_USE =>
        accept SEIZE do
          IN_USE := TRUE;
        end SEIZE;
   or
     when IN_USE =>
     -- can only accept a RELEASE when the semaphore is in use
        accept RELEASE do
          IN_USE := FALSE;
        end RELEASE;
   or
     terminate;
           -- allow the task to complete if the program unit in which activated
               --this task completes
   end select;
   end loop;
end SEMAPHORE;

-- we can declare task objects at this point
MY_SEMAPHORE, A, B : SEMAPHORE;
     -- creates three independent tasks that run concurrently thus giving us
         --three independent semaphores
```

```
        •
        •
        •
-- sample entry calls
MY_SEMAPHORE.SEIZE;
A.RELEASE;
B.SEIZE;
```

— Task objects can be components of other objects. In addition, task objects can be designated by access objects.

```
    type SET_OF_SEMAPHORES is array ( -10 .. 10) of SEMAPHORE;

A, B : SET_OF_SEMAPHORES;
        -- cannot initialize this array since the components are a
        -- limited type for which assignment is not a defined operation

    -- creates 42 semaphores in a structure
    -- entry calls would look like

    A(-7).SEIZE;
    B(12).RELEASE;
```

— An additional example of tasking.

```
    -- acts as a buffer between two other tasks
    task BUFFER is
        entry READ   (C  : out CHARACTER);
        entry WRITE ( C : in  CHARACTER);
    end;

    task body BUFFER is
        POOL_SIZE   : constant INTEGER := 100;
        POOL                  : array (1 .. POOL_SIZE) of CHARACTER;
        COUNT       : INTEGER range 0 .. POOL_SIZE := 0;
        IN_INDEX, OUT_INDEX : INTEGER range 1 .. POOL_SIZE :=1;
```

```
begin
  loop
      select
            when COUNT < POOL_SIZE =>
            accept WRITE (C : in CHARACTER) do
                  POOL (IN_INDEX) := C;
            end;
            IN_INDEX := IN_INDEX mod POOL_SIZE + 1;
            COUNT := COUNT + 1;
      or
            when COUNT >0 =>
            accept READ (C : out CHARACTER) do
                C:=POOL (OUT_INDEX) ;
            end;
            OUT_INDEX := OUT_INDEX mod POOL_SIZE + 1;
            COUNT := COUNT - 1;
      or
            terminate;
      end select;
  end loop;
end BUFFER;


-- the data producing task
loop
   -- produce the next character CHAR
   BUFFER.WRITE(CHAR);
   exit when CHAR = ASCII.EOT;
end loop;
-- package ASCII defines constants for all control characters; EOT -> End of
         --Transmission


-- the data consuming task
loop
   BUFFER.READ(CHAR);
   -- consume the next character CHAR
   exit when CHAR = ASCII.EOT;
end loop;
```

Examples A - 38   Generic Sampler

— The Generic Formal part identifies the types, objects, and subprograms that are used to parameterize a generic program unit.

```
generic -- parameterless

generic
    SIZE : NATURAL;   -- formal object

generic
    LENGTH : INTEGER := 200;  -- formal objects with a default expression
    AREA    : INTEGER  := LENGTH*LENGTH;

generic
    type ITEM is private;                          -- formal type
    type INDEX is (<>);                            -- formal type
    type ROW is array (INDEX range <>) of ITEM;     -- formal type
    with function "<" (X, Y : ITEM) return BOOLEAN; -- formal subprogram
```

— Declarations for generic subprograms .

```
generic
    type ELEM is private;
procedure EXCHANGE(U, V : in out ELEM);

generic
    type ITEM is private;
    with function "*"(U, V : ITEM) return ITEM is <>;
function SQUARING (X : ITEM) return ITEM;
```

— Declaration for a generic package.

```
generic
    type ITEM is private;
```

```
      type VECTOR is array (POSITIVE range <>) of ITEM;
      with function SUM(X, Y : ITEM) return ITEM;
    package ON_VECTORS is
      function SUM(A, B : VECTOR) return VECTOR;
      function SIGMA(A : VECTOR) return ITEM;
      LENGTH_ERROR : exception;
    end;
```

— Generic formal types identify which types are allowed to be used in a generic instantiation.

```
    type ITEM is private;   -- any non-limited type

    type BUFFER (LENGTH : NATURAL) is limited private; -- any type

    type ENUM    is (<>);   -- an enumeration or integer type

    type INT      is range <>; -- an integer type

    type ANGLE   is delta <>;  -- a fixed point type

    type MASS    is digits <>; -- a floating point type

    type TABLE    is array (ENUM) of ITEM;
                        -- an array type, both the index and component
```

— The generic formal part for declaring a formal integer type.

```
    generic
      type RANK is range <>;
      FIRST :  RANK := RANK'FIRST;
      SECOND : RANK := FIRST + 1;    -- the operator "+" for the type RANK
```

— Generic formal subprograms allow the passing of subprograms to the generic subprogram or package.

with function INCREASE (X : INTEGER) **return** INTEGER;

with function SUM (X, Y : ITEM) **return** ITEM;

with function "+" (X, Y : ITEM) **return** ITEM **is** <>;

with function IMAGE (X : ENUM) **return** STRING **is** ENUM'IMAGE;

with procedure UPDATE **is** DEFAULT_UPDATE;

— Example of generic program unit bodies for the declarations above.

— These program units must be written to the constraints of the generic formal parameters. For example, if ELEM (the generic formal type) is declared as a private type, then you can only use those operations defined for private types within the body of the program unit.

```
-- Example of a generic procedure body

procedure EXCHANGE (U, V : in out ELEM) is
    T : ELEM;     -- the generic formal type
begin
    T := U;
    U := V;
    V := T;
end EXCHANGE;

-- Example of a generic function body

function SQUARING (X :ITEM) return ITEM is
begin
    return X*X;          -- the formal operator "*"
end;

-- Example of a generic package body

package body ON_VECTORS is
    -- adds two vectors of the same length but with different index bounds
```

```ada
function SUM (A, B : VECTOR) return VECTOR is
        RESULT : VECTOR (A'RANGE); -- the formal type VECTOR
        BIAS : constant INTEGER := B'FIRST - A'FIRST;
                -- computes the index offset between the vectors

begin
        if A'LENGTH /= B'LENGTH then
                raise LENGTH_ERROR;
        end if;

        for N in A'RANGE loop
                RESULT(N) := SUM(A(N),B(N + BIAS));
                        -- formal function SUM
        end loop;
        return RESULT;
end;

-- sums all of the components of a vector
function SIGMA (A : VECTOR) return ITEM is
        TOTAL : ITEM := A(A'FIRST);          -- the formal type ITEM
begin
        for N in A'FIRST + 1 .. A'LAST loop
                TOTAL := SUM(TOTAL, A(N));    -- the formal function SUM
        end loop;
        return TOTAL;
end;
end;
```

— Generic instantiation creates a version of the program unit from the generic template.

```ada
procedure SWAP is new EXCHANGE (ELEM => INTEGER);
        -- a new EXCHANGE procedure that operates on objects of type
                -- INTEGER

procedure SWAP is new EXCHANGE (CHARACTER);
                -- SWAP is overloaded
```

```
     -- a new EXCHANGE procedure that operates on objects of type
     -- CHARACTER

function SQUARE is new SQUARING (INTEGER);
     -- "*" of INTEGER used by default
     -- a new SQUARING function that operates on objects of type INTEGER

function SQUARE is new SQUARING (ITEM => MATRIX, "*" =>
                                        MATRIX_PRODUCT);
     -- a new SQUARING functions that operates on objects of type MATRIX
        -- and performs a MATRIX_PRODUCT where the "*" is called in the
           -- generic subprogram body

function SQUARE is new SQUARING (MATRIX, MATRIX_PRODUCT);
     -- same as previous

package INT_VECTORS is new ON_VECTORS (INTEGER, TABLE, "+");
```

— Using the instantiated units is the same as if you wrote a special procedure, function or package for each data type.

```
SWAP(A, B);
A := SQUARE(A);

T : TABLE(1 .. 5) := (10, 20, 30, 40, 50);
N : INTEGER := INT_VECTORS.SIGMA(T);

use INT_VECTORS;
M : INTEGER := SIGMA(T);
```

— Example of a generic package, which implements a stack abstraction. This package can be used to build stack data structures and operate on them for any data types but a limited type.

```ada
generic
   SIZE : POSITIVE;
                         -- you can create stacks of any size work with
   type ITEM is private;        -- almost any type
package STACK is
   procedure PUSH (E : in ITEM);
   procedure POP   (E : out ITEM);
   OVERFLOW, UNDERFLOW : exception;
end STACK;

package body STACK is
   -- we are restricted in the package body to operations on ITEM that are
       -- defined for a private type

   type TABLE is array (POSITIVE range <>) of ITEM;

   SPACE : TABLE (1 .. SIZE);
   INDEX : NATURAL := 0;

   procedure PUSH (E : in ITEM) is
   begin
        if INDEX >= SIZE then
                raise OVERFLOW;
        end if;
        INDEX := INDEX + 1;
        SPACE (INDEX) := E;
   end PUSH;

   procedure POP ( E : out ITEM) is
   begin
        if INDEX = 0 then
                raise UNDERFLOW;
        end if;
        E := SPACE (INDEX) ;
        INDEX := INDEX - 1;
   end POP;

end STACK;

-- generic instantiation
```

```
package STACK_INT is new STACK (SIZE => 200, ITEM => INTEGER);
package STACK_BOOL is new STACK (100, BOOLEAN);

-- using the stacks

STACK_INT.PUSH(N);
STACK_BOOL.PUSH(TRUE);
```

— A different implementation of a generic stack abstraction.

```
generic
    type ITEM is private;       -- size is not a parameter
package ON_STACKS is
    type STACK (SIZE : POSITIVE) is limited private;
    procedure PUSH (S : in out STACK; E : in ITEM);
    procedure POP (S : in out STACK; E : out ITEM);
    OVERFLOW, UNDERFLOW : exception;
private
    type TABLE is array (POSITIVE range <>) of ITEM;
    type STACK(SIZE : POSITIVE) is
        record
                SPACE : TABLE(1 .. SIZE);
                INDEX : NATURAL := 0;
        end record;
end;

-- a generic instantiation

declare
    package STACK_REAL is new ON_STACKS(REAL);
    use STACK_REAL;
    S : STACK (100);
            -- note that multiple stacks for type REAL can be created and
                -- sized independently with this implementation.
begin
    ...
    PUSH(S, 2.54);
```

Language Defined Library Units

As with any other language, Ada provides services for Input and Output, predefined data types, and operations that cause the program to actually execute. These are primarily provided using the package features of Ada. Table A-15 summarizes the services provided by the Language Defined Library Units.

TABLE A-15   LANGUAGE DEFINED LIBRARY UNITS

NAME	DESCRIPTION OF SERVICES PROVIDED
STANDARD	• Defines all predefined data types and operations • Defines all predefined exceptions (except I/O) • Is the package into which all other library units are compiled
CALENDAR	• Defines data types and operations on type TIME • Used in tasking and applications that need access to real time
SYSTEM	• Defines implementation aspects of a specific Ada system
MACHINE_CODE	• Defines machine code level interface to target machine
UNCHECKED_DEALLOCATION	• Allows user control over deallocation of access objects
UNCHECKED_CONVERSION	• Allows bit level type conversions

SEQUENTIAL_IO   • Provides tape-like I/O operations

DIRECT_IO   • Provides random access disk-like I/O
                            operations

TEXT_IO   • Provides human readable I/O operations

IO_EXCEPTIONS   • Defines I/O exceptions

LOW_LEVEL_IO   • Defines low level access operations to
                            target machine I/O devices

Developmental Structure of an Ada program

One of the key concepts of Ada is its ability to effectively support the development of large applications. In order to do this, Ada provides us with facilities to:

- Manage a large number of identifiers or names.

- Support the separate development of individual program units.

- Support both top down and bottoms up development strategies.

Table A-16 identifies the unique features of Ada that support Large Scale Application Development. Figure A-5 identifies and summarizes the Ada features that support large scale development. Figure A-6 illustrates the support for separate development and the two development strategies. After the figures and table are a set of examples that illustrate the usage of these developmental aspects of Ada.

TABLE A- 16   ADA FEATURES THAT SUPPORT LARGE SCALE DEVELOPMENT

SEPARATE COMPILATION

— Allows large programs to be broken into small manageable pieces, which can be developed and compiled with a high degree of independence.

— Supports Top-Down development through the use of subunits, which allow details of a program unit to be developed independently of the program unit in which it is declared.

— Supports Bottom-Up development through the use of "Libraries" of subprograms and packages.

PROGRAM LIBRARY

— Supports separate compilation mechanism.

— Provides the same high degree of compile time checking for separately compiled program units as it would for a single large program.

NAME SPACE MANAGEMENT

— Mechanisms and rules that allow a developer to invent names for entities without concern for conflicting with another developer's invented names.

LOW LEVEL INTERFACE

— Allows the use of inline code statements to access target machine features.

— Allows interface to other languages through pragmas.

— Allows control of error checking at runtime.

COMPILATION UNITS

Generic Declarations   Package Declarations

Subprogram Declarations   Generic Instantiations

Package Bodies   Subunits

Subprogram Bodies

Compilation Order - the rules that determine the required sequence that separate compilation units must be compiled

Separate Compilation - rules by which individually developed elements of a program can be submitted to the compiler.

Program Library - the essence of the program. It holds all of the declarations needed to compile and link the full program.

Scope - for an entity, this is the region of program text where its declaration has effect.

Visibility - for an entity, this is the region of program text where its name can be seen.

Overloading - allows a single name to refer to multiple entities in the same region of program text.

Hiding - when name conflicts exist, hiding rules determine which entity is actually referenced.

NAME SPACE MANAGEMENT

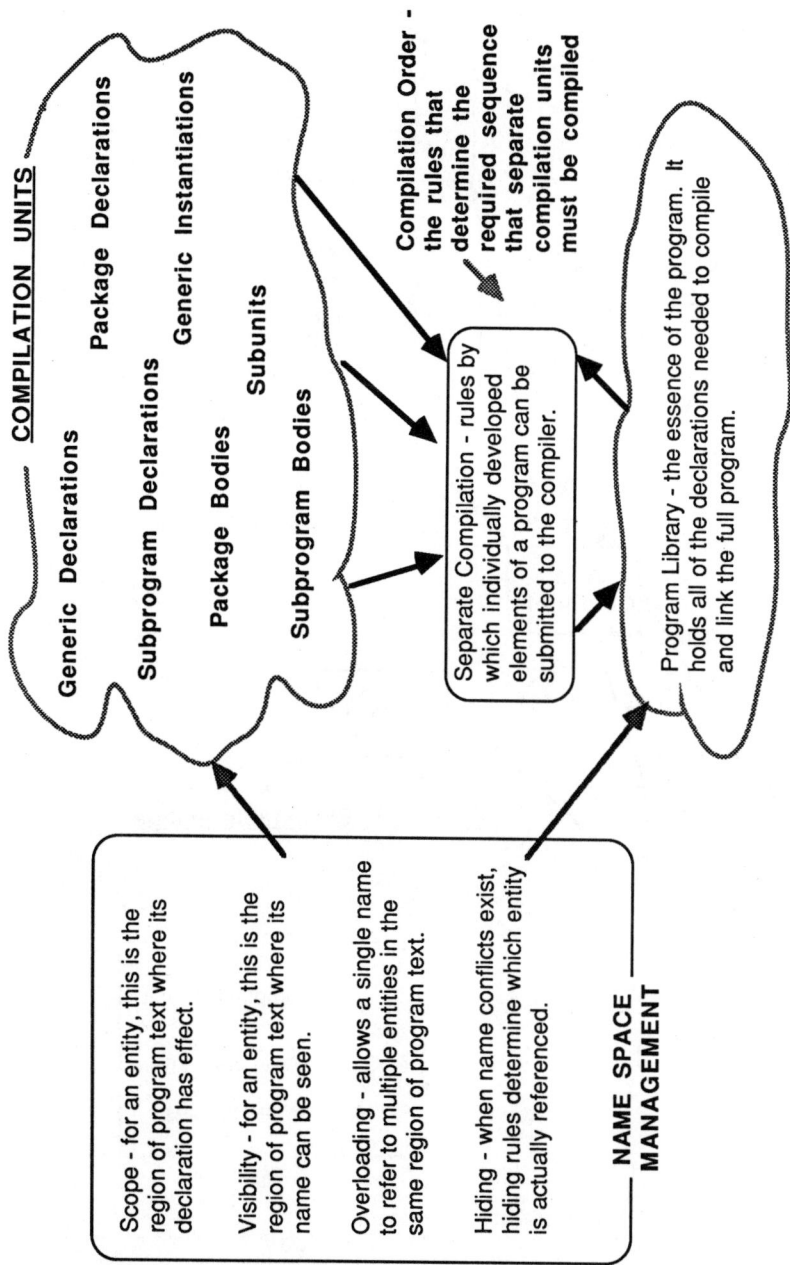

Figure A-5   Ada Features that Support Large Scale Development

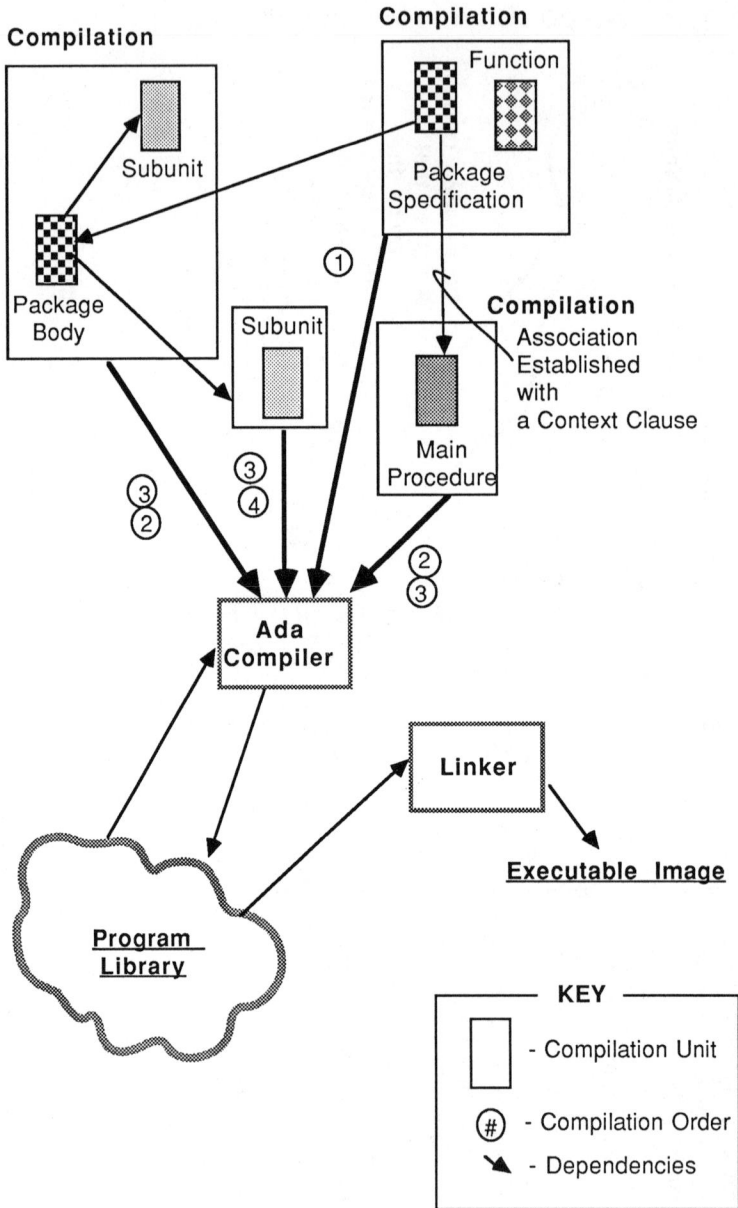

Figure A-6   **Support For Separate Development**

Examples A - 39 Developmental Structure

— Scope and Visibility rules of Ada determine where entities can be accessed in the program text. For those entities that you can access, these rules determine how you may reference them, directly or by selection.

```
procedure P is
    A, B : BOOLEAN;     -- full name of A and B :  P.A and P.B
    procedure Q is
        C : BOOLEAN;
        B : BOOLEAN;
                -- an inner homograph of B, it hides the outer B - P.B

    begin
        B := A;             -- means Q.B := P.A;
                            -- B and A directly visible
        C := P.B;           -- means Q.C := P.B;
                            -- C directly visible
                            -- B only visible by selection
    end Q;
begin
    ...
    A := B;                 -- means P.A := P.B;
end P;
```

— Further restrictions exist on where you can use a name, over and above the scope and visibility rules.

```
K : INTEGER := K * K;
                -- illegal, can't reference an object in its own declaration
T : T;                      -- illegal, name conflicts
procedure P (X : P);        -- illegal
procedure Q (X :  REAL := Q);
                -- illegal, even if there is a function named Q
procedure R (R : REAL);
                -- inner declaration is legal (though confusing)
```

— "Use clauses" cause the declaration in the referenced package to become directly visible. Some cases can exist, where the declarations made visible with a use clause will be hidden by inner declarations.

```
procedure R is
   package TRAFFIC is
        type COLOR is (RED, AMBER, GREEN);
        • • •
   end TRAFFIC;
   package WATER_COLORS is
      type COLOR is (WHITE, RED, YELLOW, GREEN, BLUE, BROWN,
                                                       BLACK);
        • • •
   end WATER_COLORS;
   use TRAFFIC;       -- COLOR, RED, AMBER, GREEN, are directly visible
   use WATER_COLORS;
        -- two homographs of GREEN are directly
            -- visible but COLOR is no longer directly  visible
   subtype LIGHT is TRAFFIC.COLOR;     -- used to resolve the
   subtype SHADE is WATER_COLORS.COLOR;
                                   -- conflicting name COLOR
   SIGNAL : LIGHT;
   PAINT : SHADE;
begin
   SIGNAL := GREEN;      -- that of TRAFFIC
   PAINT := GREEN;       -- that of WATER_COLORS
end R;

-- Example of name identification with a use clause
-- assume this is within a block statement between a declare and begin

package D is
   T, U, V : BOOLEAN;
end D;

procedure P is
   package E is
        B, W, V : INTEGER;
   end E;
```

```
    procedure Q is
            T, X : REAL;
            use D, E;
    begin
            -- the name T means Q.T, not D.T
            -- the name U means D.U
            -- the name B means E.B
            -- the name W means E.W
            -- the name X means Q.X
            -- the name V is illegal : either D.V or E.V must be used
            •
            •
            •
    end Q;
begin
    •
    •
    •
end P;
```

```
with TEXT_IO, REAL_OPERATIONS; use REAL_OPERATIONS;
procedure QUADRATIC_EQUATION is
    A, B, C, D : REAL;
    use REAL_IO,       -- achieves direct visibility of GET and PUT for REAL
            TEXT_IO,   -- achieves direct visibility of PUT for strings and of
                                        NEW_LINE
        REAL_FUNCTIONS; -- achieves direct visibility of SQRT
begin
    GET(A); GET(B); GET(C);
    D:= B**2 - 4.0 *A*C;
    if D < 0.0 then
        PUT("Imaginary Roots");
    else
        PUT("Real roots : X1 = ");
        PUT((-B-SQRT(D))/2.0*A)); PUT(" X2 = ");
        PUT((-B+SQRT(D))/2.0*A));
    end if;
    NEW_LINE;
end QUADRATIC_EQUATION;
```

— The separate compilation features of Ada allow a variety of program structuring options. This example illustrates several of the possibilities.

```ada
-- Nested Program Units Option

procedure PROCESSOR is
    SMALL : constant := 20;
    TOTAL : INTEGER := 0;
    package STOCK is
        LIMIT  : constant := 1000;
        TABLE : array (1 .. LIMIT) of INTEGER;
        procedure RESTART;
    end STOCK;

    package body STOCK is
        procedure RESTART is
        begin
            for N in 1 .. LIMIT loop
                TABLE(N) := N;
            end loop;
        end ;
    begin
        RESTART;   -- initializes the table
    end STOCK;

    procedure UPDATE (X : INTEGER) is
        use STOCK;
    begin
        •
        •
        •

        TABLE(X) := TABLE(X) + SMALL;
        •
        •
        •

    end UPDATE;
begin
        •
        •
        •
```

```
        STOCK.RESTART; -- reinitializes TABLE
            •
            •
            •


end PROCESSOR;

-- Program Units As Library Units Option

package STOCK is
    LIMIT : constant := 1000;
    TABLE : array (1 .. LIMIT) of INTEGER;
    procedure RESTART;
end STOCK;


---------------------------------------
package body STOCK is
    procedure RESTART is
    begin
            for N in 1 .. LIMIT loop
                    TABLE(N) := N;
            end loop;
    end ;
begin
    RESTART;
end STOCK;
---------------------------------------


with STOCK;
procedure PROCESSOR is
    SMALL : constant := 20;
    TOTAL : INTEGER := 0;
    procedure UPDATE (X : INTEGER) is
            use STOCK;
    begin
            •
            •
            •

            TABLE (X) := TABLE (X) + SMALL;
            •
```

```
                   .
                   .
      end UPDATE;
begin
                   .
                   .
                   .

      STOCK.RESTART; -- reinitializes TABLE
                   .
                   .
                   .


end PROCESSOR;

-- Program Units as Subunits Option - Before

with TEXT_IO;
procedure TOP is
   type REAL is digits 6;
   R, S : REAL := 1.0;
   package FACILITY is
         PI : constant := 3.14159_26536;
         function F (X : REAL) return REAL;
         procedure G (Y, Z : REAL);
   end FACILITY;

   package body FACILITY is
         -- some local declarations followed by
         function F(X : REAL) return REAL is
         begin
               -- sequence of statements of F
               .
               .
               .

         end F;
         procedure G (Y, Z : REAL) is
               -- local procedures using TEXT_IO
               .
               .
               .
```

```ada
        begin
            -- sequence of statements G
            .
            .
            .
        end G;
    end FACILITY;
procedure TRANSFORM ( U : in out REAL) is
        use FACILITY;
    begin
        U := F(U);
            .
            .
            .
    end TRANSFORM;
begin -- TOP
    TRANSFORM(R);
        .
        .
        .
    FACILITY.G(R, S);
end TOP;


-- Program Unit with Subunits - After

procedure TOP is
    type REAL is digits 6;
    R, S : REAL := 1.0;
    package FACILITY is
        PI : constant := 3.14159_26536;
        function F (X : REAL) return REAL;
        procedure G (Y, Z : REAL);
    end FACILITY;

    package body FACILITY is separate;
    procedure TRANSFORM ( U : in out REAL) is separate;
begin -- TOP
    TRANSFORM (R);
        .
        .
        .
```

```ada
      FACILITY.G (R, S);
   end TOP;

-------------------------------------------

separate (TOP)
procedure TRANSFORM ( U : in out REAL) is
   use FACILITY;
begin
   U := F(U);
   •
   •
   •
end TRANSFORM;
-------------------------------------------

separate (TOP)
package body FACILITY is
   -- some local declarations followed by
   function F (X : REAL) return REAL is
   begin
         -- sequence of statements of F
         •
         •
         •
   end F;
   procedure G (Y, Z : REAL) is separate;
end FACILITY;

-------------------------------------------

with TEXT_IO;   -- context clause only needed here not at TOP
separate (TOP.FACILITY)
procedure G (Y, Z : REAL) is
   -- local procedures using TEXT_IO
         •
         •
         •
begin
   -- sequence of statements of G
         •
         •
         •
end G;
```

Examples A-40   Other Developmental Support Features

— Machine code insertions allow you to directly code in machine language. This should only be used in a very limited manner.

```
M : MASK;

procedure SET_MASK;
pragma INLINE(SET_MASK);

procedure SET_MASK is  -- can not have any parameters
   use MACHINE_CODE;
begin
   SI_FORMAT'(CODE => SSM, B => M'BASE_REG, D => M'DISP);
            -- M'BASE_REG and M'DISP are implementation-specific
                -- predefined attributes
   -- only machine code instructions can be used here
end;
```

— Interface to other languages can be supported by an implementation. Typically an assembly language interface is available with most complete implementations.

```
package FORT_LIB is
   function SQRT( X: FLOAT) return FLOAT;
   function EXP( X: FLOAT) return FLOAT;
            -- all calls to these functions will be to the
            -- FORTRAN library for this implementation

private
   pragma INTERFACE (FORTRAN, SQRT);
   pragma INTERFACE (FORTRAN, EXP);
end FORT_LIB;

-- a typical call
```

X_RESULT := FORT_LIB.SQRT (9.99) + FORT_LIB.EXP (3.0);

— Unchecked Programming allows you to inform the implementation that you want to control the conversion between two data types or to control the time when objects designated by an access type are deallocated.

```
generic
    type SOURCE is limited private;
    type TARGET is limited private;
function UNCHECKED_CONVERSIONS (S : SOURCE) return TARGET;

generic
    type OBJECT is limited private;
    type NAME  is access OBJECT;
procedure UNCHECKED_DEALLOCATION (X : in out NAME);

-- you can create instants of these generics for any data types
```

This static view is not the only view one can take of Ada features. Another view illustrates the dynamic nature of these static features — in other words, the execution time effects of the static features. The next part of this appendix highlights the dynamics of an Ada program.

The Dynamic Framework of Ada

In the definition of Ada found in the Language Reference Manual, there is a considerable amount of discussion about the execution time effects of a program. For a language like Ada, this dynamic view is important to understand, because it determines the true effect of the program statements, as well as how program units are interrelated. In this section, we are going to focus on those aspects of the dynamics of Ada that are different or at least not commonplace in all languages. The remainder of this section will focus on presenting a general view of the Ada execution model, error condition processing, and tasking, from a dynamic perspective.

General Execution Model

The general execution model for Ada is not as simple as the model for other languages since Ada is a highly dynamic language. This dynamic nature is seen directly with the inclusion of Tasking features in Ada, but also indirectly by the manner in which objects come into existence (become usable within a program) and go out of existence (are no longer usable in the program). To give you some insight into the dynamics of Ada, we have contrived a simple procedure that will be used as the framework for the discussion of the life of a program unit. The example below is a simple procedure that is called from the main procedure.

Examples A - 41 Execution Model

```
procedure DYNAMIC_EXAMPLE ( A : in INTEGER; RESULT : out
                                              INTEGER) is

     R : INTEGER range  0 .. 300  := A - 32;
     task X_TASK;  task Z_TASK;
     task  body  X_TASK is
           B : INTEGER := 100;
     begin
           B := A + B;
     end X_TASK;

     task  body  Z_TASK is
           C : INTEGER := 200;
     begin
           loop
                 C := A/10;
           end loop;
     end Z_TASK;
```

```
begin
  RESULT := A + R;
end DYNAMIC_EXAMPLE;
```

    •

    •

    •

-- some place in the main program a call is made that looks like

```
DYNAMIC_EXAMPLE ((300 - 10),  MY_NEW_RESULTS);
```

The dynamic life of an Ada program unit, in this case a procedure, starts with the procedure call which transfers control to the called procedure and causes it to be executed. Then control is transferred back to the main procedure. The basic steps of execution are outlined below :

- The effect of the procedure call is to associate the actual parameters from the caller procedure with the formal parameters (A and Result) of the called procedure.

  — The calling actual parameter expressions are evaluated which yield 290 and the name MY_NEW_RESULTS. During this evaluation, the value of the first expression is checked to determine that it is in the range of allowed values for the subtype of the formal parameter. If it were not, then a CONSTRAINT_ERROR would be raised at the point of the call.

  — These expressions are then associated with A and RESULT, which means A will assume the value 290 and the out mode parameter Result value will be passed back to the caller at the completion of the procedures execution, if it completes.

- Next, the declarations in the declarative region of the called procedure are elaborated using the elaboration process defined for each type of declaration. In Ada, elaboration is defined as "the process by which a declaration achieves its effect (such as the creation of an object)." Elaboration only occurs during program execution. In this example we have three items in the declarative region, an object , R, and two tasks, X_TASK and Z_TASK. The effects of elaborating these declarations is summarized below:

— For object R, the object's subtype is elaborated establishing its base type as INTEGER and that only values within the range 0 to 300 are allowed when assigning to R. Then the intialization expression (A-32) is evaluated, checking that the value is within the range from 0 to 300; if it were outside of this range a CONSTRAINT_ERROR exception would be raised. Then the object is created, space allocated, etc. Finally, the value of the initialization expression is assigned to R.

— For the tasks X_TASK and Z_TASK, elaboration just establishes that the body of the tasks can be executed but does not affect the starting of their execution.

• Now we have completed the elaboration process and we can visualize ourselves sitting at the **begin.** If we had no tasks declared in this procedure we would just start to execute the statements in the executable part of the procedure. But since we have tasks, they must be activated at this point (this is not the only way in which tasks can be activated). The activation of these tasks takes place in parallel — at least to the application programmer it seems to happen that way. Activation consists of elaboration of the declarative regions of the two tasks followed by the execution of the statements in the executable part of the task body. At this point three program threads, procedure DYNAMIC_EXAMPLE, X_TASK, and Z_TASK, can be viewed as executing in parallel even on a single processor.

• Let's look at only the execution of the procedure statements which consists of a single statement. The expression is evaluated and checked to determine if the value is within the range of an INTEGER then it is assigned to RESULT.

• At this point, if we did not have tasks declared inside the procedure we would assign the value of RESULT which is a formal parameter to MY_NEW_RESULTS, after the appropriate constraint check. Then control would be transferred back to the calling procedure.

At this point all of the internally declared items in procedure DYNAMIC_EXAMPLE would not be assessable. But again the internal declared tasks affect the execution sequence.

- Even though procedure DYNAMIC_EXAMPLE has completed its execution (i.e., finished the execution of its sequence of statements), it must wait for X_TASK and Z_TASK to complete their execution. If you look at X_TASK it can complete its execution and terminate. But Z_TASK cannot since its sequence of statements is never completed. What this means is that DYNAMIC_EXAMPLE cannot complete because Z_TASK has not and will not complete and control is never returned to the caller. In this case the main procedure and Z_TASK just keeps on executing the statement in the loop forever.

This example hopefully gives some insight into the dynamic nature of Ada.

Error Handling

Ada provides a fairly complete mechanism for the development of programs which effectively handle exceptional or error conditions which can occur in the execution of a program. Earlier in this appendix we touched on the static nature of exceptions. Here we plan to cover the more dynamic aspects of error handling: those conditions that cause the language defined exceptions to occur and the manner in which exceptions propagate from one program unit to another.

Table A-17 identifies the language defined exceptions and the conditions that can cause some of them to occcur.

TABLE A-17   CONDITIONS THAT CAUSE PREDEFINED EXCEPTIONS

EXCEPTION	RAISING CONDITIONS/SITUATIONS
Constraint_Error	• attempt to assign to an object an out of range value

	• actual parameter not in subtype of formal parameter • index value being out of bounds • logical operation on array objects of different lengths
Data_Error	• when I/O reads an element that is not of the correct type
Device_Error	• when I/O hardware malfunctions
End_Error	• attempt to read past an end of file
Layout_Error	• attempt to set an I/O column number that exceeds the line length
Numeric_Error	• execution of a predefined numeric operation that cannot deliver the correct mathematical result - overflow, for example
Program_Error	• attempt to exit a function with other than a return statement • calling a subprogram whose body has not been elaborated • other erroneous program behavior
Storage_Error	• insufficient memory to allocate new objects or activate new program units
Tasking_Error	• at an entry call to an abnormal task or completed task • when a task fails during activation

Exceptions can be generated at nearly any point in the execution of a program, but the net effect of the exceptions on the program sequence is determined by the exact place of occurrence and the type of unit or statement structure (the frame) in which the exception was raised within. The effect we are talking about is the manner in which control will be transferred between program units in the process of trying to find an exception handler to handle the exception. This process is called propagation of an exception and to a limited extent can be viewed as follows:

- When an exception occurs, normal program execution is suspended.

- If there is an exception handler for the exception in the innermost subprogram body, block statement, or package body (frame) for the statement that caused the exception, then control is transferred to that handler.

- If no handler is found, then the exception is propagated to the frame which caused the frame above to be executed. If a handler for the exception is found, control is transferred there. If not, this step is repeated.

- If an exception handler is not found anywhere in the calling sequence associated with the occurrence, then execution of the program is stopped and control is transferred back to the operating system or the runtime environment.

- When a handler is found, the execution of the handler completes the execution of the frame the handler is in, then execution of the normal program flow continues from that point.

The important point of this discussion is that exceptions will modify the normal program sequence, but Ada allows the programmer or application designer to determine what form of recovery or error handling is needed in order to continue processing or handle the exception.

The examples that follow illustrate the dynamic aspects of exceptions.

Example A - 42   Exceptions During Execution

— Exceptions are raised during execution. They can occur during the elaboration of declarations or within execution of the executable part.

— Where an exception is handled is determined by where it is raised, the calling sequence, and where exception handlers are placed.

```ada
function FACTORIAL (N : POSITIVE) return FLOAT is
begin
    if N = 1 then
        return 1.0;
    else
        return FLOAT(N) * FACTORIAL(N-1);
        -- NUMERIC_ERROR can occur if initial N is too large
    end if;
exception
    when NUMERIC_ERROR => return FLOAT'SAFE_LARGE;
    -- handled by returning the maximum allowed floating point number
end FACTORIAL;

procedure P is
    ERROR : exception;
    procedure R;
    procedure Q is
    begin
        R;
        • • •                       -- error situation (2), ERROR is raised
    exception
        • • •
        when ERROR =>    -- handler E2, for situation (2) and (3)
        • • •
    end Q;
    procedure R is
    begin
        • • •                       -- error situation (3), ERROR is raised
    end R;
begin
    • • •                           -- error situation (1), ERROR is raised
    Q;
    • • •
exception
    • • •
```

```ada
    when ERROR =>   -- handler E1, for situation (1)
    . . .
end P;
```

— Exceptions raised during the elaboration of declarations are handled differently.

```ada
procedure P is
    . . .
begin
    declare
        N : INTEGER := F;   -- the function F may raise ERROR
                    -- handled by E2
    begin
        . . .               -- if ERROR raised here
                            -- handled by E1

    exception
        when ERROR =>   -- handler E1
    end;
    . . .
exception
    when ERROR =>   -- handler E2
end P;
```

— Here is an example of various exception handler locations for the same procedure. This illustrates how you can control the handling of error conditions in various ways. The procedure is called from the runtime environment directly.

Case 1 - No local exception handler; any exception will transfer control back to the runtime environment, thus terminating execution.

```ada
with TEXT_IO; use TEXT_IO;
procedure X is
    type INPUT_TYPE is (A, B, C, D);
    INPT : INPUT_TYPE;
```

```
   package X_IO is new ENUMERATION_IO (INPUT_TYPE); use X_IO;
begin
   GET (INPT);  -- if you type F,  DATA_ERROR is raised
   PUT (INPT);
end X;
```

Case 2 - Local exception handler handles the DATA_ERROR exception by printing a message to the user. But the procedure still returns control to the runtime environment.

```
with TEXT_IO; use TEXT_IO;
procedure X is
   type INPUT_TYPE is (A, B, C, D);
   INPT : INPUT_TYPE;
   package X_IO is new ENUMERATION_IO (INPUT_TYPE); use X_IO;
begin
   GET (INPT);
   PUT (INPT);
exception
   when DATA_ERROR =>  PUT_LINE ("Invalid Entry");
end X;
```

Case 3 - Exception Handler in block statement nested inside of a loop requires the user to retry until he inputs one of the allowed values.

```
with TEXT_IO; use TEXT_IO;
procedure X is
   type INPUT_TYPE is (A, B, C, D);
   INPT : INPUT_TYPE;
   package X_IO is new ENUMERATION_IO (INPUT_TYPE); use X_IO;
begin
  loop
    begin
   GET (INPT);
   exit;
    exception
```

```
      when DATA_ERROR => PUT_LINE ("Invalid Entry - Try Again");
        end;
      end loop;
      PUT (INPT);
   end X;
```

Tasking

Tasking represents the most complex set of Ada features and as such is difficult to describe in a limited manner. Since the objective of this appendix is to give you an insight into the features of Ada, we are going to use a series of figures to illustrate the dynamic aspects of tasking. The more static aspects of tasking have been covered earlier in this appendix. Before we introduce the figures, let us summarize some of the key features of tasking in general:

- Tasks represent parallel threads of program control which will run concurrently in real time on a multiprocessor or in apparent real time on a single processor.

- From an application point of view, all tasks can be viewed as running on their own dedicated logical processor which can share data and interact with other logical processors to accomplish the program's intent.

- All runtime scheduling of tasks is handled by the runtime environment whose characteristics and implementation are hidden from the application programmer.

- Interaction, communication, and controlled data sharing between tasks is accomplished through a single mechanism called a rendezvous. The rendezvous takes place between two statement types only, an entry call and an accept statement.

- Activation of a task is controlled by the location of the declaration of the task in the program and the type of declaration associated with the task.

- Tasks are program units as well as object types. They derive their features from both.

- You can declare task types and objects of that type which can be treated like an object. This means that task objects can be passed as parameters in procedure calls, declared as components in arrays or records, and designated by access objects.

Figures A-7 through A-13 following illustrate various interaction sequences associated with tasking.

- When the calling task and the called task have both arrived at a point where they expect communication to take place, this point is called a rendezvous.

  — The point is the entry call for the calling task and an accept for the called task.

  — Each entry has a queue associated with it.

  — When a task makes an entry call, it goes on the queue for that entry.

  — When an accept statement is executed by a task, the task it rendezvous with is removed from the queue of the entry specified in the accept statement.

  — If the called task reaches an accept statement first, it waits for some task to call that entry.

  — If a task issues an entry call before the called task reaches an accept statement, the calling task waits.

  — Several different tasks might call the same entry of a task before the called task reaches an accept statement for that entry. Each calling task waits, and entry calls are accepted in order of arrival.

Figure A-7   **Rendezvous Concept**

---

1. The **in** and **in out** actual parameters of the entry call are copied into the formal parameters of the accept statement.

2. The statements inside the accept statement are executed.

3. The **in out** and **out** formal parameters of the accept statement are copied back to the actual parameters of the entry call, completing execution of the entry call statement.

TASK X: TASK T :
                        rendezvous
T.Entry_A   ::::::::::::::::::::::::::::::::::   **accept** Entry_A

    (Data_In,   ----------------->   (Input : **in** ... ; Output : **out** ...) **do**
                                                    -- Statements, assign
                        -- value to output

    Data_Out); <-----------------   **end** Entry_A;

Following a rendezvous, both tasks resume asynchronous execution.

Figure A-8   **Steps in a Rendezvous**

•   Simple selective wait statements allow tasks to accept calls on any one of several specified entries. Form of the statement is:

        select
                accept alternative
        {**or**
                accept alternative}
        end select;

    Where accept alternative has the form :

        accept statement

[sequence of statements]

- In executing the selective wait, one of two cases can occur :

1. None of the entries have been called:
   — wait at select until one is called and accept that call.

2. One or more of the entries has been called:
   — one accept statement that can be executed immediately is
   selected arbitrarily and executed.

- The method of arbitrary selection depends on the runtime system, but a
  good runtime system will be fair. The programmer should view the
  choice as random.

```
loop
   select
         accept SET_DESTINATION (DESTINATION : in
                                       POSITION_TYPE) do
               CURRENT_DESTINATION := DESTINATION;
         end SET_DESTINATION;

   or

         accept REPORT (NEW_POSITION: in POSITION_TYPE) do
               CURRENT_POSITION := NEW_POSITION;
         end REPORT;

         if WITHIN_RANGE(CURRENT_POSITION,
                  CURRENT_DESTINATION) then
               ALERT_PILOT;
         end if;

   end select;
end loop;
```

Figure A-9   **Simple Selective Wait**

- Selective waits with guards allow conditional selection of an accept statement. This version of the selective wait has the form :

```
select
[when  condition  =>]
        accept alternative
{or
[when  condition  =>]
        accept alternative }
end  select;
```

The condition is called a Guard.

- An alternative is said to be open if

   — it has no guard, or
   — it has a guard, and its condition is true.

- Execution of a selective wait statement

   — first causes all guards to be evaluated
   — and then proceeds as with the simple selective wait using only the open alternatives.

```
subtype BUFFER_RANGE_TYPE is NATURAL range 1 ..
                                        TOTAL_BUFFERS;

task type BUFFER_ALLOCATION_TYPE is
    entry REQUEST(BUFFER : out BUFFER_RANGE_TYPE);
    entry RELEASE(BUFFER : in BUFFER_RANGE_TYPE);
end BUFFER_ALLOCATION_TYPE;

task body BUFFER_ALLOCATION_TYPE is
    AVAILABLE : array (BUFFER_RANGE_TYPE) of BOOLEAN :=
        (others => TRUE);
    NUMBER_OF_BUFFERS_AVAILABLE : NATURAL range
        0 .. TOTAL_BUFFERS := TOTAL_BUFFERS;
begin
```

```
loop
  select
  when NUMBER_OF_BUFFERS_AVAILABLE > 0 =>
  accept REQUEST (BUFFER : out BUFFER_RANGE_TYPE) do
    SEARCH_LOOP:
      for CANDIDATE_BUFFER in RESOURCE_RANGE_ TYPE'RANGE
      loop
        if AVAILABLE(CANDIDATE_BUFFER) then
          AVAILABLE(CANDIDATE_BUFFER) := FALSE;
          BUFFER := CANDIDATE_BUFFER;
          exit SEARCH_LOOP;
        end if;
      end loop SEARCH_LOOP;
    NUMBER_OF_BUFFERS_AVAILABLE :=
                    NUMBER_OF_BUFFERS_AVAILABLE - 1;
  end REQUEST;
  or
  accept RELEASE(BUFFER : in BUFFER_RANGE_TYPE) do
    AVAILABLE(BUFFER) := TRUE;
    NUMBER_OF_BUFFERS_AVAILABLE :=
                    NUMBER_OF_BUFFERS_AVAILABLE + 1;
  end RELEASE;
  end select;
  end loop;
end BUFFER_ALLOCATION_TYPE;
```

Figure A-10   **Selective Wait with Guards**

- When a task wants to <u>delay itself</u> it uses the delay statement :

  delay expression;

Where expression is a simple expression of type DURATION.

- DURATION is a predefined fixed point type whose values are expressed in seconds.

- The delay statement delays the task for <u>at least</u> the DURATION specified.
  —The runtime system might not allocate the CPU to a task the instant that its delay expires, so the effective delay can be longer.

- The delay statement treats a negative DURATION as a zero DURATION.

- Operations on objects of the type DURATION are defined in the predefined package CALENDAR.

- An implementation provides for DURATION values of at least -86,400 seconds to +86,400 seconds (one day).

- The smallest increment of DURATION must be no greater than 20 milliseconds. The LRM expects a value of 50 microseconds typically.

EXAMPLE:

        delay 5.0 -- delay for a minimum of 5 seconds
        delay 0.5 -- delay for a minimum 1/2 second

EXAMPLE :

        for I in 1 .. NUMBER_OF_ROCKETS **loop**
            SIMULATE_ROCKET_LAUNCH;
            delay TIME_BETWEEN_LAUNCHES;
        end loop;

EXAMPLE:

             • • •
        TIME_OF_NEXT_AOS : TIME;
             • • •

     begin
             • • •
        TIME_OF_NEXT_AOS :=
                        COMPUTE_NEXT_EXPECTED_AOS;
        delay TIME_OF_NEXT_AOS - CALENDAR.CLOCK;
        ESTABLISH_COMMUNICATIONS;
             • • •
     end;

Figure A-11   **Delay Statements**

- Timed entry calls allow a task to perform some other actions if its entry call is not accepted in time.

```
select
      entry call statement ;
      [ sequence of statements ]
or
      delay  delay expression ;
      [ sequence of statements ]
end  select;
```

- Execution of the timed entry call proceeds as follows:

— the actual parameters, if any, are evaluated.

— the delay expression is evaluated and then the entry call is issued.

- If the rendezvous can be started within the specified delay, then it is performed and the first sequence of statements, if any, is executed.

- Otherwise, the entry call is <u>cancelled</u> after the specified delay has expired, after which the second sequence of statements is executed.

- Cancelling the entry call removes the call from the entry's queue. The called task never sees the call.

```
loop
  select
    TEMPERATURE_TASK.READ (TEMPERATURE =>
                                CURRENT_TEMPERATURE);
    if CURRENT_TEMPERATURE >= STANDARD_TEMPERATURE then
        WATER_CONTROL_TASK.INCREASE_WATER_FLOW;
    while CURRENT_TEMPERATURE >=
      STANDARD_TEMPERATURE - 10 loop
      select
        TEMPERATURE_TASK.READ (TEMPERATURE =>
                                    CURRENT_TEMPERATURE);
      or
        delay 0.1;
```

```
      raise TEMPERATURE_EXCEPTION;
    end select;
    end loop;
       WATER_CONTROL_TASK.NORMAL_WATER_FLOW;
    end if;
  or
    delay 0.1;
    raise TEMPERATURE_EXCEPTION;
  end select;
end loop;
```

Figure A-12 **Timed Entry Call**

• Conditional entry calls allow a task to perform some other action if the entry call cannot result in an immediate rendezvous.

```
select
       entry call statement;
       [ sequence of statements ]
else
       sequence of statements
end select;
```

• Execution of a conditional entry call proceeds as follows :

— the actual parameters, if any, are evaluated.
— the entry call is issued.

• If the called task can establish a rendezvous with the calling task immediately, then the rendezvous takes place, and the first sequence of statements is executed.

• Otherwise, if the rendezvous cannot take place, then the entry call is cancelled and the second sequence of statements is executed.

Figure A-13 **Conditional Entry Call**

The following example further demonstrates the dynamic aspects of tasking.

Example A - 43   Tasking during Execution

— Task activation

```
procedure P is
    A, B : RESOURCE; -- elaborate the task objects A, B
    C : RESOURCE;     -- elaborate the task object C
begin
    -- the tasks A, B, C are activated in parallel before the first statement
    ...
end P;
```

— Task dependences determine the order in which tasks terminate.

```
declare
    type GLOBAL is access RESOURCE;
    A, B : RESOURCE;
    G    : GLOBAL;
begin
    -- activation of A and B
    declare
        type LOCAL is access RESOURCE
        X : GLOBAL := new RESOURCE;   -- activation of X.all
        L : LOCAL := new RESOURCE;    -- activation of L.all
        C : RESOURCE;
    begin
        -- activation of C
        G := X;          -- both G and X designate the same task object
        • • •
    end;          -- await termination of C and L.all (but not X.all)
    • • •
end;                    -- await termination of A, B, and G.all
```

— Example using a task to implement a buffer between two other tasks.

```ada
task BUFFER is
    entry READ  (C : out CHARACTER);
    entry WRITE( C : in CHARACTER);
end BUFFER;

task body BUFFER is
    POOL_SIZE  : constant INTEGER := 100;
    POOL                 : array (1 .. POOL_SIZE) of CHARACTER;
    COUNT        : INTEGER range 0 .. POOL_SIZE := 0;
    IN_INDEX, OUT_INDEX : INTEGER range 1 .. POOL_SIZE :=1;
begin
    loop
        select
            when COUNT < POOL_SIZE =>
                accept WRITE (C : in CHARACTER) do
                    POOL(IN_INDEX) := C;
                end WRITE;
                IN_INDEX := IN_INDEX mod POOL_SIZE + 1;
                COUNT := COUNT + 1;
            or when COUNT >0 =>
                accept READ (C : out CHARACTER) do
                    C:=POOL(OUT_INDEX) ;
                end READ;
                OUT_INDEX := OUT_INDEX mod POOL_SIZE + 1;
                COUNT := COUNT - 1;
            or
                terminate;
        end select;
    end loop;
end BUFFER;

-- code fragment from producing task

loop
    -- produce the next character CHAR
    BUFFER.WRITE (CHAR);
    exit when CHAR = ASCII.EOT;
    -- writes to buffer until end of transmission character is to be sent to buffer
```

```
end loop;

-- code fragment from consuming task

loop
    BUFFER.READ(CHAR);
    -- consume the next character CHAR
    exit when CHAR = ASCII.EOT;
    -- reads from buffer until end of transmission character is received
end loop;
```

Appendix B: Ada Syntax Summary

This summary was derived from the Ada Language Reference Manual (LRM) [60]. The basic Syntax Notation used here is:

- Lower case words with underscores denote syntactic categories.

- Boldface words are reserved words.

- Square brackets enclose optional item(s).

- Braces enclose repeated item(s).

- Vertical bars separate alternative items.

- Open brace followed by a vertical bar stands for a vertical bar.

- Italicized parts of syntactic categories are added to enhance readability and give semantic information only and are not part of the element.

Also identified with the syntax is the LRM section and page numbers associated with a particular element of syntax.

Character Set {2.1 page 2-1}

```
graphic_character ::=
        basic_graphic_character
      | lower_case_letter
      | other_special_character
```

```
basic_graphic_character ::=
        upper_case_letter
    | digit
    | special_character
    | space_character
basic_character ::=
        basic_graphic_character
    | format_effector
```

Identifiers {2.3 page 2-4}

```
identifier ::=
        letter {[underline] letter_or_digit}
letter_or_digit ::=
        letter
    | digit
letter ::=
        upper_case_letter
    | lower_case_letter
```

Numeric Literals {2.4   page 2-4}

```
numeric_literal ::=
        decimal_literal
    | based_literal
```

Decimal Literals {2.4.1   page 2-4}

```
decimal_literal ::=
        integer [.integer] [exponent]
integer ::=
        digit {[underline] digit}
exponent ::=
        E [+] integer
    | E - integer
```

Based Literals {2.4.2   page 2-5}

```
based_literal ::=
      base # based_integer [.based_integer] # [exponent]
base ::=
      integer
based_integer ::=
      extended_digit {[underline] extended_digit}
extended_digit ::=
       digit
      | letter
```

Character Literals {2.5   page 2-6}

```
character_literal ::=
      'graphic_character'
```

String Literals {2.6   page 2-6}

```
string_literal ::=
      "{graphic_character}"
```

Pragmas {2.8   page 2-8}

```
pragma ::=
      pragma identifier [(argument_association {, argument_association})];
argument_association ::=
      [argument_identifier =>] name
      | [argument_identifier =>] expression
```

Declarations {3.1   page 3-1}

```
basic_declaration ::=
       object_declaration
      | number_declaration
      | type_declaration
      | subtype_declaration
```

| subprogram_declaration
| package_declaration
| task_declaration
| generic_declaration
| exception_declaration
| generic_instantiation
| renaming_declaration
| deferred_constant_declaration

Objects and Named Numbers {3.2   page 3-2}

```
object_declaration ::=
      identifier_list : [constant] subtype_indication [:= expression];
      | identifier_list : [constant] constrained_array_definition [:=
      expression];
number_declaration ::=
      identifier_list : constant := universal_static_expression;
identifier_list ::=
      identifier {, identifier}
```

Type Declarations {3.3.1   page 3-7}

```
type_declaration ::=
      full_type_declaration
      | incomplete_type_declaration
      | private_type_declaration
full_type_declaration ::=
      type identifier [discriminant_part] is type_definition;
type_definition ::=
      enumeration_type_definition
      | integer_type_definition
      | real_type_definition
      | array_type_definition
      | record_type_definition
      | access_type_definition
      | derived_type_definition
```

Subtype Declarations {3.3.2   page 3-8}

```
subtype_declaration ::=
      subtype identifier is subtype_indication;
subtype_indication ::=
      type_mark [constraint]
type_mark ::=
        type_name
      | subtype_name
constraint ::=
        range_constraint
      | floating_point_constraint
      | fixed_point_constraint
      | index_constraint
      | discriminant_constraint
```

Derived Types {3.4   page 3-10}

```
derived_type_definition ::=
      new subtype_indication
```

Scalar Types {3.5   page 3-12}

```
range_constraint ::=
      range range
range ::=
        range_attribute
      | simple_expression .. simple_expression
```

Enumeration Types {3.5.1   page 3-13}

```
enumeration_type_definition ::=
      (enumeration_literal_specification {,
      enumeration_literal_specification})
enumeration_literal_specification ::=
      enumeration_literal
```

```
enumeration_literal ::=
        identifier
      | character_literal
```

Integer Types {3.5.4   page 3-15}

```
integer_type_definition ::=
        range_constraint
```

Real Types {3.5.6   page 3-19}

```
real_type_definition ::=
        floating_point_constraint
      | fixed_point_constraint
```

Floating Point Types {3.5.7   page 3-20}

```
floating_point_constraint ::=
        floating_accuracy_definition [range_constraint]
floating_accuracy_definition ::=
        digits static_simple_expression
```

Fixed Point Types {3.5.9   page 3-24}

```
fixed_point_constraint ::=
        fixed_accuracy_definition [range_constraint]
fixed_accuracy_definition ::=
        delta static_simple_expression
```

Array Types {3.6   page 3-27}

```
array_type_definition ::=
        unconstrained_array_definition
      | constrained_array_definition
```

```
unconstrained_array_definition ::=
    array(index_subtype_definition {, index_subtype_definition}) of
                                    component_subtype_indication
constrained_array_definition ::=
    array index_constraint of component_subtype_indication
index_subtype_definition ::=
    type_mark range <>
index_constraint ::=
    (discrete_range {, discrete_range})
discrete_range ::=
    discrete_subtype_indication
    | range
```

Record Type {3.7   page 3-33}

```
record_type_definition ::=
    record
        component_list
    end record
component_list ::=
        component_declaration {component_declaration}
    | {component_declaration} variant_part
    | null;
component_declaration ::=
    identifier_list : component_subtype_definition [:= expression];
component_subtype_definition ::=
    subtype_indication
```

Discriminants {3.7.1   page 3-34}

```
discriminant_part ::=
    (discriminant_specification {; discriminant_specification})
discriminant_specification ::=
    identifier_list : type_mark [:= expression]
```

Discriminant Constraints {3.7.2　page 3-36}

```
discriminant_constraint ::=
    (discriminant_association {, discriminant_association})
discriminant_association ::=
    [discriminant_simple_name {| discriminant_simple_name} =>]
    expression
```

Variant Parts {3.7.3　page 3-38}

```
variant_part ::=
    case discriminant_simple_name is
        variant
        {variant}
    end case;
variant ::=
    when choice {| choice} =>
        component_list
choice ::=
        simple_expression
    | discrete_range
    | others
    | component_simple_name
```

Access Types {3.8　page 3-40}

```
access_type_definition ::=
    access subtype_indication
```

Incomplete Type Declaration {3.8.1　page 3-41}

```
incomplete_type_declaration ::=
    type identifier [discriminant_part];
```

Declarative Part {3.9　page 3-43}

```
declarative_part ::=
      {basic_declarative_item} {later_declarative_item}
basic_declarative_item ::=
        basic_declaration
      | representation_clause
      | use_clause
later_declarative_item ::=
        body
      | subprogram_declaration
      | package_declaration
      | task_declaration
      | generic_declaration
      | use_clause
      | generic_instantiation
body ::=
        proper_body
      | body_stub
proper_body ::=
        subprogram_body
      | package_body
      | task_body
```

Names {4.1　page 4-1}

```
name ::=
        simple_name
      | character_literal
      | operator_symbol
      | indexed_component
      | slice
      | selected_component
      | attribute
simple_name ::=
      identifier
prefix ::=
        name
      | function_call
```

Indexed Components {4.1.1   page 4-2}

```
indexed_component ::=
     prefix(expression {, expression})
```

Slices {4.1.2   page 4-3}

```
slice ::=
     prefix(discrete_range)
```

Selected Components {4.1.3   page 4-3}

```
selected_component ::=
     prefix.selector
selector ::=
      simple_name
     | character_literal
     | operator_symbol
     | all
```

Attributes {4.1.4   page 4-5}

```
attribute ::=
     prefix'attribute_designator
attribute_designator ::=
     simple_name [(universal_static_expression)]
```

Aggregates {4.3   page 4-7}

```
aggregate ::=
     (component_association {, component_association})
component_association ::=
     [choice {| choice} => ] expression
```

Expressions {4.4   page 4-11}

```
expression ::=
        relation {and relation}
      | relation {and then relation}
      | relation {or relation}
      | relation {or else relation}
      | relation {xor relation}
relation ::=
        simple_expression [relational_operator simple_expression]
      | simple_expression [not] in range
      | simple_expression [not] in type_mark
simple_expression ::=
      [unary_adding_operator] term {binary_adding_operator term}
term ::=
      factor {multiplying_operator factor}
factor ::=
        primary [** primary]
      | abs primary
      | not primary
primary ::=
        numeric_literal
      | null
      | aggregate
      | string_literal
      | name
      | allocator
      | function_call
      | type_conversion
      | qualified_expression
      | (expression)
```

Operators and Expression Evaluation {4.5   page 4-12}

```
logical_operator  ::=
        and
      | or
      | xor
```

```
relational_operator  ::=
        =
      | /=
      | <
      | <=
      | >
      | >=
binary_adding_operator  ::=
        +
      | -
      | &
unary_adding_operator  ::=
        +
      | -
multiplying_operator  ::=
        *
      | /
      | mod
      | rem
highest_precedence_operator  ::=
        **
      | abs
      | not
```

Type Conversions {4.6   page 4-21}

```
type_conversion ::=
       type_mark(expression)
```

Qualified Expressions {4.7   page 4-24}

```
qualified_expression ::=
       type_mark'(expression)
     | type_mark'aggregate
```

Allocators {4.8   page 4-24}

```
allocator ::=
       new subtype_indication
       | new qualified_expression
```

Simple and Compound Statements {5.1   page 5-1}

```
sequence_of_statements ::=
       statement {statement}
statement ::=
       {label} simple_statement
       | {label} compound_statement
simple_statement ::=
       null_statement
       | assignment_statement
       | procedure_call_statement
       | exit_statement
       | return_statement
       | goto_statement
       | entry_call_statement
       | delay_statement
       | abort_statement
       | raise_statement
       | code_statement
compound_statement ::=
       if_statement
       | case_statement
       | loop_statement
       | block_statement
       | accept_statement
       | select_statement
label ::=
       <<label_simple_name>>
null_statement ::=
       null;
```

Assignment Statements {5.2   page 5-2}

```
assignment_statement ::=
    variable_name := expression;
```

If Statements {5.3   page 5-4}

```
if_statement ::=
    if condition then
        sequence_of_statements
    {elsif condition then
        sequence_of_statements}
    [else
        sequence_of_statements]
    end if;
condition ::=
    boolean_expression
```

Case Statements {5.4   page 5-5}

```
case_statement ::=
    case expression is
        case_statement_alternative
        {case_statement_alternative}
    end case;
case_statement_alternative ::=
    when choice {| choice } =>
        sequence_of_statements
```

Loop statements {5.5   page 5-7}

```
loop_statement ::=
    [loop_simple_name:]
        [iteration_scheme] loop
            sequence_of_statements
        end loop [loop_simple_name];
```

```
iteration_scheme ::=
        while condition
      | for loop_parameter_specification
loop_parameter_specification ::=
        identifier in [reverse] discrete_range
```

Block Statements {5.6   page 5-9}

```
block_statement ::=
      [block_simple_name:]
          [declare
                declarative_part]
          begin
                sequence_of_statements
          [exception
                exception_handler
                {exception_handler}]
          end [block_simple_name];
```

Exit Statements {5.7   page 5-10}

```
exit_statement ::=
        exit [loop_name] [when condition];
```

Return Statements {5.8   page 5-10}

```
return_statement ::=
        return [expression];
```

Goto Statements {5.9   page 5-11}

```
goto_statement ::=
        goto label_name;
```

Subprogram Declarations {6.1   page 6-1}

```
subprogram_declaration ::=
        subprogram_specification;
subprogram_specification ::=
        procedure identifier [formal_part]
        | function designator  [formal_part] return type_mark
designator ::=
        identifier
        | operator_symbol
operator_symbol ::=
        string_literal
formal_part ::=
        (parameter_specification {; parameter_specification})
parameter_specification ::=
        identifier_list : mode type_mark [:= expression]
mode ::=
        [in]
        | in out
        | out
```

Subprogram Bodies {6.3   page 6-4}

```
subprogram_body ::=
        subprogram_specification is
            [declarative_part]
        begin
            sequence_of_statements
        [exception
            exception_handler
            {exception_handler}]
        end [designator];
```

Subprogram Calls {6.4   page 6-7}

```
procedure_call_statement ::=
        procedure_name [actual_parameter_part];
```

```
function_call ::=
      function_name [actual_parameter_part]
actual_parameter_part ::=
      (parameter_association {, parameter_association})
parameter_association ::=
      [formal_parameter =>] actual_parameter
formal_parameter ::=
      parameter_simple_name
actual_parameter ::=
       expression
     | variable_name
     | type_mark(variable_name)
```

Package Structure {7.1   page 7-1}

```
package_declaration ::= package_specification;
package_specification ::=
         package identifier is
            {basic_declarative_item}
         [private
            {basic_declarative_item}]
          end [package_simple_name]
package_body ::=
         package body package_simple_name is
            [declarative_part]
         [begin
             sequence_of_statements
         [exception
             exception_handler
             {exception_handler}]]
         end [package_simple_name];
```

Private Type and Deferred Constant Declarations {7.4   page 7-5}

```
private_type_declaration ::=
      type identifier [discriminant_part] is [limited] private;
deferred_constant_declaration ::=
      identifier_list : constant type_mark;
```

Use Clauses {8.4 page 8-6}

```
use_clause ::=
    use package_name {, package_name};
```

Renaming Declarations {8.5 page 8-8}

```
renaming_declaration ::=
        identifier : type_mark renames object_name;
        | identifier : exception renames exception_name;
        | package identifier renames package_name;
        | subprogram_specification renames subprogram_or_entry_name;
```

Task Specifications and Bodies {9.1 page 9-1}

```
task_declaration ::=
        task_specification;
task_specification ::=
        task [type] identifier [is
            {entry_declaration}
            {representation_clause}
        end [task_simple_name]]
task_body ::=
        task body task_simple_name is
            [declarative_part]
        begin
            sequence_of_statements
        [exception
            exception_handler
            {exception_handler}]
        end [task_simple_name];
```

Entries, Entry Calls and Accept Statements {9.5 page 9-8}

```
entry_declaration ::=
        entry identifier [(discrete_range)] [formal_part];
entry_call_statement ::=
        entry_name [actual_parameter_part];
```

```
accept_statement ::=
    accept entry_simple_name [(entry_index)] [formal_part] [do
        sequence_of_statements
    end [entry_simple_name]];
entry_index ::=
    expression
```

Delay Statements, Duration, and Time {9.6   page 9-10}

```
delay_statement ::=
    delay simple_expression;
```

Select Statements {9.7   page 9- 12}

```
select_statement ::=
    selective_wait
    | conditional_entry_call
    | timed_entry_call
```

Selective Waits {9.7.1   page 9-12}

```
selective_wait ::=
    select
        select_alternative
    {or
        select_alternative}
    [else
        sequence_of_statements]
    end select;
select_alternative ::=
    [when condition =>] selective_wait_alternative
selective_wait_alternative ::=
    accept_alternative
    | delay_alternative
    | terminate_alternative
accept_alternative ::=
    accept_statement
    [sequence_of_statements]
```

```
delay_alternative ::=
    delay_statement
    [sequence_of_statements]
terminate_alternative ::=
    terminate;
```

Conditional Entry Calls {9.7.2   page 9-14}

```
conditional_entry_call ::=
    select
        entry_call_statement
        [sequence_of_statements]
    else
        sequence_of_statements
    end select;
```

Timed Entry Calls {9.7.3   page 9-15}

```
timed_entry_call ::=
    select
        entry_call_statement
        [sequence_of_statements]
    or
        delay_alternative
    end select;
```

Abort Statements {9.10   page 9-18}

```
abort_statement ::=
    abort task_name {, task_name};
```

Compilation Units - Library Units {10.1   page 10-1}

```
compilation ::=
    {compilation_unit}
compilation_unit ::=
        context_clause library_unit
    | context_clause secondary_unit
```

```
library_unit ::=
        subprogram_declaration
        | package_declaration
        | generic_declaration
        | generic_instantiation
        | subprogram_body
secondary_unit ::=
        library_unit_body
        | subunit
library_unit_body ::=
        subprogram_body
        | package_body
```

Context Clauses - With Clauses {10.1.1   page 10-2}

```
context_clause ::=
        {with_clause {use_clause}}
with_clause ::=
        with unit_simple_name {, unit_simple_name};
```

Subunits of Compilation Units {10.2   page 10-6}

```
body_stub ::=
        subprogram_specification is separate;
        | package body package_simple_name is separate;
        | task body task_simple_name is separate;
subunit ::=
        separate (parent_unit_name) proper_body
```

Exception Declarations {11.1   page 11-1}

```
exception_declaration ::=
        identifier_list : exception;
```

Exception Handlers {11.2   page 11-3}

```
exception_handler ::=
    when exception_choice {| exception_choice} =>
        sequence_of_statements
exception_choice ::=
    exception_name
    | others
```

Raise Statements {11.3   page 11-4}

```
raise_statement ::=
    raise [exception_name];
```

Generic Declarations {12.1   page 12-1}

```
generic_declaration ::=
    generic_specification;
generic_specification ::=
    generic_formal_part   subprogram_specification
    | generic_formal_part   package_specification
generic_formal_part ::=
    generic
        {generic_parameter_declaration}
generic_parameter_declaration ::=
    identifier_list : [in [out]] type_mark [:= expression];
    | type identifier is generic_type_definition;
    | private_type_declaration
    | with subprogram_specification [is name];
    | with subprogram_specification [is <>];
generic_type_definition ::=
    (<>)
    | range <>
    | digits <>
    | delta <>
    | array_type_definition
    | access_type_definition
```

Generic Instantiation {12.3   page 12-8}

```
generic_instantiation ::=
        package identifier is new generic_package_name
                                [generic_actual_part];
        | procedure identifier is new generic_procedure_name
                                [generic_actual_part];
        | function designator is new generic_function_name
                                [generic_actual_part];
generic_actual_part ::=
        (generic_association {, generic_association})
generic_association ::=
        [generic_formal_parameter =>] generic_actual_parameter
generic_formal_parameter ::=
        parameter_simple_name
        | operator_symbol
generic_actual_parameter ::=
        expression
        | variable_name
        | subprogram_name
        | entry_name
        | type_mark
```

Representation Clauses {13.1   page 13-1}

```
representation_clause ::=
        type_representation_clause
        | address_clause
type_representation_clause ::=
        length_clause
        | enumeration_representation_clause
        | record_representation_clause
```

Length Clauses {13.2   page 13-3}

```
length_clause ::=
        for attribute use simple_expression;
```

Enumeration Representation Clauses {13.3   page 13-5}

```
enumeration_representation_clause ::=
    for type_simple_name use aggregate;
```

Record Representation Clauses {13.4   page 13-5}

```
record_representation_clause ::=
    for type_simple_name use
      record [alignment_clause]
          {component_clause}
      end record;
alignment_clause ::=
    at mod static_simple_expression;
component_clause ::=
    component_name at static_simple_expression range static_range;
```

Address Clauses {13.5   page 13-7}

```
address_clause ::=
    for simple_name use at simple_expression;
```

Machine Code Insertions {13.8   page 13-4}

```
code_statement ::=
    type_mark'record_aggregate;
```

GLOSSARY

This glossary has been derived from two sources: The Ada Language Reference Manual, Appendix D [60] and the IEEE Standard Glossary of Software Engineering Terminology[80].

Accept statement. A statement that specifies the actions to be performed when the entry is called. See entry.

Access type. A value of an access type (an access value) is either a null value or a value that designates an object created by an allocator. The designated object can be read and updated via the access value. The definition of an access type specifies the type of the objects designated by values of the access type. See also collection.

Actual parameter. A particular entity associated with the corresponding formal parameter by a subprogram call, entry call, or generic instantiation. See parameter.

Aggregate. The evaluation of an aggregate yields a value of a composite type. The value is specified by giving the value of each of the components. Either positional association or named association may be used to indicate which value is associated with which component.

Allocator. The evaluation of an allocator creates an object and returns a new access value which designates the object.

Application Software. Software specifically produced for the functional use of a computer system; for example, software for navigation, gunfire control, payroll, general ledger. Contrast with system software.

Architectural design. (1) The process of defining a collection of hardware and software components and their interfaces to establish a framework for the development of a computer system. (2) The result of an architectural design process.

Array type. A value of an array type consists of components which are all of the same subtype (and hence, of the same type). Each component is uniquely distinguished by an index (for a one-dimensional array) or by a sequence of indices (for a multidimensional array). Each index must be a value of a discrete type and must lie in the correct index range.

Assignment. Assignment is the operation that replaces the current value of a variable by a new value. An assignment statement specifies a variable on the left, and on the right, an expression whose value is to be the new value of the variable.

Attribute. The evaluation of an attribute yields a predefined characteristic of a named entity; some attributes are functions.

Block statement. A block statement is a single statement that may contain a sequence of statements. It may also include a declarative part, and exception handlers; their effects are local to the block statement.

Body. A body defines the execution of a subprogram, package, or task. A body stub is a form of body that indicates that this execution is defined in a separately compiled subunit.

Cohesion. The degree to which the functions performed by a single program module are functionally related.

Collection. A collection is the entire set of objects created by evaluation of allocators for an access type.

Compilation unit. A compilation unit is the declaration or the body of a program unit, presented for compilation as an independent text. It is optionally preceded by a context clause, naming other compilation units upon which it depends by means of one more with clauses.

Complexity. The degree of complication of a system or system component, determined by such factors as the number and intricacy of conditional branches, the degree of nesting, the types of data structures, and other system characteristics.

Component. A component is a value that is a part of a larger value, or an object that is part of a larger object.

Composite type. A composite type is one whose values have components. There are two kinds of composite type: array types and record types.

Constant. An object whose value once initialed does not change. See object.

Constraint. A constraint determines a subset of the values of a type. A value in that subset satisfies the constraint.

Context clause. An optional clause that precedes a compilation unit, naming other compilation units upon which the compilation unit depends. See compilation unit.

Coupling. A measure of the independence among modules in a program.

Data. A representation of facts, concepts or instructions in a formalized manner suitable for communication, interpretation, or processing by human or automatic means.

Data abstraction. The result of extracting and retaining only the essential characteristic properties of data by defining specific data types and their associated functional characteristics, thus separating and hiding the representation of details.

Declaration. A declaration associates an identifier (or some other notation) with an entity. This association is in effect within a region of text called the scope of the declaration. Within the scope of a declaration, there are places where it is possible to use the identifier to refer to the associated declared entity. At such places the identifier is said to be a simple name of the entity; the name is said to denote the associated entity.

Declarative Part. A declarative part is a sequence of declarations. It may also contain related information such as subprogram bodies and representation clauses.

Derived Type. A derived type is a type whose operations and values are replicas of those of an existing type. The existing type is called the parent type of the derived type.

Direct visibility. At a given point in a program text, the declaration of an entity with a certain identifier is said to be visible if the entity is an acceptable meaning for an occurrence at that point of the identifier. The declaration is visible by selection at the place of the selector in a selected component or at the place of the name in a named association. The declaration is directly visible if the identifier alone has that meaning.

Design. The process of defining the software architecture, components, modules, interfaces, test approach, and data for a software system to satisfy specified requirements.

Design language. A language with special constructs and, sometimes, verification protocols used to develop, analyze, and document a design.

Design methodology. A systematic approach to creating a design, consisting of the ordered application of a specific collection of tools, techniques, and guidelines.

Detailed design. The process of refining and expanding the preliminary (architectural) design to contain more detailed descriptions of the processing logic, data structures, and data definitions, to the extent that the design is sufficiently complete to be implemented.

Discrete Type. A discrete type is a type which has an ordered set of distinct values. The discrete types are the enumeration and integer types. Discrete types are used for indexing and iteration, and for choices in case statements and record variants.

Discriminant. A discriminant is a distinguished component of an object or value of a record type. The subtypes of other components, or even their presence or absence, may depend on the value of the discriminant.

Discriminant constraint. A discriminant constraint on a record type or private type specifies a value for each discriminant of the type.

Elaboration. The elaboration of a declaration is the process by which the declaration achieves its effect (such as creating an object); this process occurs during program execution.

Embedded computer system. A computer system that is integral to a larger system whose primary purpose is not computational; for example, a computer system in a weapon, aircraft, command and control, or rapid transit system.

Encapsulation. The technique of isolating a system function within a module and providing a precise specification for the module. See also information hiding.

Entry. An entry is used for communication between tasks. Externally, an entry is called just as a subprogram is called; its internal behavior is specified by one or more accept statements specifying the actions to be performed when the entry is called.

Enumeration type. An enumeration type is a discrete type whose values are represented by enumeration literals which are given explicitly in the type declaration. These enumeration literals are either identifiers or character literals.

Evaluation. The evaluation of an expression is the process by which the value of the expression is computed. This process occurs during program execution.

Exception. An exception is an error situation which may arise during program execution. To raise an exception is to abandon normal program execution so as to signal that the error has taken place. An exception handler is a portion of program text specifying a response to the exception. Execution of such a program text is called handling the exception.

Expanded name. An expanded name denotes an entity which is declared immediately within some construct. An expanded name has the form of a selected component: the prefix denotes the construct (a program unit, or a block, loop, or accept statement); the selector is the simple name of the entity.

Expression. An expression defines the computation of a value.

Fixed point type. A real type whose values represent approximations to the real numbers. Fixed point types are specified by absolute error bound.

Floating point type. A type whose values represent approximations to the real numbers. Floating point types are specified by a relative error bound expressed as a number of significant decimal digits.

Formal parameter. An identifier used to denote the named entity within the body. See parameter.

Function. Specifies a sequence of actions and also returns a value called the result. See subprogram.

Generic unit. A generic unit is a template either for a set of subprograms or for a set of packages. A subprogram or package created using the template is called an instance of the generic unit. A generic instantiation is the kind of declaration that creates an instance. A generic unit is written as a subprogram or package but with the specification prefixed by a generic formal part which may declare generic formal parameters. A generic formal parameter is either a type, a subprogram, or an object. A generic unit is one of the kinds of program unit.

Handler. A portion of program text specifying a response to the exception. See exception.

Index. Each component of an array type is uniquely distinguished by an index (for a one-dimensional array) or by a sequence of indices (for a multidimensional array). Each index must be a value of a discrete type and must lie in the correct index range. See array type.

Index constraint. An index constraint for an array type specifies the lower and upper bounds for each index range of the array type.

Indexed component. An indexed component denotes a component in an array. It is a form of name containing expressions which specify the values of the indices of the array component. An indexed component may also denote an entry in a family of entries.

Instance. A subprogram or package created using the template of a generic program unit. A generic instantiation is the kind of declaration that creates an instance. See generic unit.

Integer type. An integer type is a discrete type whose values represent all integer numbers within a specific range.

Integration. The process of combining software elements, hardware elements, or both into an overall system.

Interface. A shared boundary. An interface might be a hardware component to link two devices or it might be a portion of storage or registers accessed by two or more computer programs.

Interface specification. A specification that sets forth the interface requirements for a system or system component.

Interrupt. A suspension of a process such as the execution of a computer program, caused by an event external to that process, and performed in such a way that the process can be resumed. Synonymous with interruption.

Iteration. The process of repeatedly executing a given sequence of programming until a given condition is met or while a given condition is true.

Lexical element. A lexical element is an identifier, a literal, a delimiter, or a comment.

Limited type. A limited type is a type for which neither assignment nor the predefined comparison for equality is implicitly declared. All task types are limited. A private type can be defined to be limited. An equality operator can be explicitly declared for a limited type.

Literal. A literal represents a value literally, that is, by means of letters and other characters. A literal is either a numeric literal, an enumeration literal, a character literal, or a string literal.

Maintainability. The ease with which maintenance of a functional unit can be performed in accordance with prescribed requirements.

Mode. Specifies whether the associated actual parameter in a subprogram or entry call supplies a value for the formal parameter, or the formal supplies a value for the actual parameter, or both. See parameter.

Model number. A model number is an exactly representable value of a real type. Operations of a real type are defined in terms of operations on the model numbers of the type. The properties of the model numbers and of their operations are the minimal properties preserved by all implementations of the real type.

Modular. Pertaining to software that is organized into limited aggregates of data and contiguous code that perform identifiable functions.

Modularity. (1) The extent to which software is composed of discrete modules and identifiable with respect to compiling, combining with other units, and loading; for example, the input to, or output from, an assembler, compiler, linkage editor, or an executive routine. (2) A logically separ-ate part of a program.

Name. A name is a construct that stands for an entity: it is said that the name denotes the entity, and that the entity is the meaning of the name. See also declaration, prefix.

Named association. A named association specifies the association of an item with one or more positions in a list, by naming the positions.

Object. An object contains a value. A program creates an object either by elaborating an object declaration or by evaluating an allocator. The declaration or allocator specifies a type for the object; the object can only contain values of that type.

Operation. An operation is an elementary action associated with one or more types. It is either implicitly declared by the declaration of the type, or it is a subprogram that has a parameter or result of the type.

Operator. An operator is an operation which has one or two operands. A unary operator is written before an operand; a binary operator is written between two operands. This notation is a special kind of function call. An operator can be declared as a function. Many operators are implicitly declared by the declaration of a type (for example, most type declarations imply the declaration of the equality operator for values of the type).

Overloading. An identifier can have several alternative meanings at a given point in the program text: this property is called overloading. For example, an overloaded enumeration literal can be an identifier that appears in the definitions of two or more enumeration types. The effective meaning of an overloaded identifier is determined by the context. Subprograms, aggregates, allocators, and string literals can also be overloaded.

Package. A package specifies a group of logically related entities, such as types, objects of those types, and subprograms with parameters of those types. It is written as a package declaration and a package body. The package declaration has a visible part, containing the declarations of all entities that can be explicitly used outside the package. It may also have a private part containing structural details that complete the specification of the visible entities, but which are irrelevant to the user of the package. The package body contains implementations of subprograms (and possibly tasks as other packages) that have been specified in the package declaration. A package is one of the kinds of program unit.

Parameter. A parameter is one of the named entities associated with a subprogram, entry, or generic unit, and used to communicate with the corresponding subprogram body, accept statement or generic body. A formal parameter is an identifier used to denote the named entity within the body. An actual parameter is the particular entity associated with the corresponding formal parameter by a subprogram call, entry call, or generic instantiation. The mode of a formal parameter specifies whether the associated actual parameter supplies a value for the formal parameter, or the formal supplies a value for the actual parameter, or both. The association of actual parameters with formal parameters can be specified by named associations, by positional associations, or by a combination of these.

Performance. A measure of the ability of a computer system or subsystem to perform its functions; for example, response time, throughput, number of transactions.

Parent type. A derived type is a type whose operations and values are replicas of those of an existing type. The existing type is called the parent type of the derived type.

Portability. The ease which software can be transferred from one computer system to another.

Positional association. A positional association specifies the association of an item with a position in a list, by using the same position in the text to specify the item.

Pragma. A pragma conveys information to the compiler.

Prefix. A prefix is used as the first part of certain kinds of name. A prefix is either a function call or a name.

Private part. Part of a package specification containing structural details that complete the specification of the visible entities, but which are irrelevant to the user of the package. See package.

Private type. A private type is a type whose structure and set of values are clearly defined, but not directly available to the user of the type. A private type is known only by its discriminants (if any) and by the set of operations defined for it. A private type and its applicable operations are defined in the visible part of a package, or in a generic formal part. Assignment, equality, and inequality are also defined for private types, unless the private type is limited.

Procedure. Specifies a sequence of actions and is invoked by a procedure call statement. See subprogram.

Program. A program is composed of a number of compilation units, one of which is a subprogram called the main program. Execution of the program consists of execution of the main program, which may invoke subprograms declared in the other compilation units of the program.

Program unit. A program unit is any one of a generic unit, package, subprogram, or task unit.

Programming Support Environment. An integrated collections of tools accessed via a single command language to provide programming support capabilities throughout the software life cycle. The environment typically includes tools for designing, compiling, loading, testing, configuration management, and project management.

Prototype. A model suitable for evaluation of design, performance, and product potential or an instance of a software version that does not exhibit all the properties of the final system; usually lacking in terms of functional or performance attributes.

Qualified expression. A qualified expression is an expression preceded by an indication of its type or subtype. Such qualification is used when, in its absence, the expression might be ambiguous (for example as a consequence of overloading).

Quality. The totality of features and characteristics of a product or service that bears on its ability to satisfy given needs.

Quality Assurance. A planned and systematic pattern of all actions necessary to provide adequate confidence that the item or product conforms to established technical requirements.

Queue. A list that is accessed in a first-in, first-out manner. Contrast with stack.

Raising an exception. To abandon normal program execution so as to signal that the error has taken place. See exception.

Range. A range is a contiguous set of values of a scalar type. A range is specified by giving the lower and upper bounds for the values. A value in the range is said to belong to the range.

Range constraint. A range constraint of a type specifies a range, and thereby determines the subset of the values of the type that belong to the range.

Real time. Pertaining to the processing of data by a computer in connection with another process outside the computer according to time requirements imposed by the outside process. This term is also used to describe systems operating in conversational mode, and processes that can be influenced by human intervention while they are in progress.

Real type. A real type is a type whose values represent approximations to the real numbers. There are two kinds of real type: fixed point types are specified by absolute error bound; floating point types are specified by a relative error bound expressed as a number of significant decimal digits.

Record type. A value of a record type consists of components which are usually of different types or subtypes. For each component of a record value or record object, the definition of the record type specifies an identifier that uniquely determines the component within the record.

Reliability. The ability of an item to perform a required function under stated conditions for a stated period of time.

Renaming declaration. A renaming declaration declares another name for an entity.

Rendezvous. A rendezvous is the interaction that occurs between two parallel tasks when one task has called an entry of the other task, and a corresponding accept statement is being executed by the other task on behalf of the calling task.

Representation clause. A representation clause directs the compiler in the selection of the mapping of a type, an object, or a task onto features of the underlying machine that executes a program. In some cases, representation clauses completely specify the mapping; in other cases, they provide criteria for choosing a mapping.

Requirement. A condition or capability that must be met or processed by a system component to satisfy a contract, standard, specification, or other formally imposed document. The set of all requirements forms the basis for subsequent development of the system or system component.

Reusability. The extent to which a module can be used in multiple applications.

Scalar type. An object or value of a scalar type does not have components. A scalar type is either a discrete type or a real type. The values of a scalar type are ordered.

Scope. The region of program text in which an identifier is associated with an entity. See declaration.

Selected component. A selected component is a name consisting of a prefix and of an identifier called the selector. Selected components are used to denote record components, entries, and objects designated by access values; they are also used as expanded names.

Semantics. The relationships between symbols and their meanings.

Semaphore. A shared variable used to synchronize concurrent processes by indicating whether an action has been completed or an event has occurred.

Simple name. A name that denotes an entity. See declaration, name.

Simulation. The representation of selected characteristics of the behavior of one physical or abstract system by another system. In a digital computer system, simulation is done by software; for example, (a) the representation of physical phenomena by means of operations performed by a computer system, (b) the representation of operations of a computer system by those of another system.

Statement. A statement specifies one or more actions to be performed during the execution of a program.

Stub. A dummy program module used during the development and testing of a higher-level module.

Subcomponent. A subcomponent is either a component, or a component of another subcomponent.

Subprogram. A subprogram is either a procedure or a function. A procedure specifies a sequence of actions and is invoked by a procedure call statement. A function specifies a sequence of actions and also returns a value called the result, and so a function call is an expression. A subprogram is written as a subprogram declaration, which specifies its name, formal parameters, and (for a function) its result; and a subprogram body which specifies the sequence of actions. The subprogram call specifies the actual parameters that are to be associated with the formal parameters. A subprogram is one of the kinds of program unit.

Subtype. A subtype of a type characterizes a subset of the values of the type. The subset is determined by a constraint on the type. Each value in the set of values of a subtype belongs to the subtype and satisfies the constraint determining the subtype.

Subunit. A body stub is a form of program unit body that indicates that this execution is defined in a separately compiled subunit. See body.

System. A collection of people, machine, and methods organized to accomplish a set of specific functions.

Task. A task operates in parallel with other parts of the program. It is written as a task specification (which specifies the name of the task and the names and formal parameters of its entries), and a task body which defines its execution. A task unit is one of the kinds of program unit. A task type is a type that permits the subsequent declaration of any number of similar tasks of the type. A value of a task type is said to designate a task.

Top-Down. Pertaining to an approach that starts with the highest level of a hierarchy and proceeds through progressively lower levels — for example, top-down design, top-down coding, top-down testing.

Type. A type characterizes both a set of values, and a set of operations applicable to those values. A type definition is a language construct that defines a type. A particular type is either an access type, an array type, a private type, a record type, a scalar type, or a task type.

Use clause. A use clause achieves direct visibility of declarations that appear in the visible parts of named packages.

Validation. The process of evaluating software at the end of the software development process to ensure compliance with software requirements.

Variable. An object that contains a value that can change during program execution. See object.

Variant part. A variant part of a record specifies alternative record components, depending on a discriminant of the record. Each value of the discriminant establishes a particular alternative of the variant part.

Verification. The process of determining whether or not the products of a given phase of the software development cycle fulfill the requirements established during the previous phase. See also validation.

Visibility. At a given point in a program text, the declaration of an entity with a certain identifier is said to be visible if the entity is an acceptable meaning for an occurrence at that point of the identifier. The declaration is visible by selection at the place of the selector in a selected component or at the place of the name in a named association. Otherwise, the declaration is directly visible, that is, if the identifier alone has that meaning.

Visible part. Part of package specification that contains the declarations of all entities that can be explicitly used outside the package. See package.

Walk-Through. A review process in which a designer or programmer leads one or more other members of the development team through a segment of design or code that he or she has written, while the other members ask questions and make comments about style, technique, possible errors, violation of development standards, and other problems. Contrast with inspection.

With clause. A clause that precedes a compilation unit that indicates which other program units this unit depends on. See compilation unit.

Selected Reading List

Included in this list are references and sources for further reading on the various topics covered in this book. I have attempted to highlight those references and sources that would be most informative to the practitioner. For a complete list of references used in this book see the reference section that follows.

Introduction to the Ada Effort (Chapter 1)

Booch, G., *Software Engineering with Ada*, The Benjamin/Cummings Publishing Company Inc., California, 1983.

Druffel, L. E., "The Potential Effect of Ada on Software Engineering in 1980's," *Software Engineering Notes*, Volume 7, Number 3, July 1982, pp 5 - 11.

Fisher, D. A., "DoD's Common Programming Language Effort," *Computer*, March 1978, pp 24 - 33.

Martin, J., "Answering the Software Crisis," *Defense Sciences and Electronics*, Oct. 1985, pp 22 - 32.

"Ada: Past, Present, Future - An Interview with Jean Ichbiah, the Principle Designer of Ada," *Communications of the ACM*, Volume 27, Number 10 , Oct. 1984, PP 990 - 997.

Ada As A Language (Chapter 2 and Appendix A)

Barnes, J., *Programming in Ada*, Addison-Wesley, London, 1981.

Booch, G., *Software Engineering with Ada*, The Benjamin/Cummings Publishing Company Inc., California, 1983.

Cohen, N., *Ada as a Second Language*, McGraw Hill Book Company, New York, 1986.

Downes, V.A., Goldsack, S.J., *Programming Embedded Systems with Ada*, Prentice/Hall International, New Jersey, 1982.

Tucker, A.B., *Programming Languages*, McGraw Hill Book Company, New York, 1986.

"Reference Manual for the Ada Programming Language, ANSI/MIL-STD-1815A," Department of Defense, Jan. 1983.

The Rationale for the Design of the Green Programming Language, Honeywell and Cii Honeywell Bull, 1978.

Ada Environments (Chapter 3)

Coyne, S., E. Kean, "Evaluation Criteria/Questionaire for Ada Compilers," AJPO, July 1984.

Nissen, J. C. D., B. A. Wichmann, "Ada-Europe Guidelines for Ada Compiler Specification and Selection," *National Physical Laboratory Report DTIC 10/82*, Oct.1982.

Oberndorf, P.A., M.H. Penedo, "Future Ada Environment Workshop, Summary of Project Database Working Group Discussions," *Ada Letters*, Volume IV, Number 5, March/April. 1985, pp 65 - 78.

"Ada Language System Users Reference Manual", Volumes 1 and 2, SofTech Inc., Waltham, Mass., 1984.

"Requirements for the Programming Environment for the Common High Order Languages, STONEMAN," Department of Defense, Feb. 1980.

Ada Letters - A publication of the ACM Special Interest Group on Ada. (see chapter 5 for access information)

Ada Policies and Related Standards (Chapter 4)

Fischer, H., "MIL-STD-SDS Review Issues: Ada and Design Methodologies," *Ada Letters*, Volume IV, Number 1, July/Aug. 1984, pp 7 - 17.

"Ada Compiler Validation Summary Report (VADS)," Ada Validation Facility Report, June 1985.

"Guidelines for Use of the Trademark Ada," AJPO.

"DoD Directive 5000.29, Management of Computer Resources in Major Defense Systems," Department of Defense.

"DoD Directive 5000.31, Interim List of DoD Approved High Order Languages," Department of Defense.

"Reference Manual for the Ada Programming Language, ANSI/MIL-STD-1815A," Department of Defense, Jan. 1983.

Ada Letters - A publication of the ACM Special Interest Group on Ada. (see chapter 5 for access information)

Who's Who in Ada (Chapter 5)

Ada Letters - A publication of the ACM Special Interest Group on Ada (see chapter 5 for access information)

Making the Transition to Ada (Chapter 6)

Barbacci, M., A. Habermann, M. Shaw, "The Software Engineering Institute: Bridging Practice and Potential," *IEEE Software*, Nov. 1985.

Ehrlich, K., "Factors Influencing Technology Transfer," *SIGCHI Bulletin*, Volume 17, Number 2, Oct. 1985, pp 20 - 23.

Wegner, P., "Ada Education and Technology Transfer Activities," *Ada Letters*, Volume II, Number 2, Sept/Oct. 1982, pp 51 - 60.

Ada Design and Implementation Methodologies (Chapter 7)

Booch, G., "Object-Oriented Development," *IEEE Transaction on Software Engineering, Special Issue on Software Design Methods*, Volume SE - 12, Number 2, Feb. 1986, pp 211 - 221.

Buhr, R.J.A., *System Design with Ada*, Prentice-Hall Inc., New Jersey, 1984.

Buhr, R.J.A., G.M. Karam, "An Informal Overview of CADA: A Design Environment for Ada," *Ada Letters*, Volume IV, Number 5, March/April. 1985, pp 49 - 58.

Cameron, J. R., "An Overview of JSD," *IEEE Transaction on Software Engineering, Special Issue on Software Design Methods*, Volume SE - 12, Number 2, Feb. 1986, pp 222 - 240.

Gardner, M. R., N. Brubaker, C. Dahlke, B. Goodhart, D. L. Ross, "Ada Programming Style," Intellimac Inc., Jan. 1983.

Jackson, M., *System Development*, Prentice/Hall International, N.J., 1983.

Jones, B., S. Litvintchouk, J. Mungle, H. Krasner, J. Mellby, H. Willman, "Issues in Software Reusability," *Ada Letters*, Volume IV, Number 5, March/April. 1985, pp 97 - 99.

An Object Oriented Design Handbook for Ada Software, EVB Software Engineering Inc, 1985.

VanNeste, K.F., "Ada Coding Standards and Conventions," *Ada Letters*, Volume VI, Number 1, Jan./Feb. 1986, pp 41 - 48.

Other Uses of Ada and Future Directions (Chapter 8)

Adelsberger, H. H., "ASSE - Ada Simulation Support Environement," *Proceedings of the 1982 Winter Simulation Conference*, 1982, pp 89 - 101.

Bryant, R. M., "SIMPAS - A simulation Language based on Pascal," *Proceedings of the 1980 Winter Simulation Conference*, 1980, pp 25 - 40.

Shahdad, M., R. Lipsett, E. Marschner, K. Sheehan, H. Cohen, R. Waxman, D. Ackley, " VHSIC Hardware Description Language," *Computer*, Feb. 1985, pp 94 - 103.

Tichy, W.F., "Adabase: A Database for Ada Programs," *Proceedings of the AdaTec Conference on Ada*, ACM, Oct. 6-8 1982, pp 57 - 65.

REFERENCES

1. Adelsberger, H. H., "ASSE - Ada Simulation Support Environment," *Proceedings of the 1982 Winter Simulation Conference*, 1982, pp 89 - 101.

2. Barbacci, M., A. Habermann, M. Shaw, "The Software Engineering Institute: Bridging Practice and Potential," *IEEE Software*, Nov. 1985.

3. Barnes, J., *Programming in Ada*, Addison-Wesley, London, 1981.

4. Berry, D.M., N. Yavne, M. Yavne, "On the Requirements for Use of A Program Design Language," *Ada Letters*, Volume VI, Number 1, Jan./Feb. 1986, pp 82 - 89.

5. Bond, R.M., "Ada as a Program Description Language," *Ada Letters*, Volume IV, Number 1, July/Aug. 1984, pp 67 - 73.

6. Booch, G., *Software Engineering with Ada*, The Benjamin/Cummings Publishing Company Inc., California, 1983.

7. Booch, G., "Object-Oriented Design," *Ada Letters*, Volume I, Number 3, March/April. 1982.

8. Booch, G., "Object-Oriented Development," *IEEE Transaction on Software Engineering, Special Issue on Software Design Methods*, Volume SE - 12, Number 2, Feb. 1986, pp 211 - 221.

9. Bruno, G., "An Ada Package for Discrete Event Simulation," *Proceedings of the AdaTec Conference on Ada*, ACM, Oct. 6-8 1982, pp 172 - 180.

10. Bryant, R. M., "SIMPAS - Asimulation Language based on Pascal," *Proceedings of the 1980 Winter Simulation Conference*, 1980, pp 25 - 40.

11. Buhr, R.J.A., *System Design with Ada*, Prentice-Hall Inc., New Jersey, 1984.

12. Buhr, R.J.A, G. M. Karam, C. M. Woodside, "An Overview and Examples of the Application of CAEDE: A New, Experimental Design Environment for Ada," *Proceedings of the Ada International Conference*, ACM, May 14 -16 1985, pp 173 - 184.

13. Buhr, R.J.A., G.M. Karam, "An Informal Overview of CADA: A Design Environment for Ada," *Ada Letters*, Volume IV, Number 5, March/April. 1985, pp 49 - 58.

14. Bulman, D. M., "Is Ada the Answer?," *The Yourdon Report*, Volume 6-6, 1982.

15. Cameron, J. R., "An Overview of JSD," *IEEE Transaction on Software Engineering, Special Issue on Software Design Methods*, Volume SE - 12, Number 2, Feb. 1986, pp 222 - 240.

16. Chase, A. I., M. S. Gerhardt, "The Case for Full Ada as a Design Language," *Ada Letters*, Volume II, Number 2, Sept./Oct. 1982, pp 51 - 59.

17. Cohen, N.H., "Tasks as Abstraction Mechanisms," *Ada Letters*, Volume V, Number 3-6, Nov./Dec. 1985, pp 30 - 44.

18. Coyne, S., E. Kean, "Evaluation Criteria/Questionaire for Ada Compilers," AJPO, July 1984.

19. Cugini, J. V., "Selection and Use of General-Purpose Programming Languages," *NBS Special Publication 500 -117*, Volume 1, Oct. 1984.

20. Downes, V.A., Goldsack, S.J., *Programming Embedded Systems with Ada*, Prentice/Hall International, New Jersey, 1982.

21. Druffel, L. E., "The Potential Effect of Ada on Software Engineering in 1980's," *Software Engineering Notes*, Volume 7, Number 3, July 1982, pp 5 - 11.

22. Ehrlich, K., "Factors Influencing Technology Transfer," *SIGCHI Bulletin*, Volume 17, Number 2, Oct. 1985, pp 20 - 23.

23. Fisher, D. A., "DoD's Common Programming Language Effort," *Computer*, March 1978, pp 24 - 33.

24. Fisher, D.A., "A Common Programming Language for the Department of Defense - Background and Technical Requirements," *Institute for Defense Analysis, Report P-1191*, June 1976.

25. Fischer, H., "MIL-STD-SDS Review Issues: Ada and Design Methodologies," *Ada Letters*, Volume IV, Number 1, July/Aug. 1984, pp 7 - 17.

26. Gardner, M. R., N. Brubaker, C. Dahlke, B. Goodhart, D. L. Ross, "Ada Programming Style," Intellimac Inc., Jan. 1983.

27. German, S.M., D.P. Helmbold, D.C. Luckman, "Monitoring for Deadlocks in Ada Tasking," *Proceedings of the AdaTec Conference on Ada*, ACM, Oct. 6-8 1982, pp 10 - 25.

28. Gilroy, K., "Ada Run-Time Environment Working Group Report," *Ada Letters*, Volume V, Number 3-6, Nov./Dec. 1985, pp 63.

29. Jackson, M., *System Development*, Prentice/Hall International, N.J., 1983.

30. Jones, B., S. Litvintchouk, J. Mungle, H. Krasner, J. Mellby, H. Willman, "Issues in Software Reusability," *Ada Letters*, Volume IV, Number 5, March/April. 1985, pp 97 - 99.

31. Lomuto, N., "Ada PDL is the Answer. (But what was the Question?)", Report TP - 162, SofTech Inc., Waltham, Mass., 1983.

32. Martin, D.G., "Non-Ada to Ada Conversion," *Ada Letters*, Volume VI, Number 1, Jan./Feb. 1986, pp 72 - 81.

33. Martin, J., "Answering the Software Crisis," *Defense Sciences and Electronics*, Oct. 1985, pp 22 - 32.

34. Musa, J. D., "Stimulating Software Engineering Progress- A Report of the Software Engineering Planning Group," *Software Engineering Notes*, Volume 8, Number 2, April 1983, pp 29 - 48.

35. Nissen, J. C. D., B. A. Wichmann, "Ada-Europe Guidelines for Ada Compiler Specification and Selection," *National Physical Laboratory Report DTIC 10/82*, Oct.1982.

36. Oberndorf, P.A., M.H. Penedo, "Future Ada Environment Workshop, Summary of Project Database Working Group Discussions," *Ada Letters*, Volume IV, Number 5, March/April. 1985, pp 65 - 78.

37. Parnas, D. L., P. C. Clements, "A Rational Design Process: How and Why to Fake It," *IEEE Transaction on Software Engineering, Special Issue on Software Design Methods* , Volume SE - 12, Number 2, Feb. 1986, pp 222 - 240.

38. Rogers, M. W., "IT Companies' Acceptance of and Attitudes Towards Ada," *Proceedings of the Ada International Conference* , ACM, May 14 -16 , pp 1 - 13.

39. Roubine, O., "Programming Large and Flexible Systems in Ada," *Proceedings of the Ada International Conference* , ACM, May 14 -16 , pp 197 - 209.

40. Shahdad, M., R. Lipsett, E. Marschner, K. Sheehan, H. Cohen, R. Waxman, D. Ackley, " VHSIC Hardware Description Language," *Computer*, Feb. 1985, pp 94 - 103.

41. Sherman, M., A. Hisgen, J. Rosenberg, "A Methodology for Programming Abstract Data Types in Ada," *Proceedings of the AdaTec Conference on Ada*, ACM, Oct. 6-8 1982, pp 66 - 75.

42. Simpson, R.T., "The ALS Compiler Front End Architecture," *Proceedings of the AdaTec Conference on Ada*, ACM, Oct. 6-8 1982, pp 98 - 106.

43. Smith, J., "Some Problems with Ada in Real-Time Embedded Systems," *Defense Sciences and Electronics*, Oct. 1985, pp 45 - 46.

44. Tichy, W.F., "Adabase: A Database for Ada Programs," *Proceedings of the AdaTec Conference on Ada*, ACM, Oct. 6-8 1982, pp 57 - 65.

45. Tucker, A.B., *Programming Languages*, McGraw Hill Book Company, New York, 1986.

46. VanNeste, K.F., "Ada Coding Standards and Conventions," *Ada Letters*, Volume VI, Number 1, Jan./Feb. 1986, pp 41 - 48.

47. Voigt, S., S. Beskenis "Space Station Software Issues," *NASA Conference Publication 2361*, 1984.

48. Walasek, J., "Source Listings with Combs," *Ada Letters*, Volume IV, Number 6, May/June. 1985, pp 32 - 34.

49. Wegner, P., "Ada Education and Technology Transfer Activities," *Ada Letters*, Volume II, Number 2, Sept/Oct. 1982, pp 51 - 60.

50. Weicker, R. P., " DHRYSTONE: A Synthetic Systems Programming Benchmark," *Communication of the ACM*, Volume 27, Number 10, Oct. 1984, pp 1013 - 1030.

51. Welch, P.H., "Structured Tasking in Ada," *Ada Letters*, Volume V, Number 1, July/Aug. 1985, pp 17 - 31.

52. "Ada: Past, Present, Future - An Interview with Jean Ichbiah, the Principle Designer of Ada," *Communications of the ACM*, Volume 27, Number 10 , Oct. 1984, PP 990 - 997.

53. "Ada Compiler Validation Summary Report (VADS)," Ada Validation Facility Report, June 1985.

54. "Guidelines for Use of the Trademark Ada," AJPO.

55. "The DoD STARS Program," *Computer, Full Issue Dedicated to STARS*, Volume 16, Number 11, Nov. 1983.

56. "DoD Directive 5000.29, Management of Computer Resources in Major Defense Systems," Department of Defense.

57. "DoD Directive 5000.31, Interim List of DoD Approved High Order Languages," Department of Defense.

58. "Requirements for High Order Languages, STEELMAN," Department of Defense, June 1978.

59. "Requirements for the Programming Environment for the Common High Order Languages, STONEMAN," Department of Defense, Feb. 1980.

60. "Reference Manual for the Ada Programming Language, ANSI/MIL-STD-1815A," Department of Defense, Jan. 1983.

61. " Using Ada as a Design Language, Draft Version 3.1" Ada as a PDL Working Group of the Technical Committee on Software Engineering of the IEEE Computer Society, IEEE Computer Society, Feb. 1985.

62. "Packages Spawn Ada's Growth," *Systems and Software*, April 1985, PP 93 - 100.

63. *An Object Oriented Design Handbook for Ada Software,* EVB Software Engineering Inc, 1985.

64. "Course Notes - Ada for Technical Overview (L102)," Department of Army, prepared by SofTech Inc., Waltham, Mass, 1984.

65. "Course Notes - Ada for Technical Managers (L201)," Department of Army, prepared by SofTech Inc., Waltham, Mass, 1984.

66. "Course Notes - Introduction to Software Engineering (M102)," Department of Army, prepared by SofTech Inc., Waltham, Mass, 1984.

67. "Course Notes - Basic Ada (L201)," Department of Army, prepared by SofTech Inc., Waltham, Mass, 1984.

68. "Course Notes - Advanced Ada Topics (L305)," Department of Army, prepared by SofTech Inc., Waltham, Mass, 1984.

69. "Course Notes - Realtime Systems in Ada (L401)," Department of Army, prepared by SofTech Inc., Waltham, Mass, 1984.

70. "Course Notes - Ada Orientation for Managers (L101)," Department of Army, prepared by SofTech Inc., Waltham, Mass, 1984.

71. "Ada Reusability Guidelines," Report 3285-2-208/2, SofTech Inc., Waltham, Mass., 1984.

72. "Ada Run Time Support Guidelines," Report 3285-2-208/4, SofTech Inc., Waltham, Mass., 1984.

73. "Designing Real Time Systems in Ada," Report 1123-1, SofTech Inc., Waltham, Mass., 1986.

74. "Jamps Runtime Benchmark Test," Report 3285-2-210/2, SofTech Inc., Waltham, Mass., 1984.

75. "Ada Language System Users Reference Manual," Volumes 1 and 2, SofTech Inc., Waltham, Mass., 1984.

76. "Ada Programming Design Language Survey- Final Report," SofTech Inc., Dayton, Ohio., 1984.

77. "Ada Design Methods Training Support - Case Studies Report," Report 1110-2-0, SofTech Inc., Waltham, Mass., 1983.

78. "Ada Design Methods Training Support - Real Time Ada Workbook," Report 1110-1 - 3, SofTech Inc., Waltham, Mass., 1984.

79. *The Rationale for the Design of the Green Programming Language,* Honeywell and Cii Honeywell Bull, 1978.

80. *IEEE Standard Glossary of Software Engineering Terminology,* IEEE, New York, N. Y., 1983.

INDEX

abstraction, 107
access types, 31
Ada Compiler Validation Capability
  (ACVC), 69-71
Ada Effort, 2-7
Ada Environment, 42
Ada Information Clearinghouse, 62,
  77-78
Ada Joint Program Office (AJPO),
  72-73, 76-77
Ada Language Feature Layer, 60
Ada National Standards Institute, 68
Ada opportunities, 87-89
Adaplex, 149-151
Ada Repository, 82
Ada trademark policy, 72-74
American National Standards
  Institute (ANSI), 68
Application Architectural Layer, 59
array types, 31

Babbage, Charles, 5
benchmarking, 57-65
Booch, G., 110
body, 29
Buhr, R.J.A., 111, 115, 119
Byron, Augusta, Ada, 5

Carleton Embedded System Design
  Environment (CAEDE), 119-120
certification, 69
classical training model, 94-97
Collection of Tools environment, 45

Command Language guidelines,
  48-49
Command Language Layer, 43
Common High Order Language
  Program, 11
Compilation Layer, 59
compiler validation process, 68-69
Cooper, Jack, 5
cultural differences, 93-94

Database Layer, 45
Database Layer guidelines, 52-54
database oriented language, 149-151
data type, 31
declarative part, 30
Defense Data Network (DDN), 82
DeLauer Letter, 71
demonstration methodology, 127-
  129
demonstration methodology process,
  128-131
design activities, 105
design definition, 105
design goals, 27-28
design guidelines, 123-125, 137
design issues, 142-144
design methodologies, 109-110
design principles, 107-108
design processes, 105-106
design representations, 131-135
Dialog Information Services, 81-82

entity action step, 112